Learn ClojureScript

Functional programming for the web

Andrew Meredith

Merry **Kraken** Press

Typeset using XeLaTeX, based on the memoir class. PT Serif was used as the primary body font, Oswald for headings and captions, and Fira Code for code listings and verbatim text.

" *Discovering Clojure has had a profound impact on my career, forever changing how I think about programming. Learn ClojureScript offers a smooth onramp and a good mix of both the practical and theoretical aspects of the language. With this book, web developers of all experience levels can enjoy their Clojure eureka moments while building on fun and interesting examples.* "

Brandon Bloom, *CEO, Deref Inc.*

" Learn ClojureScript *covers everything necessary without being overwhelming. The book is perfect for beginners to the language, and it's a resource I wished was around when I got into the world of Clojure and ClojureScript.* "

Kelvin Mai, *Full-Stack Engineer*

" *This is the gentlest introduction that the ClojureScript ecosystem offers. The capstone projects give you what you need to get a ClojureScript frontend up and running.* "

Roger Erens, *Software Engineer*

Contents

Contents   **iii**
    Acknowlegements ix

I   Why ClojureScript Matters   **1**

1   A First Look   **3**
    1.1   Introducing ClojureScript   4
    1.2   ClojureScript's Sweet Spots   6
    1.3   ClojureScript 101   9
    1.4   Summary 14

2   ClojureScript in the JavaScript Ecosystem   **15**
    2.1   Why JavaScript Needs Clojure 15
    2.2   Why Clojure needs JavaScript 19
    2.3   Summary 21

3   Building Blocks   **23**
    3.1   Parens, Parens Everywhere! 24
    3.2   Core Data Types 25
    3.3   Summary 30

4   Expressions and Evaluation   **33**
    4.1   Laying the Foundation with S-Expressions 33
    4.2   Evaluating ClojureScript Code 38
    4.3   Order of Operations 41
    4.4   Summary 41

II   Tools of the Trade   **43**

5   Bootstrapping a ClojureScript Project   **45**

5.1   Meeting clj   46
5.2   Bootstrapping a Project   49
5.3   Exploring the Project   51
5.4   Summary   54

6   Receiving Rapid Feedback With Figwheel   57
6.1   Testing Live Reloading 58
6.2   Writing Reloadable Code   61
6.3   Summary   65

7   REPL Crash Course   67
7.1   Understanding the REPL   67
7.2   Using a REPL for browser interaction   69
7.3   Summary   74

8   Capstone 1 - Weather Forecasting App   75
8.1   Creating an App With Reagent   76
8.2   Responding to User Input   80
8.3   Calling an External API   82
8.4   Summary   85

III Basic ClojureScript   87

9   Using Variables and Values   89
9.1   Understanding Vars   90
9.2   Creating Local Bindings With let   93
9.3   Summary   96

10 Making Choices   97
10.1 Example: Adventure Game   98
10.2 Making Simple Choices With if And when   98
10.3 Truthiness and Falsiness 106
10.4 More Complex Choices With cond   106
10.5 Summary 109

11 Looping   111
11.1 Manipulating Sequences with for 112
11.2 Performing Explicit Recursion with loop and recur 117
11.3 Looping for Side Effects 119
11.4 Summary 122

12 Reusing Code With Functions   123
12.1 Understanding Functions 123

12.2 Defining and Calling Functions 125
12.3 Functions as Expressions 131
12.4 Recursion 101 135
12.5 Summary 136

13 Interacting With JavaScript Data **137**
13.1 Example: Integration With Legacy Code 137
13.2 Using Conversion Functions 138
13.3 Working with JavaScript Data Directly 141
13.4 Summary 145

14 Performing I/O **147**
14.1 Manipulating The DOM 148
14.2 Getting User Input 150
14.3 Handling Events 153
14.4 Summary 155

15 Capstone 2 - Temperature Converter **157**
15.1 Creating the Markup 158
15.2 Code Walkthrough 159
15.3 Summary 163

IV Working With Data **165**

16 Grokking Collections **167**
16.1 Defining Collections and Sequences 169
16.2 Sequences 170
16.3 Using Lists for Sequential Data 172
16.4 Using Vectors for Indexed Data 173
16.5 Using Maps for Associative Data 174
16.6 Using Sets for Unique Data 176
16.7 Summary 177

17 Discovering Sequence Operations **179**
17.1 The Sequence Abstraction 180
17.2 Transforming With Map 181
17.3 Coercing Results With Into 185
17.4 Refining With Filter 186
17.5 Summary 189

18 Summarizing Data **191**
18.1 Understanding Reduce 193
18.2 Reduce Use Cases 195

18.3 Being More Concise 196
18.4 Summary 198

19 Mastering Data With Maps and Vectors   **199**
19.1 Domain Modeling with Maps and Vectors 201
19.2 Working With Associative Data 205
19.3 Working With Nested Data 209
19.4 Summary 212

20 Capstone 3 - Contact Book   **213**
20.1 Data Modeling 214
20.2 Creating the UI 219
20.3 Summary 227

V Idiomatic ClojureScript   **229**

21 Functional Programming Concepts   **231**
21.1 Composing Behavior from Small Pieces 231
21.2 Writing Pure Functions 236
21.3 Immutable Data 238
21.4 Functional Design Patterns 240
21.5 Summary 246

22 Managing State   **247**
22.1 Atoms 247
22.2 Transients 252
22.3 Using State Wisely 253
22.4 Summary 254

23 Namespaces and Program Structure   **255**
23.1 Namespace Declarations 255
23.2 Grouping Related Functions 260
23.3 Namespaces and the REPL 263
23.4 Summary 264

24 Handling Exceptions and Errors   **265**
24.1 Handling Exceptions with try/catch 265
24.2 Functional Alternatives to Exceptions 269
24.3 Summary 275

25 Intro to Core Async   **277**
25.1 Overview of CSP 277
25.2 Go Blocks as Lightweight Processes 280

25.3 Communicating Over Channels 281
25.4 Channels as Values 284
25.5 Summary 285

26 Capstone 4 - Group Chat   **287**
26.1 Thinking About Interactions 288
26.2 Building Components 293
26.3 Realtime Communication 307
26.4 Summary 312

VI ClojureScript Applications   **313**

27 React as a Platform   **315**
27.1 Functional Programming Model 315
27.2 DOM Diffing 316
27.3 Creating Fast Apps 317
27.4 Summary 320

28 Lesson 28: Using React via Reagent   **321**
28.1 Reactive Data 321
28.2 Building Components 324
28.3 Updating State 327
28.4 Writing Reactive Queries 330
28.5 Summary 332

29 Lesson 29: Separate Concerns   **333**
29.1 Connecting Components With Channels 333
29.2 Message Patterns 337
29.3 Client/Server Architecture 343
29.4 Summary 343

30 Capstone 5 - Notes   **345**
30.1 What We Are Building 346
30.2 State Management 346
30.3 Building the Application 355
30.4 Summary 377

Index   **379**

Acknowlegements

This book has been a long-running project, and many people have been instrumental in making it a reality. First, I would like to thank my loving and patient wife, Diana. She has encouraged me throughout this process, and I know that I would never have finished if it were not for her.

This book started as a project for a traditional publisher. That being the case, I had several editors who invested a ton of time and energy into taking a rough manuscript and making it something well worth readings. I would specifically like to thank Kristen Watterson and Andrew Warren for patiently working with me through multiple revisions.

Finally, I would like to thank everyone who read the book online and sent me feedback. I would especially like to thank Roger Erens for the numerous pull requests and emails that he sent with corrections and suggestions for improvements. Without Roger's help, this book would have at least 50 or 60 more ~~tyos~~ typos and grammatical mistakes. I would also like to thank everyone who pre-ordered the book and made it possible for me to create a physical book in addition to the online version.

Part I

Why ClojureScript Matters

In this section, we take our first look at ClojureScript with the goal of understanding its relationship to JavaScript as well as the Clojure language. We will discover ClojureScript's utility as a tool for modern web development. Like any tool, ClojureScript is not well suited for every task, so we will identify the areas where it may not be the best choice. Finally, we will end with a brief survey of the syntax and data types in ClojureScript and walk through its execution model.

- Lesson 1: A First Look
- Lesson 2: ClojureScript in the JavaScript Ecosystem
- Lesson 3: Building Blocks
- Lesson 4: Expressions and Evaluation

Lesson 1

A First Look

In today's technology landscape, the web is king. Web apps are everywhere, and the *lingua franca* of the web is JavaScript. Whether the task is adding interactivity to a simple web page, creating a complex single-page application, or even writing microservices, JavaScript is the defacto tool. Despite its age, JavaScript has evolved to power an entire generation of web development. The JavaScript community is also one of the most active and prolific software development communities ever, with libraries and frameworks for any conceivable use.

In this lesson:

- What is ClojureScript?
- What makes ClojureScript unique?
- What sort of problems are easier to solve in ClojureScript than in JavaScript?

However, JavaScript is not without its warts. We need books to tell us what are the "Good Parts" and what parts we had best avoid. We have to deal with the reality of varying levels of support by different browsers (yes, even today). We need expend mental cycles deciding which of many viable UI frameworks we should use on our next project... and which framework we should switch to when we grow frustrated with the first framework we chose. While JavaScript has matured to meet many of the challenges of large-scale web development, there are times when another language is a better choice for a new project.

Over the course of this book, we will learn the ClojureScript programming language and see how it is especially well-suited to developing large single-page applications. While it may take a while to get used to all the parentheses, we'll see that this odd-looking language excels at building modular, high-performance user interfaces. Finally, we will see how the simple elegance of the language makes ClojureScript a joy to work with.

1.1   Introducing ClojureScript

At the fundamental level, ClojureScript is a dialect of the Clojure programming language that compiles to JavaScript. Clojure was created in 2008 by Rich Hickey as a general-purpose programming language with the goal of being pragmatic, safe, and simple. While Clojure originally compiled only to Java Virtual Machine bytecode, ClojureScript entered the scene in 2011 as an option to bring Clojure to client side web development. While there are a few differences between Clojure and ClojureScript, they are largely the same language running on different platforms. ClojureScript inherits Clojure's pragmatism, safety, and simplicity.

ClojureScript has all the buzzwords of an obscure, academic language - immutable data structures, functional programming, Lisp, etc. - but that should not fool us into thinking that it is a language designed for academia. It is an intensely practical language that was born to address some of the issues that we as JavaScript programmers find most troubling. ClojureScript specifically addresses those pain points that we run into when building and maintaining large applications. It has presented such successful solutions to asynchronous programming, state management, and higher-level abstractions that numerous JavaScript libraries have appeared that mimic certain features of ClojureScript. It is a practical language that is especially well-suited to client-side web development.

Beyond being a practical language, ClojureScript can be a very enjoyable language to write. The terseness of a language like ClojureScript is a breath of fresh air when we have grown so accustomed to writing the same boilerplate over and over again. Additionally, Clojure-Script comes with a much more extensive standard library than JavaScript, so those simple tasks that require custom code or a third-party library can often be accomplished without ever leaving core ClojureScript.

While we will look at many features of ClojureScript that make it different from JavaScript, we should not think that it is a totally alien language. After the initial "parenthesis shock", we will see that its syntax is actually simpler than that of JavaScript. Let's take a look at a couple of examples of code translated from JavaScript to ClojureScript to get a feel for how the language is structured. Below we have an example of a JavaScript function call. Since JavaScript can be written in several different styles, we'll look at an objected oriented example as well as a functional example.

Figure 1.1: Object-Oriented JavaScript function call

This object-oriented style is very familiar to most JavaScript programmers and requires little explanation. Next, we'll look at the perhaps slightly less familiar functional style. This style is widely used in *lodash* and similar libraries.

Figure 1.2: Functional JavaScript function call

Next, let's look at a ClojureScript version of the same example. Notice that there are the same number of parentheses in the ClojureScript version as there were in the JavaScript versions. In fact, the only differences from the functional JavaScript code is that the left parenthesis is moved to the left and there is no comma between arguments.

Figure 1.3: ClojureScript function call

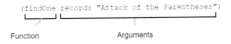

While this is a trivial example, it should be enough to see that ClojureScript should not be intimidating - different, yes, but not frightening. As we will see over the coming lessons, we need to adjust our eyes to read ClojureScript, but the process is not that different from learning a new library or programming technique.

Quick Review

- Does ClojureScript or JavaScript come with a more extensive standard library?
- Does ClojureScript encourage an object-oriented style ot a functional style like *lodash* and *ramda*?

1.2   ClojureScript's Sweet Spots

While ClojureScript is a general-purpose programming language, it is not the best tool for
every job. If we just want to animate one or two elements on a webpage or implement an
analytics snippet, ClojureScript is probably overkill (in fact, even jQuery may be overkill for
such simple examples). How are we to decide, then, when to use ClojureScript and when to
stick with JavaScript? In order decide whether to use ClojureScript on a project, we should
have an idea of the types of projects in which it excels.

Writing Single-Page Applications

Clojure started out as a general-purpose application programming language for the JVM,
so ClojureScript's heritage is based in application programming. Indeed we see that the
constructs that make ClojureScript so valuable are precisely those that are necessary for
application-type programs. Specifically, ClojureScript addresses the JavaScript's issues
that start as minor annoyances and escalate to major issues as an application grows. Anyone who has maintained a large JavaScript application knows how difficult it is to address
strategic architecture, module loading, cross-browser compatibility, library selection, tooling, and a whole host of other issues simultaneously.

The problem with JavaScript is that each of these issues must be addressed separately, but
your choice for solving one issue may affect others. For instance, the module system that
we use is a separate concern from our build tool, which in turn is separate from our testing
framework. However, we need to make sure that our build tool supports our testing framework, and both support our module system or can be easily integrated with it. Suddenly,
the awesome app that we were planning to write gets stifled by the fact that we just spent 3
days trying to get the build set up. I can tell you that scenarios like this are commonplace,
since I have experienced a number of them personally.

Paradoxically, ClojureScript makes things easier by taking away choices. The module system is built in to the language. There is a built-in test framework. Most libraries provide
an API that works on common data structures in a functional style, so they are simple to
integrate. Additionally, the Google Closure Library that is built in will cover most common concerns such as handling dates, DOM manipulation, HTML5 history, graphics, and
ajax. While building a ClojureScript application is not nearly the adventure that building
a JavaScript one is, it is certainly more productive.

Optimizing UIs

We have alluded to the fact that ClojureScript's immutable data structures make some interesting UI optimizations possible, but we have not gone into detail as to how that works.
It is really the combination of React's virtual DOM concept and ClojureScript's immutable

data structures that make such optimizations possible. Since we know that ClojureScript's data structures are immutable, we know that any structure that we create cannot change. If we have some data structure backing a UI component, we know that we will not need to re-render the component as long as it is backed by the same data structure. This knowledge allows us to create highly optimized UIs.

Consider this: we are writing a contact management app, and we have a ContactList component that contains ContactListItem components. These components are all backed by a list of contacts and should re-render whenever a contact changes. If we were writing the component using a JavaScript framework, we would either have to put our data inside special objects that the framework provides so that it can track changes, use a dirty-checking mechanism to periodically find what we need to change, or render everything to an in-memory representation of the DOM and render any changes to the actual DOM. The ClojureScript community has adopted the last method, but the story is actually better in ClojureScript, because we can be selective about which components we even need to render to the virtual DOM, saving additional CPU cycles.

Figure 1.4: Optimizing a UI with immutable data structures

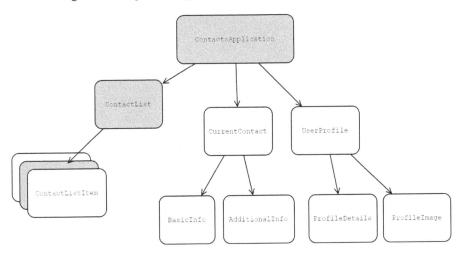

In this example, whenever a contact is changed, we replace the map modeling that contact entirely. When it comes time to render to the virtual DOM, the ContactList is going to re-render, because the contacts list is now a new object entirely. Of the ContactListItem components, only the one that that reflects the contact we edited is going to re-render. The rest of the ContactListItems can quickly see that their underlying data has not changed, so there is no work to be done. Furthermore, none of the other portions of the application need to render either. While this optimization may sound rather minor, we will see later that it can have a dramatic effect on the performance of an application.

Modernizing Async

JavaScript has now adopted `async/await` - which is a first-class syntax for dealing with promise-like objects - as the preferred way to achieve asynchronous programming. You will still find raw promises, callbacks, and generators in some places, but `async/await` has become more or less universal.

ClojureScript, on the other hand, has embraced a style of asynchronous programming called CSP, or *Communicating Sequential Processes*. This is the same style of async that has proven so effective in the Go programming language. Using CSP, we do not deal directly with promises or callbacks. Instead, we think about values and passing them around via *channels*. For now, you can think of channels as streams or promises that can deliver more than one value. Additionally, we can write asynchronous code that looks like synchronous code, tremendously reducing the cognitive load of writing async code. Performing requests or getting input sequentially or in parallel are both natural. Some ClojureScript developers consider async the single most important advantage that ClojureScript has over JavaScript. We will have to judge for ourselves when we see it in action later in this book, but know that it enables a completely new way of thinking about async.

Modularizing Design

In the early days of JavaScript, we probably wrote a single JavaScript file that we included in every page of a website that covered all of the scripting that we needed on the site. If the file got too big or different pages had entirely different requirements, we probably wrote several JavaScript files and included them on the applicable pages. Maybe eventually we heard about the "Module Pattern" or "Revealing Module Pattern" and separated our code into narrowly focused modules with one file per module. Now we had to worry about loading every file in the correct order on the page so that we would not try to reference a module that did not yet exist. At this point, we probably heard talk of module loaders that could asynchronously load only the modules we needed and figure out the correct order to load them in - they could even concatenate all of our modules into a single file for deployment. The problem was that there were once again several competing standards for module loading - AMD, CommonJS, and ES2015. Even today, finding the right tooling to integrate modules into our process can be painful, and every team needs at least one Webpack expert who is aware of the gotchas of bundling code for deployment.

ClojureScript, on the other hand, has the advantage of being a compiled language and can provide its own module system with no additional complexity. ClojureScript uses *namespaces*, which are named collections of functions and data, to organize code. Loading order, preventing circular dependencies, and compiling to a single asset for production are all part of the standard compiler toolchain. As an added benefit, the ClojureScript compiler outputs Google Closure modules, which it then passes off to the Google Closure compiler for additional optimization, including elimination of dead code paths. Having a good module system at the language level tremendously simplifies the setup process of any new project.

Quick Review

- Which of the following projects would be a good fit for ClojureScript?
    - single-page app such as a dashboard for a CMS
    - adding animations to a static page
    - web-based game with complex asynchronous user interactions
    - CPU-intensive number-crunching simulations

- Does ClojureScript use the same module systems as JavaScript (CommonJS, and ES2015)?

1.3 ClojureScript 101

Now that we have seen some of the advantages that ClojureScript can bring to front-end web development, let's take a step back and survey ClojureScript's distinct features. As with any technology that promises to bring significant improvement to the way we code, there will be new concepts. And as with any new concept, the first step towards mastery is familiarity. Let's get ready to explore what makes ClojureScript tick.

A Compile-to-JavaScript Language

In 2008, if we were to do any client-side web programming, the only viable option was JavaScript. Over the next few years, languages that compiled to JavaScript started to appear. These languages either cleaned up JavaScript's cruft or added some features that were not present in JavaScript itself. Some of these languages were modest in their approach, retaining much of the feel of JavaScript. Others were radical departures from JavaScript that fell into the category of research languages. ClojureScript made significant improvements to JavaScript while sustaining the community support required of a language intended for professional use.

In addition to the other languages that compile to JavaScript, we must consider the fact that many of us are compiling newer versions of JavaScript to older versions so that we can take advantage of language features that make JavaScript more productive and enjoyable before they are supported by the major browsers. Starting with the ES2015 standard, JavaScript has accumulated many of the best ideas from more recent programming languages, but since new features are always introduced quicker than browsers can adopt them, we are perpetually at least a year away from using "Modern JavaScript", and we must unfortunately treat JavaScript itself as a compile-to-js language! In many fields, this sort of complexity would be considered insanity, but in web development, this is the status quo. In contrast to the constant flux of JavaScript, ClojureScript has remained remarkably stable as a language, with much of the innovation happening in libraries rather than the language itself.

As with any compile-to-js language, the fact that ClojureScript exists is a statement that JavaScript is not sufficient. CoffeeScript addressed JavaScript's verbose and inconsistent syntax (it was written in just over a week, after all). TypeScript, Dart, and PureScript address it's lack of a type system, enabling developers to better reason about their code. JavaScript itself addresses the age of the language, bringing more modern features while maintaining some semblance to previous versions and providing an easy path to migrate old JavaScript applications. ClojureScript brings a simpler syntax, an arsenal of data structures that rule out a whole class of bugs, a better paradigm for asynchronous programming, and excellent integration with one of the most popular UI frameworks (React). In short, ClojureScript attempts to be a better general-purpose front-end language than JavaScript; and the larger the application, the more its benefits will be evident.

A Simple Language

JavaScript is a chameleon language. Not only is it possible to write code in imperative, object-oriented, or functional style; it is possible to mix all of these styles in the same codebase. Even if we consider a task as simple as iterating over an array, there are quite a few methods to accomplish this, all of them fairly idiomatic in JavaScript. If we are most comfortable with the imperative style, we could use a `for` loop and manually access each element of the array. On the other hand, we could use the `Array.prototype.forEach()` function (provided we do not have to worry about supporting old browsers). Finally, if we were already using *lodash* on a project, we could use one of its helper functions. Each of these methods are demonstrated below, and they should look familiar to most JavaScript programmers.

```
Listing 1.1: Iterating over an array in JavaScript

const numbers = [4, 8, 15, 16, 23, 42];

for (let num of numbers) {                               ①
  console.log(`The number is ${num}`);
}

numbers.forEach(                                         ②
  (num) => console.log(`The number is ${num}`)
);

const printNum = (num) => {                              ③
  console.log(`The number is ${num}`);
};
_.each(numbers, printNum);
```

① Imperative

② Object-oriented

③ Functional

Perhaps more problematic than allowing several styles of programming to coexist in the same codebase is JavaScript's "bad parts" - the quirks that are the subject of so many technical interview questions. When a developer first learns JavaScript, there are a number of pitfalls that she must learn to avoid. Somehow, we have learned to live with all of the additional complexity laid upon us by JavaScript because we have not had the luxury of choosing a simpler language. Consider this partial list of some of JavaScripts quirks and think whether we would be better off adopting a language without so many gotchas:

- variable hoisting
- several ways to set `this`
- `=` vs `==`
- the `void` operator
- `'ba' + + 'n' + 'a' + 's'`
- What does `xs.push(x)` return? What about `xs.concat([x])`?

When we consider all of JavaScript's complexity, we can see that we must code very cautiously or risk being bitten by one of these quirks. For some simple applications, we may be able to live with this, but as our codebases grow, the value of a simpler language becomes more and more apparent. Maintaining a consistent codebase without loads of unnecessary complexity takes a great deal of skill and discipline. While there are a lot of expert JavaScript developers out there who do have the requisite skill and discipline, it does not change the fact that it is **hard** to write good JavaScript at the application level. Thankfully, ClojureScript is a simpler option - admittedly with a learning curve - but it is generally the things with a steeper learning curve that ultimately prove the most valuable.

Whereas we have seen that JavaScript promotes a wide variety of programming styles, ClojureScript is opinionated and is designed to make the functional style of programming easy. In fact, we will see that idiomatic ClojureScript looks a great deal like JavaScript written in the functional style, but with less ceremony. Below is an example of how you could iterate over a vector, which is similar to a JavaScript array.

Listing 1.2: Iterating over a vector in ClojureScript

```
(def numbers [4, 8, 15, 16, 23, 42])

(doseq [n numbers]
  (println "The number is" n))
```

Like the JavaScript code, this defines a sequence of numbers then logs a statement to the console for each of the numbers. It even looks pretty similar to the object-oriented version with the exception that doseq is not attached to a particular object prototype. However, this - along with some minor variations - is how you can expect it to look when you need to iterate over a collection in ClojureScript. Always.

A Powerful Language

One of the spectrums in programming languages is that of how much functionality to include by default. At one extreme is assembly, which translates directly into CPU instructions and has no "standard library", and at the other end is highly-specialized languages that include everything necessary to accomplish most any given task in their problem domain. When it comes to front-end web programming languages, JavaScript leans more towards the spartan end of the spectrum, and ClojureScript leans toward the "batteries included" end, providing higher level tools by default. Between its variety of core data structures and an extensive collection API, macros that allow for extension of the language itself, and the entire Google Closure Library available by default, ClojureScript provides more powerful tools for constructing applications.

Figure 1.5: Spectrum of programming languages

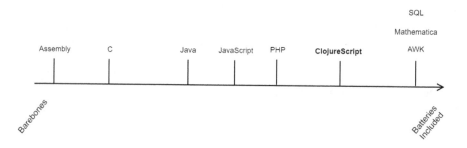

The abstractions provided by ClojureScript are higher-level than those provided by JavaScript, enabling most code to be written more concisely and descriptively. While JavaScript provides numbers, strings, arrays, objects, and simple control structures, ClojureScript provides similar primitives as well as keywords, lists, vectors, sets, maps, protocols, records, and multimethods. Don't worry if you have no idea what any of these things are - after all, that is what this book is all about! While the additional tools mean that there are more things to learn, it also means that there are fewer occasions to learn a new library or write our own data structures and generic algorithms.

A Functional Language

Love it or hate it, ClojureScript embraces the concept of functional programming. If "functional programming" sounds like an intimidating, academic topic, do not fear - we'll see that most of the functional programming concepts should be at least somewhat familiar for those of us who work with JavaScript on a regular basis. This should not be surprising, since JavaScript was heavily influenced by Scheme (a functional Lisp, just like ClojureScript). Functional programming is one of the three main styles of programming supported by JavaScript, with an emphasis on using functions in the mathematical sense of a mapping of some input value to some output value.

Figure 1.6: Comparison of JavaScript programming paradigms

Paradigm	Description	Key Concepts
Imperative	Describes a program as a sequence of statements that may modify the program state, receive input, or produce output.	Variables, loops, assignment, statements, subroutines
Object-Oriented	Models the real world in terms of objects, their behaviors, and their interactions with each other.	Objects, classes or prototypes, methods, messages, object graphs
Functional	Describes a program as a transformation of some input value to some output value using functions that can be composed.	Pure functions, immutable values, higher-order functions

While functional programming in JavaScript is gaining momentum, the majority of code that we are likely to find is either imperative or object-oriented. Without getting too far into the nitty-gritty of functional programming at this point, we can say that ClojureScript focuses on building programs by assembling small functions together that take some data and return some new data without modifying the arguments that were passed in or any global state.

One key feature of writing functions this way is that when you call a function with the same arguments, you always get the same result. While this may seem like an unimportant property for a function, it makes testing and debugging much easier. If most of a program is written as pure functions, tests can be written without any set-up. Contrast this with the typical way that object-oriented systems are tested: a number of objects must be constructed and put in to just the right state before every test, or the test will not run correctly.

Quick Review

- Is the ClojureScript language stable? Why or why not?
- List at least 3 ways in which ClojureScript improves upon JavaScript
- What is the difference between *simplicity* and *familiarity*? What are some aspects of JavaScript that are not simple?
- Does ClojureScript or JavaScript operate at a higher level of abstraction?
- Of the 3 styles of programming that are common in JavaScript (imperative, object-oriented, and functional), which is encouraged by ClojureScript?

1.4   Summary

ClojureScript is an incredible useful language, particularly for front-end web development. It shares many of JavaScript's functional programming concepts, but it is both a simpler and more productive language. ClojureScript may appear foreign with all its parentheses, but under the parenthesis-packed surface, it shares much in common with JavaScript. We should now understand:

- What ClojureScript is and what sets it apart from JavaScript
- What types of apps are the best fit for ClojureScript

Lesson 2

ClojureScript in the JavaScript Ecosystem

Now that we have a good idea of what ClojureScript is and how to use it, we will continue to pull back the curtain to get a clearer picture of how this curious language fits into its environment - the JavaScript ecosystem. While the language is quite different from JavaScript, it maintains a symbiotic relationship to its JavaScript host. JavaScript needs ClojureScript, and ClojureScript needs JavaScript. Let's explore this interesting symbiosis.

In this lesson:

- What problems in JavaScript does ClojureScript try to solve?
- How using a compiled language helps in application development
- Why is JavaScript an ideal platform for ClojureScript?

2.1 Why JavaScript Needs Clojure

Having seen ClojureScript's sweet spots, it should be apparent that there are some gains that it promises. Still, can we get a similar advantage from JavaScript itself without having to learn a new language? Also, does ClojureScript really give us that much additional leverage in our daily development tasks? ClojureScript may not be the best tool for trivial tasks, but for anything more complex, JavaScript does in fact *need* a language like Clojure to enable more productive and enjoyable development.

Clojure(Script)

λ

You may have noticed several times where I have used the terms "Clojure" and "ClojureScript" interchangeably. Clojure as a language has implementations that compile to both Java bytecode and to JavaScript. Some of the potential confusion comes from the fact that "Clojure" refers to both the language and its Java implementation. I will follow the general pattern of the Clojure community of using the two terms interchangeably when talking about the language itself and using "ClojureScript" when discussing the ecosystem or language features that are specific to ClojureScript.

Higher Level Language

ClojureScript operates with higher-level constructs than JavaScript. In JavaScript, we work largely with variables, loops, conditional branching structures, objects and arrays. In ClojureScript, we work with expressions, collections, sequences, and transformations. The journey from lower-level concepts to higher-level ones is the way that we gain productivity.

Figure 2.1: Features defining each level of abstraction

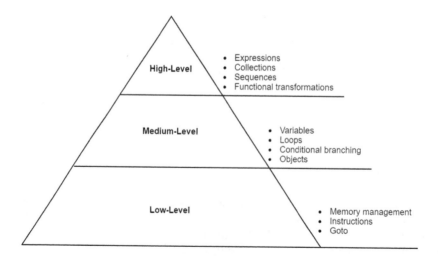

When we work at a higher level, a couple of interesting things happen. First, it takes less code to accomplish a given task, which helps with both initial development and debugging/maintenance. Second, it causes the structure of the code more closely resemble the problem domain, making it clearer for us to understand when we come back to it. Third, it frees us to think more about the problems of the domain rather than technical implementation issues. All of these factors can enable huge productivity boosts, both in the initial development and maintenance phases of an application.

When we write less code to accomplish a given task, there are a couple of benefits. First, it almost goes without saying that it is quicker to write a little code than it is a lot of code. Even though more time is usually spent designing and planning code than actually writing it, we do not want to be hampered by how many keystrokes it takes to turn our ideas into code. Second, fewer lines of code means fewer bugs. The developer who would rather spend her time fixing bugs than writing new features is either a rarity or nonexistent. The terseness of a high-level language like ClojureScript means that there are fewer places for bugs to hide, and in turn, we can spend more time making forward progress.

Less Boilerplate

I cannot count the times that I have had a simple task that I wanted to accomplish with JavaScript - say, performing a deep clone of an object - but had to do a Google search to remember how to do it either using vanilla JavaScript or the libraries that I had available. Usually, I would end up on some StackOverflow thread that I had already visited numerous times and copying and pasting the example into yet another "utils" file in yet another project. Libraries such as *lodash* (and *jQuery* for you history buffs out there) help compensate for JavaScript's lack of common utilities, but they do not solve the problem that one must look beyond the language itself to get the functionality of a robust standard library.

The problem of needing to pull in third-party libraries for most tasks is uniquely problematic for the browser because every additional library adds time to the page load. Compound this issue with the fact that most web apps at least need to consider mobile clients with slow networks. When every byte counts, as it does on the web, we are continually faced with the question of whether to include another library for limited utility or write the functions that we need from scratch.

Finally, JavaScript developers must continually face the reality of browser compatibility issues. The available options are to target the lowest common denominator of the browser that you would like to support (and miss out on the language features that improve developer productivity), pull in libraries (and add substantial page size), or implement browser-detection and write the browser-specific portions from scratch (and face the additional complexity that comes with browser hacks). The choices do not sound very attractive, and we should not have to make a trade-off between developer productivity, performance, and complexity. In order to solve the browser compatibility problem without sacrificing any of these things, we need to look outside JavaScript itself.

ClojureScript, on the other hand, has a rich set of data structures and functions for working with collections, strings, math, state management, JavaScript interoperability, and more. Additionally, ClojureScript is built on top of Google's Closure (with an "s", not a "j") library, putting the same tools that power applications like Gmail and Google Docs at your finger-tips. With so many tools at our disposal, we'll see that the amount of utility code that we need to write is minimal. Finally, ClojureScript compiles down to a widely-supported sub-set of JavaScript, making browser compatibility much less of an issue. ClojureScript takes the focus off the "plumbing", allowing us to focus more on the interesting problems of the domain in which we are working.

Immutable Data by Default

We have already looked at immutable data as one of the fundamental concepts of functional programming. While much of the JavaScript community is starting to recognize the value of immutable data, working with immutable data in JavaScript is still not native and can feel somewhat cumbersome. Libraries like *immer* and *Immutable.js* allow us to get the benefits of immutable data from JavaScript, but once again, the language currently has no native support.

In ClojureScript, however, the situation is reversed. All of the default data structures are immutable, and we have to go out of our way to work with mutable objects. This is one area where ClojureScript is very opinionated, but the style of programming that it promotes is one that will lead to fewer bugs and - as we have already seen - optimized user interfaces. Once we have become accustomed to using ClojureScript's data structures, returning to mutable objects and arrays will feel unusual - even dangerous.

Compiler Optimized

One advantage that a compiled language has is that it can implement optimizations in the JavaScript code that it produces. It is rare for a high-level language to match either the speed, resource usage, or compiled code size of a lower-level language. ClojureScript, however, can often produce JavaScript that runs as fast as hand-written JavaScript. Its im-mutable data structures do usually consume more memory and are slower than raw objects and arrays, but the UI optimizations afforded by these data structures can make Clojure-Script interfaces *effectively faster* than a corresponding JavaScript interface.

One metric that matters a great deal to JavaScript programmers is code size. When work-ing in a server-side environment, the code size is usually not a concern - the code is read from disk and immediately read into memory. However, with front-end JavaScript appli-cations, the code usually must be read over the internet, potentially over a low-bandwidth mobile network. In this situation, every byte counts, and we are used to laboring over our code and trying to make it as small as possible, even at the cost of clarity. Minification helps tremendously, but we still must be mindful about including more libraries. Often, the benefit added by a library is offset by the kilobytes that it adds to page load time.

One of the most interesting features of the ClojureScript compiler is that it produces Google Closure modules, and it then makes use of the Closure Compiler to optimize the JavaScript. Since the ClojureScript compiler guarantees that the JavaScript it produces is valid Google Closure modules, we can safely make use of the Closure Compiler's most aggressive optimizations when preparing production assets. In addition to the typical removal of whitespace and renaming variables, the Closure Compiler will analyze an entire codebase and remove any code paths that can never be called. Effectively, this means that we can pull in a large library, and if we use only a couple of functions from this library, only those functions and the functions they call are included in our codebase. In an environment where code size is so critical, this is clearly a significant advantage.

Quick Review

- Can you think of any pieces of code that you find yourself writing for almost every JavaScript project? Would any of these be solved by a more complete standard library?
- What is the advantage of working in a language that compiles to JavaScript Can you think of any disadvantages?

2.2 Why Clojure needs JavaScript

As useful as the Clojure language is, it needs JavaScript. The most significant things that JavaScript enable for the Clojure language are client-side web development, the rich ecosystem of libraries and technologies, and a much lighter-weight platform with a smaller footprint than the Java Virtual Machine. That said, ClojureScript compiles to JavaScript, so it runs where JavaScript does, including the client, server, desktop, and Internet of Things (IoT) devices.

Client-Side Development

Clojure was originally a server-side language. It was certainly possible to write desktop GUIs using Swing or another Java UI toolkit, but the vast majority of Clojure was written for the server. Clojure is excellent as a server-side programming language, but as we have discussed, it brings some significant advantages to UI development as well. With the advent of ClojureScript, Clojure is now a general-purpose language that can be used for almost any application - on the server or client. As Rich Hickey stated when he announced ClojureScript, "Clojure *rocks*, and JavaScript *reaches*."

Additionally, with technologies like Electron and NW.js, we have the option of writing desktop applications in JavaScript as well; and since ClojureScript compiles to JavaScript, we can take advantage of the same technologies to write desktop applications in ClojureScript as well. While Clojure itself enables developers to write Java GUI applications, many developers prefer the lighter-weight style afforded by these JavaScript UI technologies.

ClojureScript on the Desktop

λ

The developers of the LightTable editor - one of the most popular editors supporting the Clojure language - opted to build their UI using ClojureScript and deploy inside Electron. This enabled them to build an incredibly flexible, customizable UI without the complexity of a traditional desktop UI.

Finally, there are a few technologies that allow JavaScript applications to run as mobile apps. React Native is gaining a lot of traction in this area, making it an excellent choice for ClojureScript, since most ClojureScript UIs are built on React as a platform. While this area of JavaScript mobile native apps is relatively new territory, it is showing a lot of promise. The next generation of mobile apps may be predominantly JavaScript apps, which means that ClojureScript will be a first-class citizen for mobile clients as well.

JavaScript Ecosystem

JavaScript is more than just a language - it is a community that has opinions on best practices, libraries, tooling, and development process. It is in this community that ClojureScript lives. While we as ClojureScript developers benefit from the vast number of JavaScript libraries available, the more significant benefit provided by JavaScript is its community. We can learn from the collective experience of the community what is the good, the bad, and the ugly of front-end development. The relationship between JavaScript and Clojure is truly symbiotic, with both communities benefitting from the ideas and insights of the other.

While we have seen that ClojureScript is a very practical and useful language, let's face it - it is easy for a functional programming language to lose touch with the concerns of working programmers. Theoretical languages are useful, and most useful programming language features started out as research projects, but theoretical purity is not our top concern when writing web apps. Get-it-done-ability is a much higher priority, and from its inception, JavaScript has been about getting things done as straightforwardly as possible. Being a citizen of the JavaScript community helps ClojureScript stay focused on pragmatic concerns that help us build better web applications.

Smaller Footprint

The JVM is an excellent platform for developing high-performance cross-platform applications. It is not so excellent when it comes to running in resource-constrained environments or scripting. While the slogan "Write once, run anywhere" was used by Sun Microsystems to promote Java, it is ironically JavaScript that has become a "universal" runtime. From the browser to the server to the Raspberry Pi and embedded devices, JavaScript will run just about anywhere. Running Java on something like a Raspberry Pi, on the other hand, is a practical impossibility. ClojureScript is a great option for writing applications where Java is too much bloat. Its ability to run on almost any device is another aspect of JavaScript's "reach" that we can take advantage of from ClojureScript.

Scripting is another area where Java is fairly weak. Whether as a scripting language embedded in a larger application or as a system shell scripting language, Java is too large and complex, and the startup time of the JVM makes it impractical for short-lived programs like simple scripts. JavaScript is a great scripting language. Node.js allows us to write system scripts as well as web servers.

Quick Review

- What is the most common platform for ClojureScript - web, desktop, mobile, or IoT devices? Can it be used outside this platform?
- How well does ClojureScript interoperate with existing JavaScript tools and libraries?

2.3 Summary

In this lesson, we have explored the relationship of ClojureScript to its host, JavaScript. We have learned:

- How ClojureScript improves on JavaScript's development experience
- How JavaScript's lightweight and ubiquitous runtime allows us to write ClojureScript for practically any platform.
- Why client-side web development is a great fit for ClojureScript.

Now that we have a good understanding of both what ClojureScript is and how it is related to the JavaScript platform, we are ready to see the language in action. In the next section, we will work through the process of writing a ClojureScript application, learning the common tools and practices as we go.

Lesson 3

Building Blocks

With an understanding of what ClojureScript is and why it matters, we will begin our journey with an overview of the basics of the language. One of the biggest hurdles in learning an unfamiliar language is understanding the syntax. While there is a great deal of crossover between languages at the conceptual level, the way that those concepts are expressed can be quite different. Over the next two lessons, we will hone in on the foundational skill of reading ClojureScript code. Even though the syntax is so simple compared to JavaScript, it looks very unusual to most programmers who have cut their teeth on C-like languages (including JavaScript). The skill of reading ClojureScript will go a long way towards being able to read the longer code samples in the coming lessons with ease.

In this lesson:

- Learn the basics of ClojureScript's syntax
- Understand the purpose of all the parentheses
- Survey the core data types that are built in to the language

---

First, in this lesson, we will survey the most common syntactic elements of the language, then in the next lesson we will take a look at how ClojureScript code is actually evaluated. Understanding the evaluation model will help us both understand the code we read and write code that does exactly what we expect it to. ClojureScript is a very small language - much smaller than JavaScript - so it is very simple to understand. Despite the foreign syntax, we can reach a point of familiarity surprisingly quickly due to the relatively few syntactic elements of the language.

3.1   Parens, Parens Everywhere!

As we have seen in the examples of the previous lessons, ClojureScript code is replete with parentheses. For many, this single aspect of the language is what makes it seem intimidating. Parentheses are the primary symbols used for delineating one piece of code from another. Consider that JavaScript and other languages in the C family use both parentheses and curly brackets - parentheses to indicate parameters to a function and to specify the order of operations and curly brackets to set apart blocks of related statements. Once we get over the initial "paren shock", ClojureScript begins to look simple, even elegant.

Expressions and Function Evaluation

Parentheses are used in ClojureScript to indicate expressions to be evaluated. We will look much deeper into these so called s-expressions in the next lesson, but they are so critical that we must at least mention them here. At a high level, every ClojureScript program has basically the following form:

Listing 3.1: ClojureScript function expression

```
(some-function arg1 arg2 ...)
```

Whenever there is an open parenthesis, the next thing that the compiler expects is something that can be called - usually a function. Everything else until the next closing parenthesis is expected to be an argument.

Figure 3.1: A Simple Expression

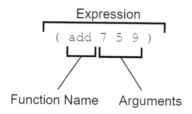

If we were to write the same general structure in JavaScript, it would look something like the following:

Listing 3.2: JavaScript function expression

```
someFunction(arg1, arg2, ...);
```

Both the ClojureScript and JavaScript code indicate that there is some function that should be called with some number or arguments. While the JavaScript code indicates a function call by putting the name of the function first, followed by some arguments enclosed in parentheses, ClojureScript indicates the same thing by enclosing both the function name and its arguments within a set of parentheses.

3.2 Core Data Types

ClojureScript has all of the primitive data types that we would expect from any programming language: numbers, strings, booleans, and the like. We refer to these simple values as scalars. Additionally, the language has a variety of useful *collection* types as well - think arrays and objects from JavaScript. These collections are so frequently used that there is special syntax for representing them. Before diving into each of the data types, it bears enumerating a complete list of data types for reference. The following table lists the types that have a literal syntactic representation, along with a brief description and an example of how it is expressed in code.

ClojureScript Data Literals

Data Type	Description	Example
Number	Integer or floating point numbers	`17.4`
String	Textual data	`"Today is the first day ... "`
Character	Textual data	`\a`
Boolean	Logical true/false	`true`
Keyword	Lightweight identifiers	`:role`
Symbol	Identifiers that are extensively used internal to ClojureScript	`'cljs-is-awesome`
List	Ordered collection supporting efficient traversal	`'(1 3 5 7 9)`
Vector	Ordered collection supporting efficient access by index	`[0 2 4 6 8]`
Map	Unordered collection associating unique keys to values	`{:name "Kayleigh", :age 29}`
Set	Unordered collection of unique values	`#{true "ubiquity" 9.2}`
nil	The empty value	`nil`
Object	JavaScript object - used for interop	`#js {"isJs" true, "isImmutable" false}`
Array	JavaScript array - user for interop	`#js ["Lions" "Tigers" "Bears"]`

We will now look at each data type in turn and see a few examples of its usage so that we can identify the various elements in any given piece of ClojureScript code.

Numbers

ClojureScript uses JavaScript's Number primitive, so it can support exactly the same integer and floating point numbers that JavaScript does. Below are examples of the different formats that ClojureScript recognizes as valid numbers.

Listing 3.3: Numbers

```
32                                    ①

012                                   ②

0xbeef                                ③

0.6                                   ④

1.719493e3                            ⑤

-0.12e-4                              ⑥
```

① Decimal integer
② Octal integer starts with a leading zero
③ Hexadecimal integer starts with leading `0x`
④ Float
⑤ Float with an exponent
⑥ Float with a sign and exponent with a sign

Strings

Strings, like numbers, use JavaScript primitives. However, ClojureScript's string syntax is more restricted than JavaScript's. Notably, strings *must* be contained in double quotes, since ClojureScript uses single quotes for other purposes. Double quotes and other special characters are escaped with a backslash.

Listing 3.4: Strings

```
"Quick! Brown foxes!"                 ①

\a                                    ②

"Column 1\tColumn 2"                  ③
```

```
"foo
bar"                                                    ④
```

① Simple string
② Single character strings can be represented by the character proceeded by a backslash
③ String with special character
④ Strings can span multiple lines

Booleans

ClojureScript also uses JavaScript booleans. Since the only possible options for a boolean are `true` or `false`, we will forego an extended example.

Keywords

We now encounter a data type that does not have a JavaScript equivalent. A keyword is represented by a name preceded by a colon. Keywords evaluate to themselves, and two keywords with the same name are considered equal. One interesting property of keywords is that they can be used as a function. When used as a function, the keyword expects a map as an argument and it will return the value in the map for which it is the key. When a keyword begins with two colons, the current namespace will be prepended to the keyword.

Listing 3.5: Keywords

```
:a-keyword                                              ①

::namespaced-keyword                                    ②

:explicit-ns/keyword                                    ③

{:name "Bill", :type "admin"}                           ④

(:type user)                                            ⑤
```

① Imperative
② Simple keyword
③ With implicit namespace - shorthand for `:cljs.user/namespaced-keyword`
④ With explicit namespace
⑤ Used as keys in a map
⑥ Used as a function to perform a map lookup

Symbols

Symbols are an interesting data type because they are closely linked to the Lisp family of programming languages from which ClojureScript is derived. Symbols are names that usually evaluate to some other object. We have seen symbols in almost every example without even thinking about it.

```
Listing 3.6: Symbols

my-function                                            ①

first                                                  ②
```

① Symbol referring to a user-defined variable
② Symbol referring to a built-in function

Of ClojureScript's data types, symbols are probably the most difficult to comprehend. They have a very meta quality about them, and they do not directly correspond to another familiar concept. Since they are not used very commonly in application code, we will not revisit symbols to the depth that we will with the other data types.

Lists

Lists are comprised of a number of expressions inside parentheses. However, remember that s-expressions are also written the same way. For this reason, we designate a list that should not be evaluated as an s-expression by placing a quote before it. It is interesting to note that ClojureScript code is actually made up of lists.

```
Listing 3.7: Lists

(+ 1 2 3 4)                                            ①

'(+ 1 2 3 4)                                           ②

'(some data)                                           ③

'()                                                    ④
```

① A list that is interpreted as an expression and evaluated
② Prevent evaluation of a list by starting it with a single quote
③ Lists can contain any ClojureScript data type
④ An empty list

Vectors

Vectors are comprised of a number of expressions contained inside square brackets. When ClojureScript encounters a vector, it will interpret it as a data structure and will not try to evaluate it as a function call. They are used in a similar manner to JavaScript arrays and are the most common data structure in ClojureScript. Vectors are also used to list the arguments that a function takes.

```
Listing 3.8: Vectors

[]                                          ①

["Alice" "Bob" "Carol"]                     ②

(defn say-hello [name]                      ③
  (println "Hello," name))
```

① An empty vector
② A vector used to define a collection of strings
③ A vector used to declare a function's argument list

Maps

Maps are collections similar to a JavaScript object. They associate unique keys with values and can subsequently be used to lookup values by key. The syntax for a map is even similar to that of a JavaScript object, since it consists of a number of key-value pairs inside curly brackets. Either commas or newlines are often used to separate pairs. Commas are whitespace in ClojureScript, and we will frequently find them omitted.

```
Listing 3.9: Maps

①
{}                                          ①

{"product" "Self-Sealing Stem Bolt"        ②
 "sku" "DS9-SB09"
 "stock" 212}

{:name "Jorge", :age 29}                    ③
```

① An empty map
② A map using strings as keys
③ A map using keywords as keys

Sets

Sets are an unordered collection of unique elements. They are often used when we want to avoid duplicates or need to quickly determine whether an element is in a collection. Sets are declared with any number of elements contained inside curly brackets that are prefixed with a pound sign.

Listing 3.10: Sets

```
#{}                                                      ①

#{"admin" "editor" "author" "subscriber"}               ②
```
---

① An empty set
② A set with several unique strings

Of the data structures that have their own syntax, sets are probably the least often used. It is still important to be able to recognize them, since at first glance they look quite similar to a map.

Nil

Nil is the empty value and is always written as `nil`. It is the equivalent of `null` in JavaScript and acts the same as `false` when used as a boolean.

The JavaScript interop forms will be covered in a later lesson, so we will defer discussion until that point.

Quick Review

- Which collection type is most similar to a JavaScript object?
- Which collection type is most similar to a JavaScript array?
- Google a ClojureScript library in a domain that is interesting to you, and look over the source code. Can you identify most of the syntactic elements?

3.3   Summary

In this lesson, we got our first real taste of ClojureScript code, surveying the basic structure and core data types of the language. We also took a first look into expressions, the core building block of ClojureScript. In fact, expressions are so critical that the entire next lesson will be devoted to them. We now know about:

- How parentheses are used to evaluate functions
- The scalar data types: number, string, boolean, keyword, and symbol
- The collection data types: list, vector, map, and set
- The empty value: `nil`

Lesson 4

Expressions and Evaluation

As we briefly touched on in the previous lesson, the concept of an *expression* is at the core of ClojureScript code. For programmers coming from a language like JavaScript, thinking in terms of expressions requires a shift in perspective, but like most aspects of ClojureScript, we will find that programming with expressions is quite simple once we get used to it.

In this lesson:

- Learn about s-expressions and identify them
- Define the difference between a statement and an expression
- Understand ClojureScript's model of evaluation

4.1 Laying the Foundation with S-Expressions

Most ClojureScript code is represented with a construct called an s-expression. S-expression is short for "symbolic expression", and the term comes from the old Lisp family of languages that inspired Clojure.

Structuring an S-Expression

An s-expression can take two forms:

1. A primitive value, such as 12, true, or "tacos"
2. A parenthesized list containing zero or more expressions separated by whitespace: (expression*)

With just these two forms, we have defined most of the ClojureScript's syntax. There is no special syntax for blocks, loops, function calls, conditionals, or almost any other part of the language. As we will discuss shortly, ClojureScript departs from most Lisps in that it adds a few additional syntactic elements to make the code more readable, but the simple s-expression is by far the most basic and prevalent syntactic construct. We will now turn to several examples of s-expressions.

Listing 4.1: S-expressions

```
5                                                          ①
;; 5

+                                                          ②
;; #object[cljs$core$_PLUS_ ...]

()                                                         ③
;; ()

(+ 5 5)                                                    ④
;; 10

(take 5 (range))                                          ⑤
;; (0 1 2 3 4)

(map inc (take 5 (range)))
;; (1 2 3 4 5)

(mk-sandwich "Bacon" "Lettuce" "Tomato")          ⑥
;; WARNING: Use of undeclared Var cljs.user/mk-sandwich at line 1 <cljs repl>
;; #object[TypeError TypeError: Cannot read property 'call' of undefined]
```

① A primitive
② A function name
③ An empty s-expression
④ An s-expression consisting of other simple s-expressions
⑤ S-expressions can be nested
⑥ Just because an s-expression is syntactically valid does not guarantee that it will run

At this point, we can begin to see that all of the parentheses serve a purpose after all (even this author had his doubts at first). They provide a consistent and explicit structure for evaluating any code. While other programming languages generally have separate syntax for function calls, math and logic operations, conditionals, method calls, etc., there is only one syntactic construct in ClojureScript, with clearly defined rules for evaluation. We will walk through the rules for how an s-expression is evaluated, but first, we will take a brief detour to discuss the emphasis on *evaluation of expressions* rather than *execution of statements*.

> **Note**
>
> Using a language based on s-expressions means that there is no such thing as operator precedence. In JavaScript, we must recall that * has higher precedence than +, that && has higher precedence than OR, and that ! has a higher precedence than any of the other operators listed here. In ClojureScript, we do not need a chart because precedence is explicit in the syntax of the language itself. For instance, there is no question about the meaning of the expression (and x (or y z)), and it is also clear that (or (and x y) z) means something else entirely. What at first looked like weird syntax is proving to be quite useful!

Understanding Expressions

Being a functional programming language, ClojureScript emphasizes *expressions* rather than statements. That is, everything in ClojureScript *evaluates* to some concrete value. Whereas JavaScript allows statements that do not yield a value and functions that do not return anything (rather, that return undefined, every piece of ClojureScript code - from a simple number to an entire program - is evaluated to produce some value.

Let us consider some JavaScript statements that are not expressions and do not return anything:

Listing 4.2: JavaScript Statements

```javascript
const x = 5;

if (10 % 2 === 0) {
  evenOrOdd = "Even";
}

for (let i = 0; i < 10; i++) {
  console.log("Looping!");
}
```

In each of these examples, we see a piece of code that performs some computation, but it does not give a specific result. One way to think about it is that if we put a const foo = before any of these statements, it would lead to a syntax error, as in the following example:

Listing 4.3: Statements are not expressions

```
const foo = if (10 % 2 === 0) {
    evenOrOdd = "Even";
}
// Uncaught SyntaxError: Unexpected token if
```

In ClojureScript, on the other hand, there are no statements, only expressions, so absolutely everything has a value (even if that value is nil). This simplifies things quite a bit, as we do not have to divide the language into expressions, which evaluate to some value, and statements, which are executed, not evaluated. *Everything* has a value. Below are the ClojureScript equivalents of the JavaScript statements that we just considered.

Listing 4.4: ClojureScript expressions

```
(def x 5)
;; #'user/x                                        ①

(if (even? 10) "Even" "Odd")
;; "Even"                                          ②

(doseq [i (range 5)]
  (println "Looping!"))
;; Looping!
;; Looping!
;; Looping!
;; Looping!
;; Looping!
;; nil                                             ③
```

① Defining a var evaluates to the var itself
② An if expression evaluates to the appropriate branch
③ doseq evaluates to nil

Imagine building a contact list app, and you would like to display the number of users missing phone numbers somewhere in the UI. A typical way to do this in JavaScript would be to create a counter variable then loop through the list of users, incrementing the counter if the phone number was missing. Finally, the contents of some element would be updated with the value of the counter.

Listing 4.5: Statement-oriented JavaScript code

```
let counter = 0;
const users = [
  /* ... */
];
```

```
for (let user of users) {
  if (isMissingPhone(user)) {
    counter++;
  }
}

someElem.innerHTML = counter;
```

This code reads like an instruction manual for the computer to follow - a list of things to execute in order to accomplish some task. When programming with expressions, on the other hand, we think about the data that we have and how we can derive from it the value that we are interested in. In this case, we have a list of users, and we are interested in the number of users missing phone numbers. With the expression-oriented approach, we would probably do something like the following, which creates a filtered list of users - containing only those missing a phone number - and then gets the number of items in that filtered list.

Listing 4.6: Expression-oriented ClojureScript code

```
(set! (.-innerHTML someElem)
      (count
        (filter missing-phone? users)))
```

In addition to being shorter, this code draws a clearer connection between the data that we start with (a collection of `users`) and the data that we want (the count). Interestingly, the *entire* expression above evaluates to the number of users missing phone numbers.

We see that the expression-oriented code returns a value at the end. However, since each expression is composed of other expressions, each step in the process has some value. Now that we have a good understanding of what expressions are and how they differ from statements, we can dig into how ClojureScript *evaluates* (derives values) from expressions.

Quick Review

- For each of the following JavaScript code snippets, identify if it is an expression or a statement:

```
if (age === 16) {                    ①
  sweetSixteen = true;
}

console.log('Regardless');           ②

'happy birthday to you'              ③
  .split(" ")
  .map(_.capitalize)
  .join(" ");
```

Figure 4.1: Comparing Expressions and Statements

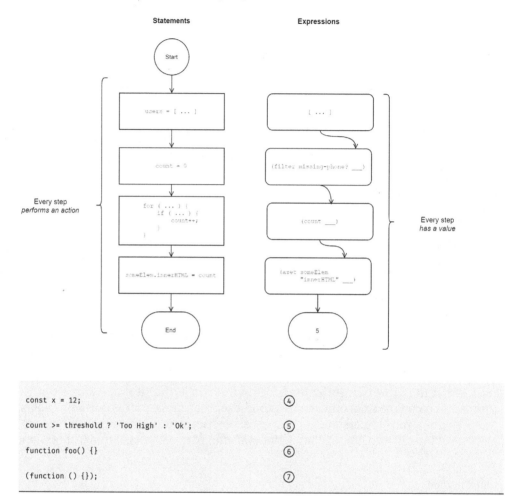

Answers: ① - Statement; ② - Statement; ③ - Expression; ④ - Statement; ⑤ - Expression; ⑥ - Statement; ⑦ - Expression

4.2 Evaluating ClojureScript Code

ClojureScript's rules for evaluating expressions are simple:

1. If the expression is a primitive element or data structure, its value *is* that element.

2. If the expression is a parenthesized list of expressions, the first expression is interpreted as a function and the rest of the expressions are interpreted as arguments.
3. Evaluate the inner expressions first and work outwards

As an example, we will look at the expression, `(map inc (take 5 (range)))`. This s-expression is a parenthesized list of expressions, so the first element, the symbol `map`, is interpreted as a function with 2 arguments: `inc` and `(take 5 (range))`.

Figure 4.2: Evaluating an expression: step 1

`inc` is a function that takes an integer and returns the next-higher number. ClojureScript can call this function directly so this argument does not need to be evaluated. However, the argument, `(take 5 (range))` must be evaluated so that its value can be passed back into the `map` expression. Remembering the rules of s-expressions, we can see the ClojureScript will interpret `take` as a function with `5` and `(range)` as its arguments.

Figure 4.3: Evaluating an expression: step 2

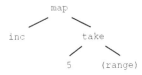

The original s-expression is almost ready to be evaluated, but first, we must evaluate the final inner s-expression, `(range)`. This s-expression has only a single expression inside it, `range`, so it will be interpreted as a function with no arguments.

Figure 4.4: Evaluating an expression: step 3

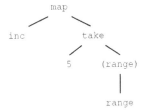

Finally, the expression will be evaluated "inside out", starting with the call to the range function and working outwards to the outermost s-expression.

Figure 4.5: Evaluating an expression: step 4

The call to range returned an *infinite* sequence of integers, starting with 0. We will get into how to work with infinite sequences later, but for now, we just need to understand that an infinite sequence is an object that can continue to produce as many values as we need. As this expression is evaluated, the infinite sequence is substituted in place of the original expression, (range), and the evaluation continues outwards.

Figure 4.6: Evaluating an expression: step 5

The next expression is interpreted as a call to the take function, with the arguments, 5 and an infinite sequence of numbers. The value of this expression is the sequence, (0 1 2 3 4), the first 5 element of the infinite sequence generated by (range). The call to take is replaced with this return value, and evaluation continues outwards again.

Figure 4.7: Evaluating an expression: step 6

(1 2 3 4 5)

Finally, the last step of the evaluation is performed, calling map with the arguments, inc and (0 1 2 3 4). This increments every element in the sequence, and returning the final value of the s-expression.

The rules of evaluating ClojureScript are simple enough that we could work out in a few steps how an expression is evaluated. The amazing thing about this is that no matter how large and involved the code that we are looking at, we can use the same process to read almost any piece of ClojureScript. Once the basic syntax is understood, most of what remains to learn is the vocabulary and common idioms.

4.3 Order of Operations

It may come as a surprise, but ClojureScript has no concept of operator prece-
dence.indexoperator precedence That is, there are no rules indicating that multiplication
should be performed before addition or any such thing. Instead of having a set of rules
that implicitly determine the order in which to evaluate an expression, we specify the order by how we nest s-expressions. For example, the following code multiplies 5 and 2 before
adding the result to 10:

Listing 4.7: Multiply then add

```
(+ 10 (* 5 2)) ; 20
```

On the other hand, the next bit of code adds 10 and 5 before multiplying the result by 2:

Listing 4.8: Add then multiply

```
(* (+ 10 5) 2) ; 30
```

The use of parentheses to determine the order of operations forces us to be more explicit
and virtually eliminates the entire class of bugs related to operator precedence.

You Try It

- Write the expression that would call a function named `make-dessert` with the arguments `"ice cream"` and `"brownies"`.
- Write the following mathematical expression in ClojureScript such that the multiplication is performed before addition and subtraction: `8 + 3 * 4 - 10`.
- Write same expression as the last exercise but such that the multiplication is performed last.

4.4 Summary

In this lesson, we learned what expressions are and how expression-oriented programming
differs from statement-oriented programming. This led us to an examination of Clojure-
Script's evaluation strategy, which simplifies expressions from the inside out. Finally, we
learned how the s-expression syntax eliminates the need for operator precedence by making the order of every operation explicit. We can now:

- Understand how ClojureScript will evaluate our code

- Define the difference between *execution* of a set of statements and *evaluation* of an expression
- Read ClojureScript's s-expression syntax

Part II

Tools of the Trade

ClojureScript is a very productive and efficient language. While these features stem largely from the language itself, ClojureScript owes quite a bit of its productivity to the tools and common practices that have developed around it (like its Lisp predecessors over the past few decades). While there are some code samples and exercises in this section - including a simple but complete application in Lesson 8 - the focus is on learning the tools that will make you an effective ClojureScript programmer. Just as a new JavaScript developer needs a basic understanding of Babel, Webpack, and the browser dev tools, a new ClojureScript developer ought to have a familiarity with the tools that we cover in this section.

Now that we have a high-level perspective on ClojureScript as a language and its place in the JavaScript ecosystem, we will walk through the process of bootstrapping a new Clojure-Script project using the ClojureScript compiler and its included build tooling. Next, we will introduce Figwheel, an invaluable tool for live-reloading code and styles, and we will learn how to write code that is conducive to live reloading. Then, we will introduce the REPL - an extremely powerful tool for experimenting with small snippets of code. Finally, we will use these tools to create a weather forecasting app that showcases and live reloading. This project is intended to convey a taste of the process of developing ClojureScript rather than giving a deep understanding of the code. Don't worry though: in the following section, we will begin our exploration of the syntax and semantics of the language!

- Lesson 5: Bootstrapping a ClojureScript Project
- Lesson 6: Receiving Rapid Feedback With Figwheel
- Lesson 7: REPL Crash Course
- Lesson 8: Capstone 1 - Weather Forecasting App

Lesson 5

Bootstrapping a ClojureScript Project

Until this point, our discussion of ClojureScript has been largely theoretical. We have an idea of why we would want to use ClojureScript, but what does it look like in action? Over the course of this section, we'll develop a small weather forecasting application from scratch. We will pay attention to the high-level concepts while leaving the discussion of the particulars until later. At this point, we are interested in getting used to the look of ClojureScript code, identifying how it makes things that are difficult in JavaScript easier, and how the tooling helps streamline the development process. Although the syntax of the application may still seem a bit foreign, we'll start to get a feel for how fun and productive a ClojureScript project can be.

In this lesson:

- Walk through setting up a project from scratch
- Learn how to use the ClojureScript compiler to build your code
- Bootstrapping with clj-new

To start out, we will learn how to create and build a ClojureScript project. Just as the carpenter must be familiar with all of his tools before he can create a masterpiece, we must get acquainted to the tools of our trade. Coming from the glut of tools that we need for JavaScript development, it should come as a relief that there are only a few key tools that we need for any ClojureScript project.

5.1   Meeting clj

Each language has its own set of tools to learn, and ClojureScript is no different. In this book, we will focus on two very important tools - clj for general-purpose build tasks, and Figwheel for live reloading of code. We'll begin by looking at our new friend clj, the built-in command-line tool for managing dependencies and building code. Like JavaScript's npm, clj is a configuration-based dependency manger as well as a simple build tool. The reader who has some familiarity with building software projects should feel at home rather quickly, but do not worry if this is your first exposure to using a build process. We will walk through the essentials in enough detail to get comfortable building ClojureScript applications.

The Clojure language comes with a command-line tool that can be used for compiling both Clojure and ClojureScript. While other build tools exist, the clj tool is the defacto option. It is a simple tool, but it is powerful enough to use even on a large project. We will use it for managing dependencies, compiling, and testing our projects. Using a single tool for all of these concerns should come as a welcome change from the proliferation of tools in the JavaScript landscape. Before proceeding any farther, we should install Java and Clojure. Since instructions change slightly with each release, readers are encouraged to follow the most recent instructions at the official Clojure Getting Started Guide[1]. One interesting feature of ClojureScript is that we do not need to install it manually - we only need to specify it as a dependency of our project. Once Clojure is installed, we can create a new project.

Creating a Project Manually

While there are tools available to create a skeleton project from a template, we will first set up our project manually so that we can better understand what is going on under the hood. First, we will need to create a new directory and enter it.

```
$ mkdir my-cljs-project
$ cd my-cljs-project
```

Next, we will need a deps.edn file in this directory. This file is the equivalent of a package.json in the JavaScript tooling community, and it specifies the list of the dependencies that our project requires as well as the location of our source code and script aliases. The .edn extension indicates that the file uses *Extensible Data Notation* - a file format containing ClojureScript data structures. Let's create a bare-bones deps file now:

Listing 5.1: deps.edn

```
{:deps {org.clojure/clojurescript {:mvn/version "1.10.773"}}}
```

---

[1]https://clojure.org/guides/getting_started

```
:paths ["src"]}
```

The `:deps` entry contains all of the dependencies that our project needs. In this case, we are requesting a recent (as of the time of this writing) version of ClojureScript. Don't worry too much about the format of the deps map, since most packages will provide you with an entry to paste into your deps file.

The `:paths` entry instructs the ClojureScript compiler where to look for code. If we had any tests, we would add the path to our tests to this vector as well.

Now, let's create our first source file and compile it! Create a file called `src/my_cljs_project/core.cljs`, and type in the following contents:

Listing 5.2: my_cljs_project/core.cljs

```
(ns my-cljs-project.core)                          ①

(js/alert "Hello World")                           ②
```

① Namespace declaration
② Trigger an alert

By default, our application will get compiled to `out/main.js`, so let's create a simple HTML page to load this application.

Listing 5.3: index.html

```
<!DOCTYPE html>
<html>
  <head>
    <meta charset="UTF-8">
  </head>
  <body>
    <script src="out/main.js" type="text/javascript"></script>
  </body>
</html>
```

Now, we will compile our ClojureScript file and load the script in a browser. All of this can be done with one command:

```
$ clj -m cljs.main --compile my-cljs-project.core --repl
```

When you run this command, you should be greeted by an empty page that pops up a "Hello World" alert! Let's break this down so that we understand what this command is doing.

- `clj` This invokes the Clojure command-line tool.
- `-m clj.main` This flag specifies the function to run. When we included `org.clojure/clojurescript` as a dependency in the `deps.edn` file, it instructed `clj` to download the ClojureScript compiler. `clj.main` is the function that invokes the compiler itself. The remaining flags are interpreted by the ClojureScript compiler rather than `clj` itself.
- `--compile my-cljs-project.core` This specifies the namespace of the "entry point" of our application. Since we only have one file, we specify its namespace. Note that the namespace matches what we specified at the top of our `core.cljs` file.
- `--repl` This flag does two things: first, it launches a web server to serve the `index.html` file and the compiled JavaScript; second, it starts a REPL, an interactive interpreter that we will learn about in Lesson .

> ### Terminal Environment
>
> The terminal examples in this book are for a Unix-like environment such as OSX or Linux. Windows users may have to make minor adaptations the commands.

Using Aliases

While the `clj` tool offers us all of the options that we need to build and run our code, it is a hassle type out `clj -m cljs.main --compile my-cljs-project.core --repl` every time we want to start up our application. A `deps.edn` file lets us specify script aliases that allow us to declare a shorthand for a number of commands or even run a Clojure file.

Listing 5.4: deps.edn

```
;; ...
:aliases
  {:dev {:main-opts ["-m" "cljs.main"
                     "--compile" "my-cljs-project.core"
                     "--repl"]}}
```

With this alias in place, we can run our application with the following command: `clj -M:dev`.

Quick Review

- What is a `deps.edn` file, and what is its equivalent in the JavaScript ecosystem?
- Explain each of the flags that were passed to `clj` to run our application.

Understanding clj

Sticking with the Clojure philosophy of composing more advanced functionality from small, simple pieces, `clj` is a building block that has a well-defined purpose: managing dependencies and running Clojure code (including the ClojureScript compiler). There are other more fully-featured tools for project management, but with more features come more complexity. For this book, we will be sticking with `clj` and a tool called Figwheel, which we will introduce in the next lesson.

When we invoke `clj -m cljs.main ...` , several things happen. First, any dependencies specified in `deps.main` will be downloaded. This download will only happen on the initial run, and the packages will be cached locally for subsequent runs. Second, the Java Virtual Machine will be started and the Clojure compiler loaded. Next, Clojure will load the code specified by the `-m` flag. In our case, we specify `cljs.main`, which is the entry point for the ClojureScript compiler. This code is available to us because we added the package for the ClojureScript compiler (`org.clojure/clojurescript`) to `deps.edn`.

After the `-m cljs.main` flag, the rest of the flags are interpreted by the ClojureScript compiler rather than `clj` itself. We will not present a reference for the ClojureScript compiler options here, but there is an excellent official reference[2]. Instead, we will discuss the options that we need as they arise through the course of the coming lessons.

5.2 Bootstrapping a Project

Now that we have had a whirlwind tour of `clj`, let's dive in and create our first simple project, a weather forecasting app. We will use a tool called clj-new[3] to create the project from a template in order to eliminate the tedium of manually configuring everything. Just like with the ClojureScript compiler, we can make use of clj-new without explicitly installing anything. One additional feature of `clj` is that it allows aliases to be defined in `~/.clojure/deps.edn` that are always available. Go ahead and create this file with the following contents:

Listing 5.5: ~/.clojure/deps.edn

```
{:aliases
 {:new {:extra-deps {seancorfield/clj-new
                     {:mvn/version "1.1.243"}}
        :exec-fn clj-new/create}
        :exec-args {}}}}
```

This will allow us to use the command `clj -X:new` to invoke the `clj-new/create` function provided by the `seancorfield/clj-new` package. clj-new requires a template name and a project

---

[2]https://clojurescript.org/reference/repl-and-main
[3]https://github.com/seancorfield/clj-new

name in order to generate the scaffolding for the project. Since we will be using Figwheel to automatically compile code and reload it as we make changes, we can use a clj-new *template*, which is a blueprint for the files and directory structure to create. By default there are several built-in templates for generating Clojure applications libraries, but we can specify other templates as well. When invoking clj-new with a template name, it will check to see if the template is a built-in one or one. If it cannot find a built-in template, it will try to find the appropriate template from a central repository, download it, and generate our project.

The Figwheel project provides a template that generates a ClojureScript project with all the plumbing required for live reloading. We will be using the Reagent library - an idiomatic ClojureScript wrapper around React - for building the UI, and thankfully the Figwheel template allows us to pass an additional argument to include Reagent boilerplate code in the generated project. We can now create the project for our app.

```
$ clj -X:new :template figwheel-main :name learn-cljs/weather :args '["+deps" "--reagent"]'
```

Since this command includes some unfamiliar syntax, let's take a moment to dissect it. As we just learned, the first part of the command, `clj -X:new`, invokes the `clj-new/create` function, and the remainder of the arguments are passed to this function. We use Clojure keyword syntax to pass `:template`, `:name`, and `:args` options. `:template` unsurprisingly specifies the name of the template to use, `:name` is the name of the project to create, and `:args` are additional arguments that the `figwheel-main` template will interpret. Since `figwheel-main` is not a built-in template, clj-new will fetch the template from Clojure's central repository, Clojars[4].

We need to understand a bit of convention in order to make sense of the structure of the generated project. Most Clojure and ClojureScript projects use a namespace-qualified package name to reduce the likelihood of naming conflicts between projects that are pushed to a central registry. The namespace is the portion before the forward slash and is commonly the GitHub username of the developer or the reverse domain name of the organization that owns the code, although it can be anything you like. For this book, we will use `learn-cljs` as the namespace for all of our projects.[5]

---

[4]https://clojars.org/

[5]You will sometimes see the namespace referred to as the "groupId" and the name as the "artifactId". This has to do with the naming conventions used by Java's Maven project management tool, which is what much Clojure tooling is built on top of.

Figure 5.1: Project namespace and name

The final argument is a bit odd-looking: `:args '["+deps" "--reagent"]'`. This passes a vector of strings as arguments to the `figwheel-main` template. The exact arguments supported vary from template to template, but Figwheel uses these to configure optional extensions to the base template. In our case, we are specifying that we want to use a `deps.edn` file to manage dependencies, and we want to include the Reagent web framework.

5.3 Exploring the Project

We now have a running (albeit skeletal) ClojureScript project. To see the application that clj-new generated, we can navigate into the project directory and see what files were generated.

```
$ cd weather
$ tree -a
.
├── .gitignore
├── README.md
├── deps.edn
├── dev.cljs.edn
├── figwheel-main.edn
├── resources
│   └── public
│       ├── css
│       │   └── style.css
│       ├── index.html
│       └── test.html
├── src
│   └── learn_cljs
│       └── weather.cljs
├── target
│   └── public
├── test
│   └── learn_cljs
│       ├── test_runner.cljs
│       └── weather_test.cljs
└── test.cljs.edn
```

Let's go ahead and explore what each of these files and directories are for. We are already familiar with the deps.edn file, and the README.md and .gitignore files should be self-explanatory, but the other EDN files could use some explanation:

- dev.cljs.edn - build file. Figwheel allows the use of separate build configurations that can be used to pass different options to the ClojureScript compiler. For example, we could use this file to configure development builds and use another file for production builds.
- figwheel-main.edn - Figwheel configuration file. This file provides configuration options to Figwheel itself.
- test.cljs.edn - build file. Like dev.cljs.edn, this file configures a specific build - in this case, the test build.

The src directory contains all of the ClojureScript source files for our project. Usually, there will be a single folder under src that shares the same name as our project's namespace, and under this folder, there can be any number of *.cljs files and other folders. By default, the figwheel-main template creates a single <project-name>.cljs file in this directory. If we open `weather.cljs` in a text editor or IDE that supports ClojureScript [6], we will see something like this:

Figure 5.2: Editing with VS Code

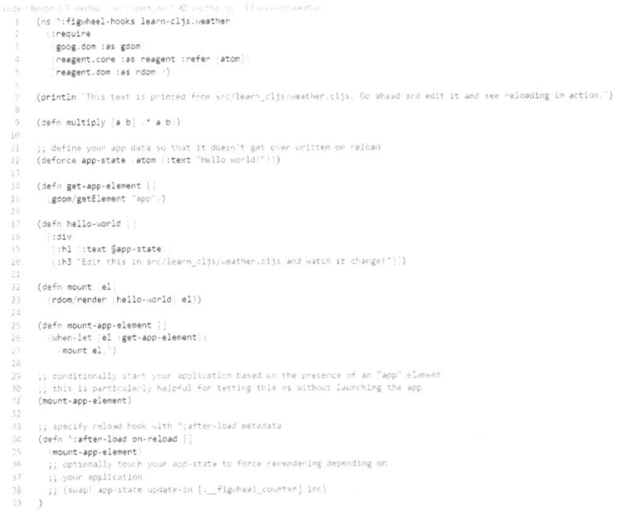

We will dig in to the rest of this file over the next couple of lessons, as we start to build out the weather forecasting app. For now, we will look at the namespace declaration at the top of the file, since it is closely tied to the structure of the project. Each ClojureScript file contains a single *namespace*, which is simply a collection of data and functions. The namespace is the unit of modularity in ClojureScript. If we open up the `weather.cljs` file that was created, we can see the namespace declared on the first line (ignoring the `^:figwheel-hooks` bit for now): `(ns ^:figwheel-hooks learn-cljs.weather)`. The ClojureScript compiler uses a simple naming convention for namespaces based on the name of the file that houses them:

1. Take the file path relative to the source directory
2. Replace the path separator ("/" on Unix-like systems and "" on Windows) with a dot,"."
3. Replace hyphens, "-", with underscores "_"

[6] Most programmers' text editors have a Clojure language package that can be used for ClojureScript, but if you prefer working with IDEs, Cursive is by far the most fully featured Clojure(Script) IDE available.

Figure 5.3: Filename to namespace convention

Hyphen or Underscore?

One detail that sometimes trips up newcomers to ClojureScript is the fact that we name directories in the project with underscores but we name namespaces with hyphens. This is a convention borrowed from Clojure, which compiles namespaces into Java classes, naming the classes according to their file path. Since hyphens are not allowed in Java class names, they are not allowed in the file paths either. ClojureScript follows Clojure's lead and requires that hyphens in a namespace be converted to underscores in the filesystem path. It is a quirk, but it is one that is easy to live with once we are aware of it.

The `resources/` directory contains all of the assets that we need to serve a website, including an `index.html`, a style sheet (which is empty by default), and once we build our project, and a page for hosting a test runner. The `index.html` was created with a single div that we can load our application into, and it includes the JavaScript file that will load our application with its dependencies.

Quick Review

- What file would you change to tweak the markup of the page that will load your app?
- What file would you change to add project dependencies?
- What file would you create to add a `learn-cljs.weather.sunny-day` namespace?

5.4   Summary

In this lesson, we have walked through the process of creating a new ClojureScript project from scratch. We were introduced to clj, the built-in Clojure (and ClojureScript) build tool. We then looked at the `clj-new` project scaffolding tool, and we explored the project structure that it generated for us. Next, we will learn about Figwheel, the other core tool that will enable us to receive immediate feedback while we are developing. After that, we will be able to jump in with both feet and start writing code. We now know:

- How to set up a brand new ClojureScript project from scratch
- What sort of tasks are handled by the `clj` tool
- How to use `clj-new` to to bootstrap a project from a template
- How a typical ClojureScript project is laid out

Lesson 6

Receiving Rapid Feedback With Figwheel

In the last lesson, we only executed one command, but we already have a basic project that will compile, and as we will see in a moment, automatically reload. Figwheel is the tool of choice in the ClojureScript community for reloading code and executing ClojureScript inside a web browser. Interactive development has been a huge priority for ClojureScript developers, and the instant feedback afforded by a tool like Figwheel delivers on making development a truly interactive experience.

In this lesson:

- Learn how interactive development is a cornerstone of ClojureScript
- Use Figwheel to compile and load it into the browser instantly
- Learn how to write reloadable code

In order to better understand how Figwheel can streamline development, let's fire it up and see it in action. Since we generated a project using the clj-new with the figwheel-main template, it included an alias that we can use to start Figwheel with a single command.

```
$ cd weather
$ clj -A:fig:build
[Figwheel] Validating figwheel-main.edn
[Figwheel] figwheel-main.edn is valid \(◠)/
```

```
# ... more output ...
Opening URL http://localhost:9500
ClojureScript 1.10.773
cljs.user=>
```

Figwheel will take a few seconds to start up and compile the existing code, but once the output indicates that Figwheel is ready to connect to our application, we can open a browser and navigate to `http://localhost:9500` and see the running application.

Figure 6.1: Reloading ClojureScript with Figwheel

What happens when we start Figwheel is that it begins watching our project for any changes to the ClojureScript source files. When any of these files are changed, Figwheel compiles them to JavaScript, sends the JavaScript to the browser, and executes it.

6.1   Testing Live Reloading

Now that we have an application running with Figwheel reloading code on any change, we can open a text editor and change some of the code. The template that we used generated a single source file at `src/learn_cljs/weather.cljs` by default, and we will restrict the exercises in this lesson to this single file. Before we make any changes, let's walk through the contents of this file at a high level.

Listing 6.1: cljs_weather/core.cljs

```
(ns ^:figwheel-hooks learn-cljs.weather        ①
  (:require
  [goog.dom :as gdom]
  [reagent.core :as reagent :refer [atom]]
  [reagent.dom :as rdom]))

(println "This text is printed from src/learn_cljs/weather.cljs. Go ahead and edit it and see reloading in action.")
```

```
(defn multiply [a b] (* a b))

;; define your app data so that it doesn't get over-written on reload
(defonce app-state (atom {:text "Hello world!"}))              ②

(defn get-app-element []
  (gdom/getElement "app"))

(defn hello-world []                                           ③
  [:div
   [:h1 (:text @app-state)]
   [:h3 "Edit this in src/learn_cljs/weather.cljs and watch it change!"]])

(defn mount [el]
  (rdom/render [hello-world] el))

(defn mount-app-element []
  (when-let [el (get-app-element)]
    (mount el)))

;; conditionally start your application based on the presence of an "app" element
;; this is particularly helpful for testing this ns without launching the app
(mount-app-element)

;; specify reload hook with ^;after-load metadata
(defn ^:after-load on-reload []                               ④
  (mount-app-element)
  ;; optionally touch your app-state to force rerendering depending on
  ;; your application
  ;; (swap! app-state update-in [:__figwheel_counter] inc)
)
```

① Namespace declaration
② Data structure to hold all UI state
③ Declare and render a Reagent component
④ Optional hook into Figwheel's reloading process

Let's start by making a minor change to the `hello-world` component. We will add a bit of extra text to it just to make sure that our changes are picked up:

Listing 6.2: "Hello World" component

```
(defn hello-world []
  [:div
   [:h1 "I say: " (:text @app-state)]])
```

Once we save the file, we should quickly see the browser update to reflect the extra text that we added. Next, let's do something slightly more interesting by changing the text inside app-state to something other than "Hello World!":

```
Listing 6.3: Changing state

(defonce app-state (atom {:text "Live reloading rocks!"}))
```

If we save the file again, we'll see that nothing in the browser changes. The reason that nothing changed is that we are using defonce to create the app-state. Using defonce ensures that whenever the cljs-weather.core namespace is reloaded, app-state is not touched. This behavior can give us a large productivity boost. Consider the scenario of building a multi-page form with some complex validation rules. If we were working on the validation for the last page in the form, we would normally make a change to the code, reload the browser, then fill in the form until we got to the last page, test our changes, and repeat the cycle as many times as necessary until we had everything to our liking. With ClojureScript and Figwheel on the other hand, we can fill in the first few pages of the form then make small changes to the code while observing the effects immediately. Since the app state would not get reset when our code is re-loaded, we would never have to repeat the tedious cycle of filling out the earlier pages.

You Try It

- Change the hello-world component to render a <p> tag instead
- Create a new component called greeter that renders, "Hello, " and update the call to rdom/render to use greeter instead of hello-world.

Do I need an IDE?

You can edit ClojureScript in any editor or IDE that you are comfortable with. Most modern text editors have Clojure/ClojureScript plugins that will provide syntax highlighting and often parenthesis balancing. Some of the more popular editors in the ClojureScript community are VS Code, Emacs, LightTable (which is itself written largely in ClojureScript), and vim. If you prefer an IDE, Cursive is a fully-featured Clojure/ClojureScript IDE built on top of IntelliJ IDEA. Whether you decide to use an IDE or simple text editor, you can find excellent ClojureScript support.

In addition to reloading ClojureScript code, Figwheel also takes care of reloading any style sheets that we may change as well. The Figwheel template that we used when creating this project configures Figwheel to watch any styles in the resources/public/css directory for changes. To test this out, we will open the default (empty) style sheet and add a couple of styles:

Listing 6.4: resources/public/css/style.css

```css
body {
  background-color: #02a4ff;
  color: #ffffff;
}

h1 {
  font-family: Helvetica, Arial, sans-serif;
  font-weight: 300;
}
```

Upon saving the style sheet, Figwheel will send the new style sheet to the browser and apply it without a full page load. The ability to instantly receive feedback on any ClojureScript or CSS change can lead to a very productive workflow.

6.2 Writing Reloadable Code

Having Figwheel reload your code is a great help, but it is not magic - we are still responsible for writing code that can be reloaded without adversely affecting the behavior of our application. Later in this book, we will be building several applications on React.js and a ClojureScript wrapper called Reagent, which strongly encourage a style of coding that is conducive to live reloading, but we should still familiarize ourselves with what makes reloadable code so that we can still take full advantage of live reloading whether we are using one of these frameworks or not.

There are many considerations that go into writing reloadable code, but they essentially boil down to three key concepts, which we will consider as the "Pillars of Reloadable Code": idempotent functions, `defonce`, and display/business logic segregation.

Figure 6.2: The pillars of reloadable code

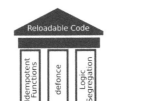

When we write code that holds to these three pillars, we will often find that not only do we end up with reloadable code, but our code often ends up being much more robust and maintainable as well. With that, we'll dig into each of these pillars and how to apply them to our code.

Idempotent Functions

An idempotent function is a function that will have the same effect whether it is called once or many times. For instance, a function that sets the innerHTML property of a DOM element is idempotent, but a function that appends a child to some other element is not:

Idempotent and Non-Idempotent Functions

```
(defn append-element [parent child]                          ①
  (.appendChild parent child))

(defn set-content [elem content]                             ②
  (set! (.-innerHTML elem) content))
```

①   Non-idempotent function
②   Idempotent function

The append-element function is definitely not idempotent because the effect will be different when we call it 100 times than when we call it once. The set-content function, on the other hand, is idempotent - no matter how many times we call it, the result is going to be the same. When working with live reloading, we should make sure that any function that is called on reload is idempotent, otherwise otherwise the side effects of that code will be run many times, leading to undesirable results.

You Try It

- Write a version of append-element that is idempotent and will only append the child if it doesn't already exist. A possible solution is given below:

```
(defn append-element [parent child]
  (when-not (.contains parent child)
    (.appendChild parent child)))
```

defonce

When we have scaffolded a Figwheel project with the `--reagent` argument, the namespace that it generates uses a construct called `defonce` to define the application state:

> **Listing 6.5: Defining once**
>
> ```
> (defonce app-state (atom {:text "Hello world!"}))
> ```

As we mentioned above, `defonce` is very similar to `def`, but as its name suggests, it only binds the var once, effectively ignoring the expression on subsequent evaluations. We often define our app state with `defonce` so that it is not overwritten by a fresh value every time our code is reloaded. In this way, we can preserve the state of the application along with any transient data while the business logic of our application is reloaded.

Another useful pattern for using defonce is to protect initialization code from running repeatedly. A `defonce` expression takes the form: `(defonce name expr)` where `name` is a symbol that names the var to bind and `expr` is any ClojureScript expression. Not only does `defonce` prevent the var from being redefined, it also prevents `expr` from being re-evaluated when the var is bound. This means that we can wrap initialization code with a `defonce` to guarantee that it will only be evaluated once, regardless of how often the code is reloaded:

> **Listing 6.6: Wrapping initialization code**
>
> ```
> (defonce is-initialized?
>   (do                                              ①
>     (.setItem js/localStorage "init-at" (.now js/Date))
>     (js/alert "Welcome!")
>     true))                                         ②
> ```

① `do` evaluates multiple expressions and takes on the value of the last expression
② Bind `is-initialized?` to `true` once the set-up is complete

In this case, we defined a var called `is-initialized?` that is only evaluated once and is bound to the value `true` once all initialization is complete. This is the first time that we have seen the `do` form. `do` evaluates each expression that is passed to it and returns the value of the final expression. It is useful when there are side effects that we want to perform (in this case, setting a value in `localStorage` and displaying an alert) before finally yielding some value. Combining `do` with `defonce` is a common pattern for ensuring that certain code will run only one time.

Quick Review

- While Figwheel is running, find the line in `core.cljs` that contains `(defonce app-state ...)`, change the text, and save the file. Does the page update? Why or why not?
- Find the line in `core.cljs` that contains `[:h1 (:text @app-state)]` and change the `h1` to `p`. Does the page update? Why is this behavior different from changing the definition of `app-state`?

Display/Business Logic Separation

The separation of display code and business logic is good practice in general, but it is even more important for reloadable code. Recall the `append-element` function that we wrote several moments back when discussing idempotent functions.

Consider that we were writing a Twitter-like application and used this function to append a new message to some feed. There are a couple of ways in which we could write this code, but not all of them are conducive to live reloading. Consider the following code, which does not separate the logic of receiving a new message from displaying it:

Listing 6.7: Combining display and business logic

```
(defn receive-message [text timestamp]
  (let [node (.createElement js/document "div")]
    (set! (.- innerHTML node) (str "[" timestamp "]: " text))
    (.appendChild messages-feed node)))
```

In this example, we combine the logic of processing an incoming message with the concern of displaying the message. Now let's say that we want to simplify the UI by removing the timestamp from the display. With this code, we would have to modify the `receive-message` function to omit the timestamp then refresh the browser, since our new code would not affect any messages already rendered. A better alternative would be something like the following:

Listing 6.8: Separating display and business logic

```
(defonce messages (atom []))                         ①

(defn receive-message [text timestamp]               ②
  (swap! messages conj {:text text :timestamp timestamp}))

(defn render-all-messages! [messages]                ③
  (set! (.- innerHTML messages-feed) "")
  (doseq [message @messages]
    (let [node (.createElement js/document "div")]
      (set! (.-innerHTML node) (str "[" timestamp "]: " text))
      (.appendChild messages-feed node))))
```

```
(render-all-messages!)                          ④
```

① All messages received are stored in a `defonce`'d atom that will not be overwritten
② The function that handles new messages is pure business logic
③ The function that renders messages is pure display logic
④ Perform a render

In this case, we could update the `render-all-messages!` function, and when Figwheel reloaded our code, the messages list would remain untouched, but the display function would behave differently, and when `render-all-messages!` is called, the display for all messages would be updated.

> **Note**
>
> λ The implementation of the above code is inefficient, since the entire list is re-rendered every time we call `render-all-messages!`. In later lessons, we will use the Reagent framework to achieve similar results much more efficiently.

Quick Review

- What are the pillars of reloadable code? Why is each one of these important?
- What is the difference between `def` and `defonce`?

You Try It

- With Figwheel running, try changing the text inside the `app-state` and saving the file. What happens? Would something different have happened if we had used `def` instead of `defonce`?
- Introduce a syntax error in the code and see what happens in the browser.

6.3   Summary

In this lesson, we examined a core feature of interactive development in ClojureScript - live reloading. We used Figwheel to reload our code whenever it changed, and we looked at the principles behind writing code that is reloadable. Equipped with this knowledge, we can take our productivity to the next level and enjoy much quicker feedback than we normally get with JavaScript. We now know:

- How to start Figwheel from the command line
- How Figwheel reloads code when it changes
- How to write code that is conducive to reloading

Lesson 7

REPL Crash Course

In the previous lesson, we learned how to use Figwheel to reload code whenever a source file changed, enabling a very quick feedback cycle. In this lesson, we will take a first look into a tool called a REPL, which stands for *Read-Eval-Print Loop* and is conceptually similar to the JavaScript console that most browsers provide. While live reloading is a great help when we already have a good idea of the code we need to write, the REPL gives us an environment for writing more exploratory code - trying out ideas and algorithms before making them part of our project. Just like unit tests, REPL development allows us to test a piece of code in isolation, examining its output and making sure that it matches our expectations. However, unlike unit tests, the REPL is more interactive and provides even quicker feedback.

In this lesson:

- Understand what a REPL is and to use it
- Use Figwheel's REPL to experiment with new code
- Learn how the REPL interacts with a web browser

7.1   Understanding the REPL

As we mentioned above, REPL stands for *Read-Eval-Print Loop* because it *Reads* each expression that we type at the prompt, *Evaluates* that expression in the context of a web browser,

Prints the result of that expression back at our command line. This process is illustrated in the figure below:

Figure 7.1: The Read-Eval-Print Loop

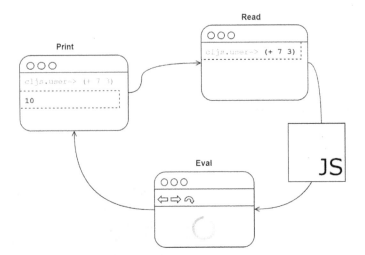

First, the REPL waits for input from the user. Once we have input a ClojureScript expression, it compiles the expression to JavaScript and sends the JavaScript code to a web browser (via a WebSocket) to be evaluated. Once the browser evaluates the JavaScript code, it sends the result back to the REPL. Finally, the REPL prints the result and waits for more input from the user. This loop continues until the REPL is killed or the browser that it is connected to is closed. Remember that the ClojureScript REPL is only in charge or the *Read* and *Print* portions, and it needs a browser to perform the *Eval* step, so if you kill the browser, the REPL will not be able to evaluate anything else until you open a browser that it can connect to again.

> **Note**
>
>
>
> There are several different REPL options with ClojureScript, but we will be using Figwheel throughout this book. Much of the information will apply to any REPL, but be aware that other REPLs may function slightly differently. Notably, it is possible to run a REPL that uses either Node.js to evaluate compiled JavaScript.

Simply providing a REPL is not all that interesting. After all, Ruby and Python have RE-PLs (or "interactive interpreters"), and every modern browser has a JavaScript REPL built into its development tools. What makes a REPL unique for ClojureScript is that Clojure-Script is a *compiled* language. That means that the REPL reads ClojureScript, compiles it to JavaScript, evaluates the JavaScript code, and prints the result back in the ClojureScript REPL all completely seamlessly. Other compile-to-JavaScript languages commonly offer an online interface for pasting in portions of code and viewing the JavaScript that the code would compile to, but ClojureScript is in a league of its own when it comes to giving the developer a dynamic, interactive programming environment. Using the REPL, we can have confidence that the code does exactly what we want it to do in the browser that we are running.

7.2   Using a REPL for browser interaction

In order to load a ClojureScript REPL, we'll use the same `learn-cljs/weather` app that we have been using through this unit:

```
$ cd weather
$ clj -A:fig:build
```

In most cases, Figwheel will be able to open a browser tab directly, but if it did not do so, please open a browser and visit `http://localhost:9500` so that our REPL can connect and start evaluating expressions.

A ClojureScript REPL instantly compiles the code that we type in to JavaScript and evaluates it in the context of a browser. In the previous lesson, we started Figwheel, opened a browser, and navigated to `http://localhost:9500`. We used this setup to reload our code every time we saved it, but Figwheel also started a REPL in the terminal that can communicate with the web page. In order to use REPL, we can simply start typing expressions into the terminal window where Figwheel is running, and it will execute in the context of the page in which our application is running. Additionally, we can interact with our application code and even change it on the fly. A typical ClojureScript development cycle follows these steps:

Figure 7.2: REPL-Driven Development Workflow

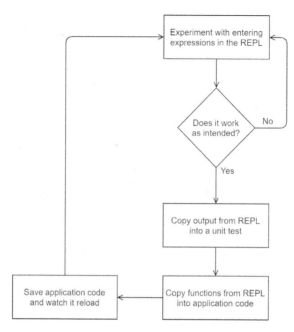

While we will not use this full workflow in this lesson, we will explore the REPL to see how we might use it for exploratory development. Once Figwheel is running and we have loaded our app in a browser, we should make sure that we can see both Figwheel and the browser. Since we we using the REPL extensively, let's take a moment to make sense of its command-line interface:

Figure 7.3: Breaking Down the REPL

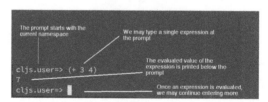

When the REPL starts up, it will display a prompt that has the namespace, `cljs.user`, followed by a fat arrow, ⇒. As mentioned in passing earlier, the namespace is the fundamental unit of modularity, which is used for grouping similar functions and data together. Whenever we define functions or data, they are added to some namespace. Unless we manually change the namespace, anything defined at the REPL gets added to the `cljs.user` namespace so that we do not accidentally overwrite the code powering the running application.

After this prompt, we can start inputting expressions one at a time. An expression can span multiple lines, but as soon as we conclude the expression, the REPL will evaluate it and display the result on the next line. There are some expressions that are only run for side effects and have no meaningful value, such as (println "Side effects!"). In this case, the REPL will print the string, "Side effects!", and return nil, indicating that the expression itself has no value.

Strings in the REPL

Note that the REPL displays special characters as they were entered complete with backslash, but if we print the string with println, the special characters are printed in the intended manner for display:

```
cljs.user=> "New\nLine"
"New\nLine"

cljs.user=> (println "New\nLine")
New
Line
nil
```

In order to change to a different namespace, we can use the in-ns function. This function takes as an argument a *symbol* with the name of the namespace to enter and changes the REPL's environment to that namespace. For example, to change into the main namespace of our application, we can simply enter, (in-ns 'learn-cljs.weather). To draw an analogy to a filesystem, a namespace is like a directory, defining a var with def or defn is like creating a new file, and in-ns is like using cd to change into a new directory. Once in the new namespace, we have access to all the vars defined in it, and any new vars that we define will be defined in that namespace.

You Try It

- Start a Figwheel REPL from the command line
- Enter some basic expressions - remember that things like numbers and strings are expressions.
- Enter the learn-cljs.weather namespace, then return to the cljs.user namespace.

Running Code in a Browser

Notice that when we start Figwheel, it opens a web browser before it can load a REPL. Why did we need a browser to use a REPL? Figwheel itself does not execute the ClojureScript code. Instead, it orchestrates the process of compiling the code to JavaScript, sending it to the web browser for execution using the browser's JavaScript engine, then displaying the results back in the terminal window.

Figure 7.4: Figwheel client/server communication

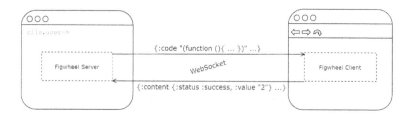

When we enter an expression in the REPL, Figwheel invokes the ClojureScript compiler to generate a piece of JavaScript code. It then sends this JavaScript code over a WebSocket to the web browser, which the browser evaluates and passes back over the WebSocket to the Figwheel server. If there are any exceptions raised while running the compiled JavaScript, the error output is sent back to Figwheel for us to look at.

This may seem like unnecessary indirection, but it is actually very useful for a couple of reasons. First, we can have confidence that our code will actually do the right thing in the context of a web browser, and second, we can manipulate the browser directly from the Figwheel REPL. We will now try a few more examples, this time with some DOM manipulation.

Listing 7.1: Browser interaction from the REPL

```
(in-ns 'learn-cljs.weather)                                ①
;; nil


(def input (.createElement js/document "input"))           ②
;; #'learn-cljs.weather/input                              ③


(.appendChild (.-body js/document) input)
;; #object[HTMLInputElement [object HTMLInputElement]]


(set! (.-placeholder input) "Enter something")             ④
;; "Enter something"


(defn handle-input [e]                                     ⑤
  (swap! app-state assoc :text (-> e .-target .-value)))
;; #'learn-cljs.weather/handle-input


(set! (.-onkeyup input) handle-input)
;; #object[learn_cljs$weather$handle_input ...]
```

(1) Enter our app's main namespace
(2) Create an `input` element and add it to the DOM
(3) `def` evaluates to the var that was defined
(4) Change the `placeholder` property of the element
(5) Create an event handler and attach it to the `input`. Note that this expression spans multiple lines.

After evaluating all of these expressions in the REPL, we will have a heading and an input in our app, and whenever we type something in it, the `h1` will be updated with whatever we type. This is powerful because now we have some code that we know works, and we could simply copy statements from our REPL session and paste them into our application. However, we could even do some refactoring in the REPL before pasting the code into our application. Whenever we redefine something in the REPL, it will affect the running application, so there is no need to refresh the page before we start redefining code. However, if we have added any event listeners or have otherwise modified the DOM, we may want to refresh the page to return to a "clean slate". In our case, we will only be refactoring the `handle-input` function, so we can continue without reloading the page.

Quick Review

- In your words, explain what happens after you input `(+ 40 2)` in the REPL and hit enter.
- Look up `https://clojuredocs.org/` and try running some of the examples in the REPL. Most of ClojureScript's library is identical to Clojure's, so most of the examples will work the same in either language.

Important

Anything that we have defined in the REPL will only last until we close or refresh the web browser, so if we want to discard everything that we have defined in the REPL, we can simply refresh the browser. Conversely, when in the middle of an involved REPL session, we should take care to not refresh the browser, lest we lose the state that we have built up.

We will probably want to get the value of some input that triggered an event in multiple places, so we can extract that into its own function. We can also make the intent of the event handler clearer if we extract the updating of the app state into its own function as well.

Listing 7.2: Refactored code

```
(defn event-value [e] (-> e .-target .-value))
;; #'learn-cljs.weather/event-value

(defn update-text [value]
  (swap! app-state assoc :text value))
;; #'learn-cljs.weather/update-text

(defn handle-input [e]
  (update-text (event-value e)))
;; #'learn-cljs.weather/handle-input
```

From this short REPL section, we now have some clean, refactored code that we could use
in our application. Almost all code needs to be refactored, but the REPL-driven style of
development enables us to refactor very early in the development process so that by the
time we write a unit test or paste the code from the REPL into an application, it is already
clean and concise. The earlier we are able to clean up our code, the less technical debt we
accumulate, and ultimately, the more productive our development becomes.

7.3   Summary

In this lesson, we explored how to use the REPL to interact with a web page. We used it
both to try out new code and to interact with code in our application's main namespace.
As with any skill, practice is key to developing the competence that eventually leads to
mastery, and ClojureScript's REPL is one of the best ways to practice new skills. Moving
forward, we will introduce almost every topic with a REPL session. We can now:

- Start a Figwheel REPL from the command line
- Understand how code entered in the REPL gets evaluated
- Write and refactor code in the REPL before committing it to our project

Lesson 8

Capstone 1 - Weather Forecasting App

Over the past couple of lessons, we have been getting familiar with the most common tools for the ClojureScript developer. While we have written a smattering of code, the focus has been on the project itself. This lesson will change course slightly and focus on writing a minimal app. This lesson will be a bit more difficult, and we will gloss over most of the detail of the code. The intent here is to present a picture of what a typical ClojureScript development workflow looks like without getting into the nitty-gritty details of the code. After learning the basic syntax and idioms of the language, we should be able to come back to this lesson with a much deeper understanding of what is going on.

In this lesson:

- Apply our knowledge of ClojureScript tools to create a new project
- Develop a ClojureScript application with a REPL-driven workflow
- Get a taste of the Reagent framework

In this lesson, we'll take the skills that we have learned over the past few lessons and put them to use developing a simple weather forecasting app that will accept user input, get data from a third-party API, and make use of React and the *Reagent* ClojureScript library for efficient rendering. This app will be simple enough to understand with only a minimal knowledge of ClojureScript yet will be representative enough to give us a clear picture of ClojureScript development. With that, let's roll up our sleeves and start writing code!

Figure 8.1: A ClojureScript single-page app in action

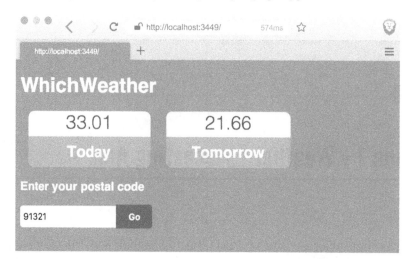

8.1   Creating an App With Reagent

We have seen how a typical ClojureScript application is laid out, and we have used clj-new to bootstrap a ClojureScript project. We have also explored the live reloading functionality and REPL that Figwheel provides to quickly iterate on small pieces of code. We will complete this high-level introduction to ClojureScript development by walking through a simple ClojureScript app. We will return to the application that we generated. We will see how quickly we can compose a ClojureScript application. The complete code for this lesson is available at the book's GitHub repository[1], so feel free to simply pull the code and follow along. The goal here is not to learn the ins and outs of ClojureScript as a language but rather to get a feel for what production ClojureScript looks like.

Creating Reagent Components

Let's begin by simplifying the core namespace so that it only contains a single Reagent component and renders it.

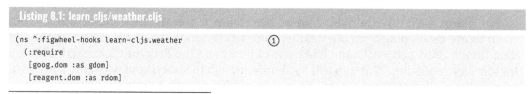

Listing 8.1: learn_cljs/weather.cljs

```
(ns ^:figwheel-hooks learn-cljs.weather          ①
  (:require
    [goog.dom :as gdom]
    [reagent.dom :as rdom]
```

---

[1]https://github.com/kendru/learn-cljs

```
    [reagent.core :as r]))

(defn hello-world []                                    ②
  [:div
   [:h1 {:class "app-title"} "Hello, World"]])

(defn mount-app-element []                              ③
  (rdom/render [hello-world] (gdom/getElement "app")))
(mount-app-element)

(defn ^:after-load on-reload []                         ④
  (mount-app-element))
```

① Declare the namespace and load the Reagent framework
② Declare a simple Reagent component
③ Render the Reagent component to the DOM
④ Instruct Figwheel to re-mount the app whenever reloading code

Most ClojureScript user interfaces prioritize declarative components. That is, components describe how they should render rather than manipulating the DOM directly. The hello-world component in our application looks something like Clojurized HTML. In fact, the syntax of Reagent components is designed to emulate HTML using ClojureScript data structures. Like with other aspects of ClojureScript, Reagent encourages small components that can be combined from small structures into larger, more useful pieces.

This hello-world component is simply a function that returns a ClojureScript data structure. Imagining a JavaScript equivalent of this function is straightforward:

Listing 8.2: A similar component in JavaScript

```
const helloWorld = () => {
    return ["h1", {"class": "title"}, "Hello, World"];
};
```

Before moving on, we should remove the "test" directory from the :watch-dirs entry in our build configuration:

Listing 8.3: dev.cljs.edn

```
^{:watch-dirs ["src"] ;; Previously contained "test" as well
  :css-dirs ["resources/public/css"]
  :auto-testing true
  }
{:main learn-cljs.weather}
```

We must remove the test directory because the scaffolded test contains a test case for a `multiply` function that we removed from the `learn-cljs.weather` namespace. If we did not remove this watch, Figwheel would not reload our code.

Quick Review

- The `hello-world` component now has a class of `app-title`. Add an id attribute to the component as well and use your browser's development tools to verify that the change worked.

Managing State in an Atom

Reagent runs this function and turns it into a structure that parallels the structure of the DOM. Any time that the function returns a different value, Reagent re-renders the component. However, in the case of this component, everything is static. For a component to be dynamic, it must render some data that could change. In Reagent, we keep all of the data that we use to render the app inside an atom, which is simply a container for data that might change. We have already seen an atom in use in the boilerplate code that we scaffolded in Lesson 5:

```
(defonce app-state (r/atom {:text "Hello world!"}))
```

Any Clojure data structure can be wrapped in an atom simply by wrapping it with (`atom` ...). Reagent components that make use of an atom will automatically re-render whenever the data inside the atom changes. This automatic re-rendering process is what enables us to write declarative components without worrying about tedious DOM manipulation.

For the weather forecasting app, we will keep the entire app state inside an atom wrapping a ClojureScript map: (`atom` {}). This will enable us to manage all of the data that we will need in a single location. This approach, when contrasted with the various approaches for managing data in some of the most popular JavaScript frameworks, is quite simple. The state for our weather forecast app will be quite simple, consisting of a title, a postal code that will be entered by the user, and several temperatures that we will retrieve from a remote API. We can create a skeleton of this app state in the `cljs-weather.core` namespace.

```
Listing 8.4: Initial application state

(defonce app-state (r/atom {:title "WhichWeather"
                            :postal-code ""
                            :temperatures {:today {:label "Today"
                                                   :value nil}
                                           :tomorrow {:label "Tomorrow"
                                                      :value nil}}}))
```

With the basic data structure in place we can identify and define the components that will
make up our interface:

Figure 8.2: The components of our app

Listing 8.5: Reagent components

```
(defn title []
  [:h1 (:title @app-state)])

(defn temperature [temp]                                  ①
  [:div {:class "temperature"}
   [:div {:class "value"}
    (:value temp)]
   [:h2 (:label temp)]])

(defn postal-code []
  [:div {:class "postal-code"}
   [:h3 "Enter your postal code"]
   [:input {:type "text"
            :placeholder "Postal Code"
            :value (:postal-code @app-state)}]
   [:button "Go"]])

(defn app []
  [:div {:class "app"}
   [title]                                                ②
   [:div {:class "temperatures"}
    (for [temp (vals (:temperatures @app-state))]         ③
      [temperature temp])]
   [postal-code]])

(defn mount-app-element []                                ④
  (rdom/render [app] (gdom/getElement "app")))
```

① A Reagent component that expects temp to be passed in
② Nesting a component inside another component

③ Render a `temperature` component from each of the `:temperatures` in the app state
④ Instruct Reagent to render `app` instead of the `hello-world` component

8.2   Responding to User Input

Now that we have an app running and rendering data, the next step is to let the user interact with the page. We will allow the user to input their postal code so that we can fetch weather data for their location. As we would in JavaScript, we attach an event handler to the input element. This handler will update the app state on every keystroke. The `postal-code` component already gets it value from the app state. The only step that we need to take is to attach the handler, and the input will stay synchronized.

Listing 8.6: Handling input with Reagent

```
[:input {:type "text"
         :placeholder "Postal Code"
         :value (:postal-code @app-state)
         :on-change #(swap! app-state assoc :postal-code (-> •-target •-value))]
```

Note that this flow is different from the "2-way" data binding of JavaScript frameworks like Vue or Angular 1. For example, to achieve a similar effect in AngularJS, we would create a controller that manages some piece of state called `postalCode` and bind this state to an input. Internally, the framework ensures that whenever the state is updated, the input element is updated with the new value, and whenever the input value is changed by the user, the state is updated. Since the framework ensures that changes propagate in the direction of UI to model as well as model to UI, it is termed 2-way binding.

Listing 8.7: Handling input with AngularJS

```
<div ng-app="whichWeather" ng-controller="inputCtrl">        ①
  <input ng-model="postalCode">                              ②
</div>

<script>
var app = angular.module('whichWeather', []);
app.controller('inputCtrl', function($scope) {               ③
    $scope.postalCode = '';                                  ④
});
</script>
```

① Provide indicators in our markup so that the framework knows which state to manage in the child elements.
② Create an input element and declare the state that it is bound to
③ Create an app and controller to handle data and process interactions

④ Initialize the state that will be bound to the input

While 2-way binding is convenient for very simple applications, it tends to have performance issues, and it can be more difficult for large applications with a lot of state, particularly derived data. The approach that we will be taking in most of the applications in this book is a little different and in fact, simpler. Instead of automatically syncing the application state and the UI in a bidirectional fashion, Reagent (and the underlying React framework) only updates the UI when the underlying state changes. Thus, we describe our components in terms of our data model, update that model when we receive input, and let the framework ensure that the UI reflects the new state.

Figure 8.3: Data binding strategies

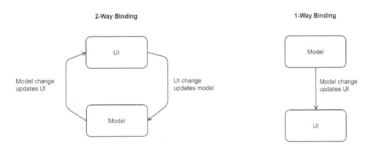

With the one-way data binding, the model is considered the single source of truth, and all changes to the model are explicit. While this may seem like an inconvenience when compared to the more automatic 2-way binding, it is much easier to reason about and debug, and it enables much simpler logic in larger applications.

Quick Review

- Let's assume that the postal code should always be a number. Change the component to use an HTML5 `number` input type.
- Two way data binding actively updates a model whenever some input changes and also updates the view when the model changes. Explain how this process is different.

In order to verify that the input is actually updating the app state, we can use the REPL to inspect the current value of the app-state. Although the name of the app state variable is `app-state`, the UI components refer to it as `@app-state`. We will explore this operator in great detail later, but for our purposes now, we need to know that it will extract the current value of an atom. We can use this operator from the REPL just as we would from a UI component to view the current app state.

```
@learn-cljs.weather/app-state
;; {:title "WhichWeather", :postal-code "81235", :temperatures
;;  {:today {:label "Today", :value nil}, :tomorrow {:label "Tomorrow", :value nil}}}
```

8.3 Calling an External API

The final piece of our weather forecast app is getting data from a remote API. While it is entirely possible to make an Ajax request using only the Google Closure libraries that are built in to ClojureScript, using an external library will greatly simplify the process. We simply need to add the `cljs-ajax` library to the `:deps` section of `deps.edn` and restart Figwheel. At that point, we can require the library in our namespace and start making requests.

Listing 8.8: deps.edn

```
{:deps {org.clojure/clojure {:mvn/version "1.10.0"}
        org.clojure/clojurescript {:mvn/version "1.10.773"}
        reagent {:mvn/version "0.10.0" }
        cljs-ajax {:mvn/version "0.8.1"} ;; Added
        }
  ;; ...
}
```

For the purpose of this application, we will use OpenWeatherMap's forecast data API. Use of the API is free, but an account is required to obtain an API key[2].

With just 2 additional functions, we can enable communication with a remote API and hook the results into our user interface. While there is some unfamiliar ground in the code ahead, we can quickly understand the basics. First, we'll consider how to process the results from the OpenWeatherMap API:

Listing 8.9: Handling the response

```
(defn handle-response [resp]
  (let [today (get-in resp ["list" 0 "main" "temp"])        ①
        tomorrow (get-in resp ["list" 8 "main" "temp"])]
    (swap! app-state                                         ②
      update-in [:temperatures :today :value] (constantly today))
    (swap! app-state
      update-in [:temperatures :tomorrow :value] (constantly tomorrow))))
```

---

① Extract data from the response
② Update the app state with the retrieved data

---

[2]https://home.openweathermap.org/users/sign_up

There are 2 pieces of data that we care about the data that the API provides - the current temperature and the forecasted temperature for 1 day in the future. `handle-response` takes care of extracting these pieces of data nested deep in the response and updates the values for today's and tomorrow's temperatures in the app state. Next, we'll look at the code necessary to make the remote API request.

Listing 8.10: Performing a request

```
(defn get-forecast! []
  (let [postal-code (:postal-code @app-state)]            ①
    (ajax/GET "http://api.openweathermap.org/data/2.5/forecast"
        {:params {"q" postal-code
                  "appid" "API_KEY"
                  "units" "imperial"}
         :handler handle-response})))                     ②
```

① Get the postal code from the `app-state` and supply it as an API request parameter
② Handle the response with the `handle-response` function above

In the `get-forecast!` function, we extract the `postal-code` from our app state in order to request a localized forecast from the OpenWeatherMap API. Notice that we specify the `handle-response` function as the response handler, so when the API returns data, we will process it and update the app state accordingly. Finally, we want to create a UI component that the user can use to fetch data. In our case, we'll use a simple button that will initiate the API request when clicked:

```
[:button {:on-click get-forecast!} "Go"]
```

We simply attach the `get-forecast!` function as an event handler on a button, and our work is done. The entire code from this lesson is printed below for reference. In order to correctly communicate with the API, please replace `"API_KEY"` in the listing below with the actual key from your OpenWeatherMap account.

Listing 8.11: Complete weather forecasting app

```
(ns ^:figwheel-hooks learn-cljs.weather
  (:require
    [goog.dom :as gdom]
    [reagent.dom :as rdom]
    [reagent.core :as r]
    [ajax.core :as ajax]))

(defonce app-state (r/atom {:title "WhichWeather"         ①
                            :postal-code ""
                            :temperatures {:today {:label "Today"
```

```
                                                    :value nil}
                                   :tomorrow {:label "Tomorrow"
                                               :value nil}}}))

(def api-key "API_KEY")

(defn handle-response [resp]                        ②
  (let [today (get-in resp ["list" 0 "main" "temp"])
        tomorrow (get-in resp ["list" 8 "main" "temp"])]
    (swap! app-state
           update-in [:temperatures :today :value] (constantly today))
    (swap! app-state
           update-in [:temperatures :tomorrow :value] (constantly tomorrow))))

(defn get-forecast! []                              ③
  (let [postal-code (:postal-code @app-state)]
    (ajax/GET "http://api.openweathermap.org/data/2.5/forecast"
      {:params {"q" postal-code
                "units" "imperial" ;; alternatively, use "metric"
                "appid" api-key}
       :handler handle-response})))

(defn title []                                      ④
  [:h1 (:title @app-state)])

(defn temperature [temp]
  [:div {:class "temperature"}
   [:div {:class "value"}
    (:value temp)]
   [:h2 (:label temp)]])

(defn postal-code []
  [:div {:class "postal-code"}
   [:h3 "Enter your postal code"]
   [:input {:type "text"
            :placeholder "Postal Code"
            :value (:postal-code @app-state)
            :on-change #(swap! app-state assoc :postal-code (-> % .-target .-value))}]
   [:button {:on-click get-forecast!} "Go"]])

(defn app []
  [:div {:class "app"}
   [title]
   [:div {:class "temperatures"}
    (for [temp (vals (:temperatures @app-state))]
      [temperature temp])]
   [postal-code]])

(defn mount-app-element []                          ⑤
  (rdom/render [app] (gdom/getElement "app")))

(mount-app-element)

(defn ^:after-load on-reload []
```

```
(mount-app-element))
```

---

① Initialize the app state on load
② Handle API responses
③ Perform API requests
④ Define UI components
⑤ Instruct Reagent to render the UI

While this app may not be a shining example of single-page application design, it is representative of the types of apps that we will be creating with ClojureScript. While its design is simple, this app demonstrates the major concerns that we are likely to face in any frontend app: component design, user interaction and communication with a data source. All said and done, we have created a complete weather forecast app in under 70 lines of code, including the pseudo-markup of the Reagent components.

You Try It

- Modify the app to display a forecast for the next 4 hours
- Separate the "Go" button into its own Reagent component

8.4 Summary

In this lesson, we have surveyed a typical ClojureScript application. While the details of the application that we developed in this lesson will become clearer as we get a better handle on the syntax and idioms, we have a concrete example of how ClojureScript brings joy to the development process. We have seen:

- How a Reagent application defines UI components
- The difference between 2-way and 1-way data binding
- How to interact with an API

Part III

Basic ClojureScript

In this section, we take our first look at ClojureScript with the goal of understanding its relationship to JavaScript as well as the Clojure language. We will discover ClojureScript's utility as a tool for modern web development. Like any tool, ClojureScript is not well suited for every task, so we will identify the areas where it may not be the best choice. Finally, we will end with a brief survey of the syntax and data types in ClojureScript and walk through its execution model.

In this section, we will begin our exploration of ClojureScript as a language, discussing the essential elements that we will need for every application: variables, control flow, functions, JavaScript interop, and I/O. First, we will take a quick look at how functional programming languages view variables (after all, if data is immutable, it cannot *vary*, right?). Next, we will consider ClojureScript's constructs for branching (if/else, etc.) and looping. Then we will learn how to extract common patterns into separate functions for reusability and clarity. Finally, we will cover the *impure* - or not purely functional - topics that are necessary in most ClojureScript code, JavaScript interoperability and user interaction via I/O. In the final lesson of this section, we will put these skills to use in building a temperature conversion app.

- Lesson 9: Using Variables and Values
- Lesson 10: Making Choices
- Lesson 11: Looping
- Lesson 12: Reusing Code with Functions
- Lesson 13: Interacting With JavaScript Data
- Lesson 14: Performing I/O
- Lesson 15: Capstone 2 - Temperature Converter

Lesson 9

Using Variables and Values

ClojureScript takes what we think we know about variables and turns it on its head. Instead of thinking about variables that may be modified, we should start thinking about values that cannot be changed. While ClojureScript has the concept of a variable (called a var), we cannot usually change that value that a variable refers to. ClojureScript is careful to draw a distinction between a var and its *value*. Just like in JavaScript, variables may be redefined to refer to a different object; but unlike JavaScript, the object that the variable refers to cannot be changed. It is this core idea of programming with *values* that makes ClojureScript so interesting. In fact, values are at the core of every functional programming language, and we will find the the combination of immutable values and pure functions (which we will discuss in lesson 12 then again in Unit 4) enable a style of programming that is very easy to reason about.

In this lesson:

- Understand the difference between an immutable value and a mutable variable
- Learn the two primary ways of naming values - def and let
- Explain the value or programming with values

9.1   Understanding Vars

A var is very similar to a JavaScript variable. It is a mutable reference to some value. The fact that it is mutable means that we can have it refer to one value initially and later refer to someone else.

Imagine going to a party where every person is a stranger to everyone else. When you walk in the door, you are given a name tag on which to write your name. Chances are, the name that you write on your name tag will be the name that the other party-goers will use to address you. Now imagine that you swap name tags with another attendee who had a different name. You as a person will remain unchanged. Receiving a new name tag does not change your identity, only the name that others will use to refer to you. Additionally, people are now using the name from your original name tag to refer to someone else. Just because the name tag does not belong to you anymore does not mean that it is invalid.

Figure 9.1: Binding a var to a value

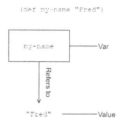

This fictional situation is an analogy to how vars and values work - the values are the people at the party, and the vars are the name tags. Just as names may be changed without affecting the people who bear them, vars may be changed without affecting the values that they name. The process of associating a var and a value is called *binding* the var to a value. Please feel free to follow along in the REPL.

Listing 9.1: Defining vars

```
(def my-name "Fred")                              ①
;; #'cljs.user/my-name

my-name
;; "Fred"

(defn mk-global [value]
   (def i-am-global value))
;; #'cljs.user/mk-global

mk-global                                         ②
;; #object[ ... ]
```

```
(mk-global [4 8 15 16 23 42])
;; #'cljs.user/i-am-global

i-am-global                                    ③
;; [4 8 15 16 23 42]

(def ten 10)
;; #'cljs.user/ten

(def twenty (* ten 2))                         ④
;; #'cljs.user/twenty

twenty
;; 20

ten                                            ⑤
;; 10
```

① Binding the var, `my-name` to the value `"Fred"`
② `defn` created a function and bound it to the var, `mk-global`
③ Even though the `i-am-global` var was defined *inside* the `mk-global` function, it is global to the `cljs.user` namespace
④ Since expressions evaluate to values, `twenty` gets bound to the result of (`* ten 2`), or `20`
⑤ We verify that the value of ten was not changed when we multiplied it by 2

Symbols

In Lesson 3, we looked very briefly at symbols, which are essentially names that refer to something else, usually a var. In the REPL session above, `my-name`, `mk-global`, `i-am-global`, `ten`, and `twenty` are all symbols. That is, they are names that refer to the var that we have bound. When ClojureScript is evaluating our program code and comes across a symbol, it will try to evaluate the symbol to whatever it refers to, and if it cannot resolve the symbol to any known value, it will display a warning.

Listing 9.2: Symbols

```
(def x 7)                                      ①
;; #'cljs.user/x

x                                              ②
;; 7

'x                                             ③
;; x
```

```
(defn doubler [x] (* 2 x))                              ④
;; #'cljs.user/doubler

(doubler 3)
;; 6

y                                                       ⑤
;; WARNING: Use of undeclared Var cljs.user/y at line 1 <cljs repl>
;; nil
```

① Use the symbol x to refer to a var
② The symbol evaluates to the thing it refers to
③ A quote before the symbol causes ClojureScript to evaluate the symbol *itself*, not the
    thing it refers to
④ Within the function, the symbol x refers to the function parameter, not the global var
⑤ Warning when trying to evaluate a symbol that does not refer to anything

λ

You Already Know How to Use It

In JavaScript, we already work with immutable data on a daily basis. Strings
and numbers in JavaScript are immutable - they are values that can not be
changed. We can *derive* new values from them, but we (thankfully) can't
say that 1 = 2 or "Unchangeable" += " ... or not". It is perfectly natural for us
to think about these sorts of values as immutable, but we have a more difficult time thinking about collections as immutable. More seasoned programmers who have encountered immutable data structures may tend to think of
them as "bulky" or resource-intensive (and many implementations of them
are indeed inefficient). Whether we are simply used to mutable collections
from other languages or have a notion of immutable collections as being impractical, it takes a while to get into the habit of working with immutable
collections However, once we get used to it, thinking of maps, vectors, et
al. as values becomes as natural as thinking about strings and numbers in
the same way.

You Try It

Almost everything in ClojureScript is a value, and a var can be bound to any value. With
this knowledge, use def to create a var that refers to this function:

```
(fn [message]
  (js/alert (.toUpperCase (str message "!!!!!!!!!!!!!!!!!!")))))
```

Can you use the var that you created to call this function? E.g. `(my-var "inconceivable")`

9.2 Creating Local Bindings With let

While `def` creates a var that is visible to an entire namespace, we sometimes want to name and use values that are more temporary or focused in scope. ClojureScript uses `let` to create these local bindings. Like vars, `let` maps a name to some value, but they do not stick around after the contents of the `let` are evaluated. This can be useful for when we want to name things for convenience in the middle of a function without polluting the namespace with a bunch of unnecessary vars. The form of a `let` expression is as follows:

Listing 9.3: Let expression

```
(let [bindings]
  expr1
  expr2
  ...
  expr-n)
```

`bindings` are pairs of names and values, such as `[a 20, b 10, c (+ a b)]`, and the entire `let` expression evaluates to the value of the last expression inside the body of the `let`. Since only the value of the last expression is considered, the other expressions are only used for side effects, such as printing to the console or doing DOM manipulation. Here is an example of how we might use `let` in a real application:

Listing 9.4: Using let

```
(defn parse-msg [msg-raw]
  (let [msg-types {:c ::control
                   :e ::event
                   :x ::error}
        msg (reader/read-string msg-raw)
        type (:t msg)
        data (:d msg)]
    (println "Got data:" data)
    [(get msg-types type) data]))
```

There are a couple of important things to notice here. First, the names that we created with the `let` - `msg-types`, `msg`, `type`, and `data` - are only defined for code inside the `let` and will be garbage collected when the `let` completes evaluation. Second, the names that we declare first are available in later bindings. For example, we defined `msg` as the result of evaluating the expression, `(reader/read-string msg-raw)`, and then we defined `type` and `data` in terms of `msg`. This is perfectly normal and allows us to write much clearer and more concise code.

Quick Review

- What happens when `let` creates a binding with the same name as a var that is already defined? What will be the output of the following code?

```
(def name "Napoleon")

(let [name "Pedro"]
  (println "Vote 4" name))
```

- Fill in the following function so that it tells you the name of your favorite dessert:

```
(let [desserts ["Apple Pie" "Ice Cream Sandwiches" "Chocolates" "Berry Buckle"]
      favorite-index 1
      favorite-dessert (get desserts favorite-index)]
  (println "All desserts are great, but I like" favorite-dessert "the best"))
```

Destructuring Bindings

The `let` form allows us to do more than bind a single name at a time. We can use it to assign names to elements in a list or vector as well as entries in a map. In the simplest case, we can declare a vector of names on the left-hand side of the binding and a sequence on the right-hand side. The nth name in the vector will be bound to the nth element in the sequence on the right (or `nil` if no such element exists):

Listing 9.5: Vector bindings

```
(let [[id name rank extra] [420 "Pepper" "Sgt."]]
  (println "Hello," rank name "- you have ID =" id "and extra =" extra))

;; Hello, Sgt. Pepper - you have ID = 420 and extra = nil
```

If we are not interested in assigning a name of a particular element, we can use an _ as its name, as in the following example:

Listing 9.6: Discarding a value

```
(let [[_ name rank] [420 "Pepper" "Sgt."]]
  (println "Hello," rank name))

;; Hello, Sgt. Pepper
```

Another common case is assigning some trailing portion of a sequence to a name. This can be done by inserting a & other at then end of the binding:

Listing 9.7: Rest bindings

```
(let [[eat-now & eat-later] ["nachos" "salad" "apples" "yogurt"]]
  (println "Please pass the" eat-now)
  (println "I'm saving these for later:" eat-later))

;; Please pass the nachos
;; I'm saving these for later: (salad apples yogurt)
```

In addition to destructuring lists and vectors, we can also destructure maps by providing a map on the left-hand side of the binding whose keys are the names to which the properties should be bound and whose values are the keys in the map on the right-hand side to bind:

Listing 9.8: Map bindings

```
(let [{x :x
       y :y} {:x 534 :y 497 :z -73}]
  (println "Inspecting coordinates:" x "," y))

;; Inspecting coordinates: 534 , 497
```

However, since we often work with maps of keywords, there is a more succinct way to bind specific values from a map to names that are similar to their key:

Listing 9.9: Binding keys

```
(let [{:keys [x y z]} {:x 534 :y 497 :z -73}]
  (println "x = " x "| y = " y "| z = " z))

;; x =  534 | y =  497 | z =  -73
```

For maps with string keys there is a similar syntax that uses :strs instead of :keys in the binding.

Finally, when destructuring maps, we may provide default values using :or inside the binding form followed by a map of name to default value:

Listing 9.10: Default values

```
(let [{:keys [fname lname profession]
       :or {profession "professional"}} {:fname "Sasha" :lname "Simonova"}]
  (println fname lname "is a" profession))

;; Sasha Simonova is a professional
```

There are more variations to ClojureScript's destructuring forms[1], but we have covered the most common ones that we will use for the rest of this book.

You Try It

- What happens when you use the & `other` form when there are no more elements in a list/vector?

```
(let [[one two & the-rest] [1 2]]
  the-rest)
```

9.3 Summary

We have now gone over the two primary means of naming things in ClojureScript `def` for namespace-level bindings and `let` for local bindings - so we are ready to tackle one of "the only two hard problems in computer science"[2]. Combining this knowledge with what we will learn in the next few lessons, we will be able to start writing some interesting applications. We can now:

- Explain what a var is and how it is referred to by a symbol
- Define global bindings using `def`
- Define local bindings using `let`
- Destructure sequences and maps

---

[1]The official Destructuring in Clojure guide - located at https://clojure.org/guides/destructuring - is an excellent reference

[2]Did you catch the reference to Phil Karlton's famous quote, "There are only two hard things in Computer Science: cache invalidation and naming things."

Lesson 10

Making Choices

Up to this point, we have mostly been writing code that has some starting point and progresses until it is complete.[1] It has a well-defined task and must follow a well-defined series of instructions to accomplish this task. What we have been missing is the concept of a *choice* - being able to take a different path depending on some condition. Imagine a road that stretched for hundreds and hundreds of miles without ever intersecting with another road. If we were to drive along that road, it would be easy because we would never have to decide whether to take another route; however, the drive would also be fairly uneventful. It is the same with the code that we write: we could write scripts that simply run from top to bottom and have a clear linear execution, but then we would be missing out on the most interesting and rewarding programs.

In this lesson:

- Apply `if` and `when` to make simple choices
- Become familiar with the concept of truthiness and how it is defined
- Choose between multiple options with `cond`

---

[1]We have come across some code samples that have used conditionals because they are almost unavoidable for any interesting program.

10.1   Example: Adventure Game

Figure 10.1: Text-based adventure game

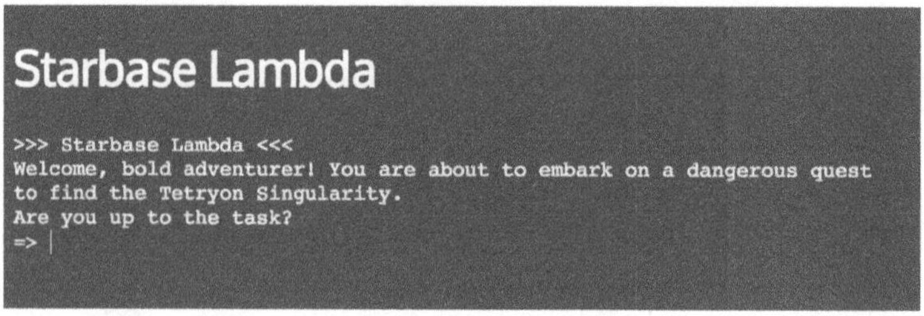

In this lesson, we will build a simple text-based adventure game. Adventure games are
perfect for learning the concept of conditionals, since they are built around letting the user
make a series of choices of how to navigate a virtual environment. So that we can focus
on learning one building block at a time, we will use the author's *bterm* terminal emulator
library[2]. This will allow us to focus on the core concepts of control structures without
getting mired in DOM manipulation and event handling or learning a large framework.

10.2   Making Simple Choices With if And when

When we are making choices, we usually need to determine if something is true or false:
is a particular checkbox selected? Is the account balance below some threshold? Does the
player have some particular potion in their inventory? These kinds of questions can only
have one of 2 answers - "yes" or "no". Remember that ClojureScript works by *evaluating
expressions*, so these questions usually take the form of an expression that evaluates to
something that is either true or false. We could imagine the above questions translated to
ClojureScript expressions:

Listing 10.1: Expressions that ask questions

```
;; Is the checkbox checked?
(aget my-checkbox "checked")


;; Is the account balance below a threshold?
(< (:balance account) low-balance-threshold)


;; Does the player have the potion of wisdom in their inventory?
(some #(= (:name %) "Potion of Wisdom")
      (get-inventory player))
```

---

[2]https://github.com/kendru/bterm

When we evaluate one of these expressions (assuming that the vars we reference are actually defined), the value will be something that we can consider to be either *true* or *false*.

Selecting With if

We often want to make one choice when the answer is true and another choice when the answer is false - in this situation, we can use ClojureScript's if special form. An if expression takes the following form:

```
(if test-expr then-expr else-expr)
```

if takes 3 expressions: a test, a value to use if the test is true, and a value to use if the test is false. The entire if expression will evaluate to the value of either the second or third expression depending on the value of the first expression. To use the account balance example from above, we could write the following:

```
(def account-status
  (if (< (:balance account) low-balance-threshold)     ①
    :low-balance                                        ②
    :ok))                                               ③
```

① Test whether the balance is below some point
② If the test is true, evaluate to :low-balance
③ If the test is false, evaluate to :ok

Special Forms

When we write an s-expression, ClojureScript will evaluate it as long as the first symbol in the expression resolves to the name of a function, a macro, or a *special form*. While the call to if looks just like a function call, if is actually a special form rather than a function. We have now been writing functions for a while, and we will learn to write macros in a later lesson, but special forms are baked into the language because they are so fundamental that they cannot be implemented as a library function (or at least not efficiently). Thankfully, from our perspective as developers, we do not need to be concerned whether the specific thing that we are calling is a function, macro, or special form, since there is no difference in the way that they are called.

While the idea of an if statement should be familiar to any developer, there is a key difference between most languages' if statement and ClojureScript's if: in ClojureScript, if is an expression, so it always evaluates to a specific value. In an imperative language like JavaScript, the `if` statement usually makes a choice between which code branch to *execute*. The actual if statement does not yield a value. For instance, the following is not valid JavaScript:

Listing 10.2: JavaScript ifs are not expressions

```javascript
// This will throw a SyntaxError
const answer = if (someCondition) {
   'Yes';
} else {
   'No';
}
```

However, JavaScript does provide the ternary operator, which is an expression. Clojure-Script's `if` expression is very similar to JavaScript's ternary operator, but there is one less piece of syntax to deal with!

Listing 10.3: ...but ternaries are

```javascript
const answer = someCondition ? 'Yes' : 'No';
```

In JavaScript - as in most imperative languages - we use `if` statements to perform side effects such as conditionally setting a variable, prompting the user for input, or manipulating the DOM. In ClojureScript, we usually use the `if` expression to decide between two values. The entire expression will take the value of either the `then` expression or the `else` expression. Selecting between more than 2 values can also be accomplished by replacing either the `then` or `else` expression with another (nested) `if` expression.

Figure 10.2: Conditional evaluation

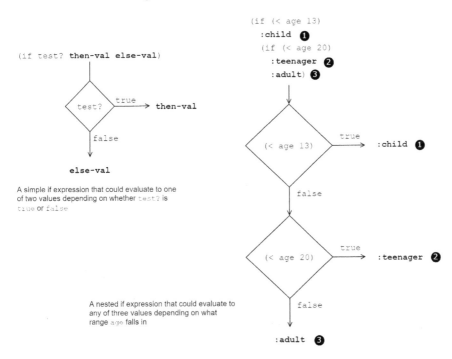

A simple if expression that could evaluate to one of two values depending on whether `test?` is `true` or `false`

A nested if expression that could evaluate to any of three values depending on what range `age` falls in

Take care, however, as deeply nested if expressions can be difficult to read and can usually be replaced with a `cond`, which we will learn about later in this lesson.

Quick Review

- Explain the difference between `if` in JavaScript and ClojureScript
- How would you write an `if` expression that - given 2 numeric values, `a` and `b` - would evaluate to `"greater"` if a > b, `"less"` if a < b, or `"same"` if they are equal?

Conditional Evaluation With when

Closely related to `if` is the `when` expression. We can think of it as an `if` without an `else` expression:

```
(when test-expr some-value)
```

When the test expression is true, the entire expression evaluates to the value given, and when the test is false, the expression evaluates to `nil`. In fact, `when` is just shorthand for an `if` where the `else` expression is `nil`:

```
(if test-expr some-value nil)
```

The two common use cases for `when` are to transform a value only when it is non-nil and to perform some side effect when a certain condition holds true. For the first case, we often see code like the following:

Listing 10.4: Operate on non-nil values

```
(defn conversion-rate [sessions]                        ①
  (let [users (user-count sessions)
        purchases (purchase-count sessions)]
    (when (> users 0)                                   ②
      (/ purchases users))))
```

① Define a function that gets the ratio of purchases to users
② Use `when` to prevent division by zero

For the second case, we will often want to perform some DOM manipulation or other side effect only in a specific case. For instance, we may want to pop up an error message when we receive a server error from a back-end API:

Listing 10.5: Conditionally perform side effect

```
(when (< 499 (:status response))
  (show-error-notification (:body response)))
```

Applying if and when

Considering the example of the adventure game, we can use use an `if` expression to determine what to do after prompting the user for a yes/no question. Let's take a quick step back to discuss the overall architecture of the game. We will represent the entire game as a map where the keys are the name of each state and the values are maps that represent a specific screen. The general shape of our game data structure is below:

We will represent our game as a collection of states with rules that determine how to move between states when the user makes some decision:

Listing 10.6: Game states

```
{:start { ... }
```

```
:state-1 { ... }
:state-2 { ... }
:state-3 { ... }
:win { ... }}
```

Our game will start with the user in a spaceship at Starbase Lambda, and their goal is to uncover the location of the **Tetryon Singularity**. They will issue simple commands as well as answer "yes" or "no" questions.

Each state in the game (which we filled in with { ... } above) will contain a `:type`, `:title`, `:dialog`, and `:transitions`. The type determines what sort of state the game is in - e.g. `:start`, `:win`, or `:lose` - title and dialog determine what we display onscreen, and the transitions determine which state the user should transition to depending on the choice that they make. For example:

Listing 10.7: Example game state

```
{:type :start
 :title "Starbase Lambda"
 :dialog (str "Welcome, bold adventurer! You are about to embark on a dangerous "
              "quest to find the Tetryon Singularity.\nAre you up to the task?")
 :transitions {"yes" :embarked,
               "no" :lost-game}}
```

When the user is in this state, we will print the title and dialog to the screen and prompt them for input. If they type "yes", we'll advance to the `:embarked` state; otherwise, we'll move on to the `:lost-game` state.

Instead of walking through scaffolding a new project, we can checkout a skeleton project from the book's GitHub repo, which already has the necessary dependencies configured in `deps.edn` as well as some basic markup and styles. We will be working from Git tag `lesson10.1`.

Prompting for Input

The first thing that we will want to do is display the title and dialog from whatever scene the user is currently in and prompt them for input. We'll handle the input later, so for now let's just think about how we can display the scene. The bterm library that we are using provides several useful functions for controlling output:

- `print` - prints a screen to the terminal
- `println` - prints a screen to the terminal with a trailing newline character
- `clear` - clears any existing output from the terminal

With this in mind, let's think about how to display the scene. We always want to print the title and dialog, but we should also indicate if they have won or lost the game. In this case, we can display either, "You've Won!" or "Game Over". To accomplish this, we can first test the type of the current scene and only display the end game message if the type is either `:win` or `:lose`:

Listing 10.8: Checking for game end

```
(when (or (= :win type)                                    ①
          (= :lose type))
  ;; Display message                                       ②
  )
```

① Check if user is in an end-game state
② Perform the side effect of printing some message

Furthermore, we want to use a different message depending on whether the user has won or lost. We can accomplish this with `if`:

```
(io/println term
            (if (= :win type) "You've Won!" "Game Over"))
```

The `if` expression will evaluate to either "You've Won!" or "Game Over" depending on the value of `type`.

Putting these pieces together with the printing of the title and dialog gives us something like this:

Listing 10.9: Prompting for input

```
(defn prompt [game current]                                ①
  (let [scene (get game current)                           ②
        type (:type scene)]
    (io/clear term)
    (when (or (= :win type)                                ③
              (= :lose type))
      (io/print term
                (if (= :win type)                          ④
                    "You've Won! "
                    "Game Over ")))
    (io/println term (:title scene))                       ⑤
    (io/println term (:dialog scene))
    (io/read term #(on-answer game current ))))) \circled{6}
```

① This function takes the entire game data structure and the current scene
② Create 2 local bindings with `let` that we will use in the rest of the function
③ Conditionally print an end-game message

④ Determine which message to print
⑤ Print the title and dialog no matter what the scene type is
⑥ Handle whatever the user types using the on-answer function that we are about to write

Handling Input

Now that we have taken care of the display side of things, we will want to handle user input. In the previous snippet, we passed control to the `on-answer` function when the user entered an answer. This function, like `prompt`, is passed the entire game data structure as well as the key identifying the current scene; however, it is also passed the string that the user entered at the prompt. Using this information, we need to determine which scene to display next then prompt the user for input once more. Here is the skeleton of what this code should look like:

```
(defn on-answer [game current answer]
  (let [scene (get game current)
        next ;; TODO: determine the next state
        ]
    (prompt game next)))
```

To start, we only need to handle responses of "yes" or "no". Since we are only deciding between 2 options, a single `if` expression will suffice:

```
(if (= "yes" answer)
  (get-in scene [:transitions "yes"])
  (get-in scene [:transitions "no"]))
```

You Try It

There is another type of game state that we need to handle = `:skip`, which has the following shape:

```
{:type :skip
 :title "..."
 :dialog "..."
 :on-continue :next-state}
```

Add another conditional to the `on-answer` function that will proceed to the next state regardless of what the user enters. A possible solution is given below:

```
(defn on-answer [game current answer]
  (let [scene (get game current)
        next (if (= :skip (:type scene))
```

```
                    (:on-continue scene)
                    (if (= "yes" answer)
                      (get-in scene [:transitions "yes"])
                      (get-in scene [:transitions "no"]))))]
    (prompt game next)))
```

10.3   Truthiness and Falsiness

Before continuing, let's take a brief step back to talk about the concept of truthiness in
ClojureScript. The test expression that we pass to `if` or `when` can be an actual boolean value
- `true` or `false` - but it does not have to be. As in JavaScript, we can pass any value as the
test. Even if it is not a boolean, the language will either consider it to be "truthy" and pass
the test or "falsy" and fail it.

Unlike JavaScript, which has a number of special cases that it considers to be falsey, ClojureScript follows a very simple rule: `false` and `nil` are falsy, and *everything else* is truthy.

ClojureScript's Truthiness Rule

`false` and `nil` are falsy, and all other values are truthy.

Quick Review

- What is the value of `(if TEST "Truthy" "Falsy")` for each of the following values for
  "TEST":

    - `true`
    - `false`
    - `"false"`
    - `""`
    - `0`
    - `nil`
    - `js/NaN`
    - `[]`

10.4   More Complex Choices With cond

With `if` and `when`, we have all that we technically need to handle any sort of decision-making
that we need to do in code. However, we are often faced with cases in which `if` would be

awkward to use. Consider adding more commands to our game so that the user could type "restart" to go back to the beginning or "help" to display the commands that are available. As we add more options, we would have to keep nesting more and more if expressions - like using a pocket knife to carve a wooden sculpture, it could work, but the result would not be pleasant.

Enter cond and its cousins, condp and case. cond takes some expression and any number of test/result pairs, and the entire expression will evaluate to the "then" expression that comes after the first test that is truthy:

Listing 10.10: The structure of cond

```
(cond
  test-1 then-1
  test-2 then-2
  ;; ...
  test-n then-n)
```

It is idiomatic to use :else as the test expression for a "fall-through" value if no other test is truthy. Remember that only false and nil are falsy, so the keyword :else will always be truthy and will satisfy cond if no prior test does. Thinking about the additional commands that we would like to add to our game, this would be much simpler using cond.

Figure 10.3: Replacing nested if with cond

Enter cond and its cousins, condp and case.

Repeated Tests With condp

If this was as good as we can do, it would be a significant improvement, but we can still simplify things further with a more focused variation of cond called condp. Like cond, condp allows us to choose from among a number of options, but if there is a lot of common code in each of the test expressions, condp can usually help us factor it out. In our case, we test the value of "answer" for equality with some string in every test expression.

This is a great case for condp, which takes 1) a binary predicate – that is, a function that take two arguments and returns a boolean value, e.g. = 2) an expression to use as the right-hand side in every test, and 3) any number of left-hand test-expression/result pairs. It can also take 4) an optional default value to use if none of the prior tests were truthy.

Listing 10.11: The structure of condp

```
(condp pred expr
  test-expr-1 then-1
  test-expr-2 then-2
  ;; ...
  test-expr-n then-n
  default-expr)
```

For every test expression/result pair, it applies the predicate to the test expression and the other expression and evaluates to the first result value whose test expression passed the predicate. On paper, this can be confusing, but seeing an example can help clarify things, so here is our text-based menu re-written using condp:

Listing 10.12: Menu refactored with condp

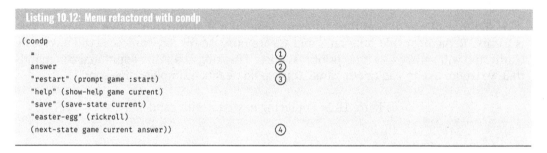

```
(condp
  =                                                    ①
  answer                                               ②
  "restart" (prompt game :start)                       ③
  "help" (show-help game current)
  "save" (save-state current)
  "easter-egg" (rickroll)
  (next-state game current answer))                    ④
```

---

① Use the = predicate function to test each option
② Pass answer as the right-hand side in every test
③ Each clause will be tested as (= "restart" answer)
④ Provide a default expression if every prior test fails

Compared to our original implementation with nested if statements, this version using condp is quite succinct and readable. For this reason, condp is widely used to test multiple values when the full flexibility of case is not required.

Quick Review

- Using cond to write some code that will evaluate to :pos when a given number is positive, :neg when it is negative, and :zero when it is exactly zero
- Write code that will do the same thing using condp

10.5 Summary

In this lesson, we learned what are usually referred to as the branching control structures. We learned that, in contrast to JavaScript and other imperative languages, these structures are used as expressions that choose between values rather than imperative statements that direct the flow of execution. We also looked at ClojureScript's concept of truthiness and how it is simpler than that of most other languages. We can now:

- Choose between two values using `if`
- Conditionally evaluate code using `when`
- Simplify multiple-choice options using `cond` and `condp`

Even though they function a little differently in ClojureScript than in other languages, these branching mechanisms are one of the most fundamental building blocks that we need to write applications. Next, we will look at the other class of control structures - loops.

Lesson 11

Looping

In the last lesson, we looked at ClojureScript's versions of we usually call branching control structure. However, we learned that things work a little bit different in ClojureScript compared to other languages that we may be used to - control structures are expressions rather than imperative controls. Now as we come to another fundamental topic - loops - we will learn that things are once again a bit different in ClojureScript.

In this lesson:

- Survey ClojureScript's various looping structures
- Learn to think in terms of sequences
- Force evaluation of loops for side effects

In imperative languages, loops are used to repeat the same instructions multiple times, usually with some small variation each time that will eventually cause the loop to exit. The classic imperative loop is a `while` loop in which the computer simply executes the same instructions over and over until some condition is met:

```
let i = 0;                                      ①

while (i < 10) {                                ②
    console.log("Counting: " + i);
```

```
    i++;                                                     ③
}
```

① Initialize a variable that will be mutated
② Set the condition for continuing the loop
③ Increment the value of `i` after every pass

Since ClojureScript emphasizes both immutability of data and expression-oriented programming - and loops are inherently both mutable and statement-oriented - one must
wonder whether there is any place in ClojureScript for loops. The answer is both "yes"
and "no" - there are several loop-like constructs, which we will look at momentarily, but
upon closer inspection, they are abstractions for other concepts that do not involve explicit
looping.

11.1   Manipulating Sequences with `for`

The first, and perhaps most common, expression that we will study in this lesson is `for`. Although it shares a name with a certain imperative loop, it is a different animal altogether.
In contrast to the iterative `for`, ClojureScript's `for` is centered around the idea of a sequence
comprehension, in which we create a new sequence by transforming, and optionally filtering, an existing one. There are multiple ways to accomplish this task in ClojureScript, but
`for` is certainly a concise and idiomatic option.

In its most basic form, `for` takes any number of sequences and a body, and it yields a new
sequence by evaluating the body for every combination of sequence elements:

Listing 11.2: `for` dissected

```
(for [elem1 sequence1                                       ①
      elem2 sequence2]                                      ②
  expr)                                                     ③
```

---

① Bind each element from `sequence1` in turn to `elem1`
② Do the same for `sequence2`
③ For every combination of elements from `sequence1` and `sequence2`, evaluate `expr` with the
bindings, `elem1` and `elem2`

Using for With a Single Sequence

Although for supports an arbitrary number of sequences, in practice it is most commonly used with just one or two. The most common usage is - as we have already mentioned - as a sequence transformation. Say we have a list of numbers and we want to find the square of each of them. What we want is to somehow describe a process that yields a new list in which each element is the square of the corresponding element in the original list. Thankfully, this is even easier to express in code than in words:

Listing 11.3: Finding the square of 0-9

```
(for [n (range 10)]                              ①
  (* n n))                                       ②
;; (0 1 4 9 16 25 36 49 64 81)
```
---

① Yield a new sequence by taking the numbers 0-9
② Make each number in the new sequence the square of the original

By now we should see that when used with a single input sequence, for describes a whole-sequence transformation. When working with ClojureScript, we should try to think whether the problem before us could be represented as a sequence transformation. If so, for provides a no-nonsense solution. Let's look at the same problem solved iteratively and with for. Imagine that we have a number of right triangles. We know the sides that are adjacent to the right angle, and we need to find the hypotenuse of each triangle. Fist, an iterative solution in JavaScript:

Listing 11.4: Get hypotenuse length iteratively

```
let sides = [[4.2, 6], [4, 4], [3, 4], [5.5, 3]];    ①
let lengths = [];                                    ②
let i;

for (i = 0; i < sides.length; i++) {                 ③
    lengths.push(
        Math.sqrt(
            Math.pow(sides[i][0], 2) +
            Math.pow(sides[i][1], 2)
        )
    );
}
```
---

① Model the triangle sides as a 2-dimensional array
② Declare an array to hold the resulting lengths

③ Iterate over the elements in sides, pushing the calculated hypotenuse length into the
  lengths array every time

This is pretty straightforward iterative code, but it is still lower-level than we would like
in ClojureScript. With loops like this, it is easy to get indices mixed up (e.g. sides[i][0]
versus sides[0][i]) or introduce off-by-1 errors. It is easy to see that this problem is just
transforming one sequence into another, so we can easily use for:

Listing 11.5: Get hypotenuse length with for

```
(let [sides-list (list [4.2 6] [4 4] [3 4] [5.5 3])]        ①
  (for [sides sides-list]                                   ②
    (Math.sqrt (+ (Math.pow (first sides) 2)                ③
                  (Math.pow (second sides) 2)))))

                                                            ④
;; (7.323933369440222 5.656854249492381 5 6.264982043070834)
```

① Declare a list or pairs that each represent 2 sides of a right triangle
② Use a for expression to apply a transformation to every pair in the list
③ Apply the Pythagorean Theorem to find the length of the hypotenuse
④ The result is a sequence with the hypotenuse of each triangle

Quick Review

- Given pairs of points as: [[x, y], [x, y]] coordinates, write a for expression that calcu-
  lates the distance between the points. *Hint: This is very similar to the previous example.*

Using for With Multiple Sequences

Some of the power of for comes in its ability to combine elements from multiple sequences.
When given multiple sequences, it will yield an element for every unique combination of
single elements from each input sequence. This type of combination is called the Cartesian
product and is an important concept in mathematical set theory. Imagine we are writing
an e-commerce app, and for any given product, there are several variations: color, size, and
style. We could use for to get all of the possible product combinations:

Listing 11.6: Generating product variations with for

```
(let [colors [:magenta :chartreuse :taupe]                 ①
      sizes [:sm :md :lg :xl]
      styles [:budget :plain :fancy]]
  (for [color colors                                       ②
        size sizes
```

```
      style styles]
    [color size style]))                                        ③
;; ([:magenta :sm :plain] [:magenta :sm :regular] [:magenta :sm :fancy]
;; ... [:taupe :xl :plain] [:taupe :xl :regular] [:taupe :xl :fancy])
```

① Declare 3 sequences
② Take every possible combination of 1 item from each collection
③ Yield a vector of each color, size, and style combination

In this example, we did not do anything with the resulting product combinations other than pack them into a vector of [color size style], but we could have performed any sort of transformation we wanted. Consider that to accomplish the same task using an iterative loop would have required us to write loops nested 3 levels deep!

Loop modifiers: let, when, and while

So far, we have been using only the basic form of for in which we take every element from one or more sequences. While this works for many use cases, there are times that we want to filter the results (say, we don't want to offer fancy products in the small size). Instead of filtering the list after for generates it, we can build the filtering logic directly into the for expression itself using the :when modifier. Again, there are times that we want to calculate some intermediate value before yielding a result. Instead of nesting a let expression inside body of the for, we can use the :let modifier. Finally, if we only want to take elements up to some cut-off point, we can use the :while modifier. To illustrate these modifiers, we will use a somewhat contrived example:

Listing 11.7: for modifiers

```
(for [n (range 100)                                             ①
      :let [square (* n n)]                                     ②
      :when (even? n)                                           ③
      :while (< n 20)]                                          ④
  (str "n is " n " and its square is " square))                ⑤

;; ("n is 0 and its square is 0"
;; "n is 2 and its square is 4"
;; "n is 4 and its square is 16"
;; ...
;; "n is 18 and its square is 324")
```

① Take n from the range of 0-99
② Declare a binding for the symbol square for each iteration as the square of n

③ Only include values for which n is even

④ Only continue until n reaches 20

To use any of these modifiers, we can simply append it to the list of sequence expressions. None of these modifiers are difficult to understand, so we will simply outline each of them below briefly before moving on.

- **:let** creates any number of bindings within the body of the `for`. It can use any of the symbols that are defined in the `for` expression as well as any other vars in scope. The usage is identical to the regular `let` form.
- **:when** determines for which inputs to emit a value. It is followed by a predicate expression, and it will emit a value if and only if the expression is truthy.
- **:while** is like `:when`, but it short-circuits the most immediate "group" when used with multiple input sequences. That is, when placed after some sequence expression, it will skip the remaining elements in the sequence after which it is placed and continue with the combination that is formed by taking the next item in the previous sequence and the first item in the sequence after which it is placed. To illustrate this behavior, consider how the placement of the while clause affects the behavior of the following example:

Figure 11.1: Behavior of `:while` modifier

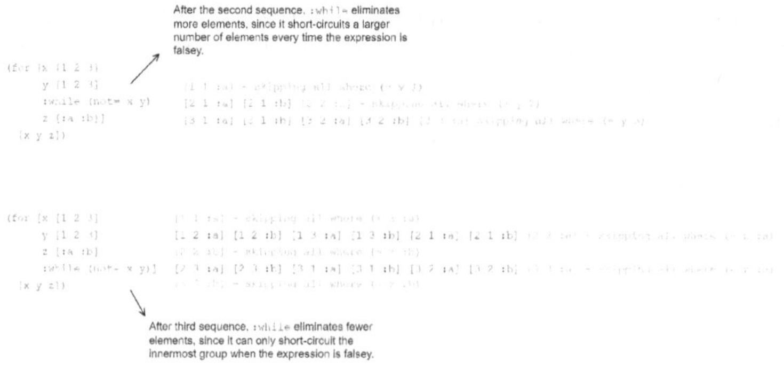

Quick Review

- White a `for` expression that takes 2 values called `x` and `y` both from (`range 50`) and yields the pairs [`x y`] for all even values of `x` and odd values of `y` when the product of `x` and `y` is less than `100`.
- Go back to the product variations example and use `:when` to filter out all variations that are both `:magenta` and `:fancy`.

11.2 Performing Explicit Recursion with loop and recur

In the next lesson, we will look in more detail at recursive functions - that is, functions that call themselves. But as a preview, below is a simple recursive function that uses the Euclidean algorithm [1] for calculating the greatest common denominator of two numbers.

Listing 11.8: A recursive function

```
(defn gcd [x y]                                ①
  (if (= y 0)
    x
    (gcd y (mod x y))))                        ②
;; #'cljs.user/gcd
(gcd 90 60)                                    ③
;; 30
```

① Define a `gcd` function using the Euclidean algorithm
② The function calls itself as the last thing it does
③ Test the function with inputs `90` and `60`

The next loop-like construct that we will look at is the dynamic duo of `loop` and `recur`. We use `loop/recur` in cases where we want to use a recursive process but do not need a separate, named function for it. The general form that we use with `loop` is as follows:

Listing 11.9: `loop` dissected

```
(loop [name-1 init-value-1                     ①
       name-2 init-value-2]
  body-exprs                                   ②
  (recur next-value-1 next-value-2))           ③
```

① Pass in any number of bindings along with their value for the first pass of the loop
② Any number of body expressions
③ Optionally recur to the beginning of the loop, supplying the values for each binding during the next iteration

This is the closest construct to an imperative loop that ClojureScript has to a traditional imperative loop. [2] Translating our `gcd` function from above into a `loop/recur` form is trivial:

---

[1] https://en.wikipedia.org/wiki/Euclidean_algorithm
[2] Interestingly, `loop` compiles down to a `while` loop in JavaScript.

Listing 11.10: Implementing gcd with loop

```
(defn gcd-loop [a b]
 (loop [x a                                        ①
        y b]
  (if (= y 0)
     x                                             ②
     (recur y (mod x y)))))                        ③
;; #'cljs.user/gcd-loop
(gcd-loop 90 60)
;; 30
```

① Initialize the loop with the function's inputs
② Return x when y is 0
③ Recur in the case that y is not 0

As we see above, we can easily control when the loop exits and when it recurses by placing the call to recur inside one branch of a conditional and another value in the other branch. This gives us the same sort of granularity that we are probably used to with imperative loops, but with less boilerplate.

recur Nuances

loop is a very useful construct that lets us simplify many types of recursive functions. However, it cannot replace all recursive functions, only a particular class known as "tail recursive" functions. These particular functions are ones that call themselves as the very last thing they do (in the "tail" position) of the function. As we mentioned in the last lesson, every time a recursive function calls itself, it consumes a stack frame, and if it recurses too deeply, the JavaScript runtime will stop execution with an error. However, recursive processes written with loop and recur can recurse arbitrarily deeply because the ClojureScript compiler is able to optimize them into an imperative loop. For this reason, loop is also usually faster than functional recursion.

Because loop only works with tail recursion, we need to be careful that no evaluation is attempted after a recur. Thankfully, the ClojureScript compiler warns us if the recur is not in the tail position, and it will not compile the code until we move the recur. Below is an example of a proper call to recur along with an illegal one.

Listing 11.11: Legal and illegal recur

```
(loop [i 0
       numbers []]
 (if (= i 10)
   numbers
   (recur (inc i) (conj numbers i))))              ①
```

```
;; [0 1 2 3 4 5 6 7 8 9]
(loop [i 7
       fact 1]
  (if (= i 1)
    fact
    (* i (recur (dec i) (* i fact))))))                    ②
;; ---- Could not Analyze  <cljs form>   line:5  column:22  ----
;;
;;   Can't recur here at line 5 <cljs repl>
;;
;;   1  (loop [i 7
;;   2         fact 1]
;;   3    (if (= i 1)
;;   4      fact
;;   5      (* i (recur (dec i) (* i fact)))))))
;;               ^---
;;
;; ---- Analysis Error  ----
;; nil
```

① It is legal to recur when it is the last thing to be evaluated in a loop
② Cannot recur here because we need to multiply by `i` after recurring

So we see that not every recursive function can be translated into a `loop`, but if it can, there is a definite performance benefit. This has been a rather brief introduction to `loop`, but we will use it quite often over the course of this book, so we will have ample opportunity to get more familiar with it.

11.3 Looping for Side Effects

Having covered `for` for sequence comprehensions and `loop/recur` for explicit recursion. There is one remaining category of looping in ClojureScript: looping for side effects. Recall that a side effect is an effect that our program causes outside the pure calculations that it performs, such as adding and removing DOM nodes or sending data to a server-side API.

One of the difficulties with ClojureScript is that many of its sequence operations (including `for`) are *lazy*. That is, they do not produce results until called on to do so. Consider this `for` expression:

```
(for [i (range 10)]
  (println i))
```

If you enter this into the REPL, it will print the numbers 0-9, just as we would expect. However, if we were to only request a few values from the sequence generated by the `for`, we would see a surprising result:

Listing 11.12: Lazy evaluation

```
(take 3                                          ①
  (for [i (range 10)]
    (println i)))
;; 0                                             ②
;; 1
;; 2
;; (nil nil nil)                                 ③
(do (for [i (range 10)]
        (println i))
      (println "Done"))
;; Done
;; nil                                           ④
```

① Only take 3 elements from the sequence given by the `for` expression
② `println` gets called only 3 times - not 10
③ Since `println` returns `nil`, the result is a sequence filed with `nil`
④ No numbers are printed, since we never need the results of the `for`

The `for` will only evaluate when the results are required to complete some other calculation - and for only as many values in the sequence as are required. This laziness is, as we will see in a later lesson, very useful for some things, but it can cause unexpected behavior when dealing with side effects, thus the need to force evaluation.

Evaluating an Existing Sequence With dorun

The first and simplest way to ensure that a sequence is fully evaluated (and thus all side effects that it may cause are run) is to wrap the sequence in a `dorun`. When just given a sequence, it will execute the code necessary to realize every value in succession, and it returns nil. For example, we could force the numbers to print in the example above simply by wrapping the `for` expression with `dorun`:

Listing 11.13: Forcing evaluation of a lazy sequence

```
(do (dorun                                       ①
      (for [i (range 10)]
        (println i)))
    (println "Done"))
;; 0                                             ②
;; 1
;; 2
;; 3
;; 4
;; 5
;; 6
```

```
;; 7
;; 8
;; 9
;; Done
;; nil
```

① Wrap the `for` in `dorun`
② All numbers are printed as expected

Looping for Effects With doseq

While `dorun` is often what we want if we have a sequence that performs side effects as each element is realized, we more often want to iterate over an existing sequence and perform a side effect for each element. In this case, we can use `doseq`. The syntax of `doseq` is identical to `for` (including the modifiers), but it evaluates immediately and returns `nil` instead of a sequence. If we think about sending a list of users to a back-end API, we certainly want to ensure that the code is evaluated when we expect it to, so we can use `doseq`, as in the example below:

```
(defn send-to-api [user]                    ①
  (println "Sending to API:" user))
;; #'cljs.user/send-to-api
(let [users [{:name "Alice"}
             {:name "Bob"}
             {:name "Carlos"}]]
  (doseq [user users]                        ②
    (send-to-api user))
  (println "Done!"))
;; Sending to API: {:name Alice}             ③
;; Sending to API: {:name Bob}
;; Sending to API: {:name Carlos}
;; Done!
;; nil
```

① Stub the `send-to-api` function
② Iterate through the `users` collection
③ Side effects are performed immediately

Here we iterate through the `users` list and call `send-to-api` for each user. Since we do not care about the return value of that function, `doseq` is the perfect option here.

Quick Review

- What would happen if we had used `for` in the previous example instead of `doseq`?
- There is a function similar to `dorun` called `doall`. Look it up online and explain when you might use one versus the other.
- DOM manipulation is a side effect. What are some use cases for using `doseq` in conjunction with the DOM?

11.4 Summary

We have now seen ClojureScript's core looping features. While `for` and `while` loops are critical in many languages, we have learned that ClojureScript does not even have these concepts. Its looping constructs center around one of three things:

- Sequence operations (`for`)
- Recursion (`loop`/`recur`)
- Forcing evaluation of side effects (`doseq`)

Even though we may at first find it difficult to solve problems without the traditional imperative loops, we will quickly discover that a "Clojure-esque" solution is often simpler. As we get more accustomed to thinking in terms of sequences and recursion, the ClojureScript way will become second nature.

Lesson 12

Reusing Code With Functions

ClojureScript is a functional programming language. The functional programming paradigm gives us superpowers, but - love it or hate it - it also makes certain demands on the way that we write code. We have already discussed some of the implications of functional code (immutable data, minimizing side effects, etc.), but up to this point we have not studied what a functions *are* - much less how to use them idiomatically. In this lesson, we define what functions are in ClojureScript, and we will study how to define and use them. Finally, we'll look at some best practices for when to break code into separate functions and how to use a special class of function that is encountered often in ClojureScript - the recursive function.

In this lesson:

- Learn ClojureScript's most fundamental programming construct
- Write beautiful code by extracting common code into functions
- Solve common problems using recursion

12.1   Understanding Functions

Think about the programs that you have written in the past. Maybe you primarily write enterprise software. Maybe you write games. Maybe you're a designer who creates amazing experiences on the web. There are so many different types of programs out there, but we can boil them all down to one common idea: a program is something that takes some sort of input as data and produces some sort of output. Enterprise software usually takes forms and generates database rows, or it takes database rows and generates some sort of user interface. Games take mouse movements, key presses, and data about a virtual environment and generate descriptions of pixels and sound waves. Interactive web pages also take user input and generate markup and styles.

Figure 12.1: Programs transform data

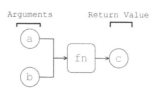

In each of these cases, a program transforms one or more pieces of data into some other piece of data. Functions are the building blocks that describe these data transformations. Functions can be composed out of other functions to build more useful, higher-level transformations.

We can think about functional programming as a description of data in motion. Unlike imperative code that makes us think about algorithms in terms of statements that assign and mutate data, we can think of our code as a description of how data flows through our program. Functions are the key to writing such declarative programs. Each function has zero or more input values (argument), and they always return some output value[1].

Figure 12.2: Functions map input to output

---

[1]In practice, many functions return nil, which is a value that denotes the absence of any meaningful value. Functions that return nil are often called for side effects.

12.2 Defining and Calling Functions

Just like strings, numbers, and keywords, ClojureScript functions are values. This means that they can be assigned to vars, passed into other functions as arguments, and returned from other functions. This should not be a new concept for JavaScript programmers, since JavaScript functions are also first-class values:

Listing 12.1: First-class functions in JavaScript

```
const removeBy = (pred) => {                                    ①
    return list =>                                              ②
        list.reduce((acc, elem) => {
            if (pred(elem)) {
                return acc;
            }
            return acc.concat([elem]);
        }, []);
}

const removeReds = removeBy(                                    ③
    product => product.color === 'Red'
);

removeReds([
    { sku: '99734N', color: 'Blue' },
    { sku: '99294N', color: 'Red' },
    { sku: '11420Z', color: 'Green' },
]);
```

① Assign a function to a variable, `removeBy`
② Return a function
③ Pass a function as an argument to another function

A direct translation[2] of this code to ClojureScript is pleasantly straightforward:

Listing 12.2: First-class functions in ClojureScript

```
(def remove-by                                                 ①
  (fn [pred]
    (fn [list]                                                 ②
      (reduce (fn [acc elem]
                (if (pred elem) acc (conj acc elem)))
              []
              list))))
```

---

[2]This code sample is intended to be a direct translation in order to illustrate the similarity between functions in ClojureScript and JavaScript. It is not idiomatic ClojureScript, and it does not take advantage of the standard library.

```
(def remove-reds                                      ③
  (remove-by (fn [product] (= "Red" (:color product)))))

(remove-reds
  [{:sku "99734N" :color "Blue"}
   {:sku "99294N" :color "Red"}
   {:sku "11420Z" :color "Green"}])
```

① Assign a function to a variable, `remove-by`
② Return a function
③ Pass a function as an argument to another function

Since JavaScript was designed with a lot of the features of Scheme - another Lisp - in mind, it should come as no surprise that functions work similarly across both languages. The primary differences are syntactical rather than semantic. So with that, let's take a look at the syntax for defining functions.

fn and defn

Functions may be defined with the `fn` special form. In its most basic version `fn` takes a vector of parameters and one or more expressions to evaluate. When the function is called, the arguments that it is called with will be bound to the names of the parameters, and the body of the function will be evaluated. The function will evaluate to the the value of the last expression in its body. As an example, let's take a function that checks whether one sequence contains every element in a second sequence:

```
Listing 12.3: Function expression

(fn [xs test-elems]                                   ①
  (println "Checking whether" xs                      ②
           "contains each of" test-elems)
  (let [xs-set (into #{} xs)]                          ③
    (every? xs-set test-elems)))
```

① Declare a function that takes 2 parameters
② The first expression is evaluated for side effects, and its result is discarded
③ The entire function takes on the value of the last expression

This example illustrates the basic form of `fn` where there is a parameter vector and a body consisting of 2 expressions. Note that the first expression logs some debug information and does not evaluate to any meaningful value. The function itself takes on the value of the final expression where `xs` and `test-elems` are substituted with the actual values with which the function is called:

```
(let [xs-set (into #{} xs)]
  (every? xs-set test-elems))
```

Anonymous Function Shorthand

There is another even terser syntax for anonymous functions that saves a few keystrokes by omitting the `fn` and the named argument list. In the next example, we use this abbreviated syntax.

Listing 12.4: Shorter anonymous functions

```
#(let [xs-set (into #{} %1)]
   (every? xs-set 2)))
```

As we can see, the function itself is defined with `#( ... )`, and each argument is referred to by its position - `%1`, `%2`, etc. If the function takes only 1 argument, then the argument may be referred to simply as `%`:

```
(#(str "Hello " %) "world")
;; => "Hello world"
```

While this syntax is handy, we should only use it for extremely small functions whose intent is readily apparent. In the normal case, we should prefer to use the slightly longer syntax for the clarity that comes with named arguments. Also, for a function that takes more than one argument, this syntax usually introduces more confusion than necessary. It is still fairly common in ClojureScript code and is often used for event callbacks.

Defining Named Functions

You may have noticed that while we have declared a useful function, we do not have any way to call it because it lacks a name. This is where `defn` comes in - it is a shorthand for declaring a function and binding it to a var at the same time:

Listing 12.5: Defining functions

```
(def contains-every?                          ①
  (fn [xs test-elems]
    ;; function body...
    ))
```

```
(defn contains-every? [xs test-elems]                    ②
  ;; function body...
  )
```

① Bind the anonymous function to a var, `contains-every?`
② Define the function and bind it at the same time with `defn`

As we can see, `defn` is a useful shorthand when we want to create a named function.

In order to keep our programs clean, we usually group related functions together into a *namespace*. When we bind a function to a var using either `def` or `defn`, the function becomes public and can be required from any other namespace. In ClojureScript, vars are exported by default unless explicitly made private[3]. Unlike object-oriented programming, which seeks to hide all but the highest-level implementation, Clojure is about visibility and composing small functions - often from different namespaces. We will look at namespaces and visibility in much greater detail in Lesson 23.

Variations of defn

The basic form of `defn` that we just learned is by far the most common, but there are a couple of extra pieces of syntax that may be used.

Multiple Arities

First, a function can be declared with multiple *arities* - that is, its behavior can vary depending on the number or arguments given. To declare multiple arities, each parameter list and function body is enclosed in a separate list following the function name.

Listing 12.6: Function arities

```
(defn my-multi-arity-fn
  ([a] (println "Called with 1 argument" a))          ①
  (                                                    ②
   [a b]                                               ③
   (println "Called with 2 arguments" a b)            ④
   )
  ([a b c] (println "Called with 3 arguments" a b c)))

(defn my-single-arity-fn [a]                           ⑤
  (println "I can only be called with 1 argument"))
```

---

[3]Functions can be made private by declaring them with `defn-` instead of `defn`.

① Unlike the basic `defn` form, each function implementation is enclosed in a list
② For each function implementation, the first element in the list is the parameter vector
③ ...followed by one or more expressions, forming the body of the implementation for that arity
④ Remember that for a single-arity function, the parameters and expressions that form the body of the function need not be enclosed in a list

Multiple arity functions are often used to supply default parameters. Consider the following function that can add an item to a shopping cart. The 3-ary version lets a quantity be specified along with the `product-id`, and the 2-ary version calls this 3-ary version with a default quantity of 1:

```
(defn add-to-cart
  ([cart id] (add-to-cart cart id 1))
  ([cart id quantity]
   (conj cart {:product (lookup-product id)
               :quantity quantity})))
```

This is one area that is surprisingly different than JavaScript because functions in Clojure-Script can only be called with an arity that is declared explicitly. That is, a function that is declared with a single parameter may only be called with a single argument, a function that is declared with two parameters may only be called with 2 arguments, and so forth.

Docstrings

A function can also contain a docstring - a short description of the function that serves as inline documentation. When using a docstring, it should come immediately after the function name:

Listing 12.7: Documenting a function

```
(defn make-inventory
  "Creates a new inventory that initially contains no items.
  Example:
  (assert
    (== 0 (count (:items (make-inventory)))))"
  []
  {:items []})
```

The advantage of using a docstring rather than simply putting a comment above the function is that the docstring is metadata that is preserved in the compiled code and can be accessed programmatically using the `doc` function that is built into the REPL:

```
dev:cljs.user=> (doc make-inventory)
```

```
------------------------
cljs.user/make-inventory
([])
  Creates a new inventory that initially contains no items.
  Example:
  (assert
    (= 0 (count (:items (make-inventory)))))
nil
```

Pre- and post-conditions

ClojureScript draws some inspiration from the *design by contract* concept pioneered by the Eiffel programming language. When we define a function, we can specify a contract about what that function does in terms of pre-conditions and post-conditions. These are checks that are evaluated immediately before and after the function respectively. If one of these checks fails, a JavaScript Error is thrown.

A vector of pre- and post-conditions may be specified in a map immediately following the parameter list, using the :pre key for pre-conditions and the :post key for post-conditions. Each condition is specified as an expression within the :pre or :post vector. They may both refer to the arguments of the function by parameter name, and post-conditions may also reference the return value of the function using %.

Listing 12.8: Preconditions and postconditions

```
(defn fractional-rate [num denom]
  {:pre [(not= 0 denom)]                             ①
   :post [(pos? %) (<= % 1)]}                        ②
  (/ num denom))

(fractional-rate 1 4)
;; 0.25

(fractional-rate 3 0)
;; Throws:
;; #object[Error Error: Assert failed: (not= 0 denom)]
```

---

① A single pre-condition is specified, ensuring that the denom is never zero
② Two post-conditions are specified, ensuring that the result is a positive number that is less than or equal to 1.

You Try It

- In the REPL, define a function that takes 1 argument, then call it with 2 arguments. What happens?
- Try enclosing the parameter list and function body of a single-arity function in a list. Is this valid?
- Combine all 3 of the advanced features of defn that we have learned to create a function with a docstring, multiple arities, and pre-/post-conditions.

12.3   Functions as Expressions

Now that we have learned how to define functions mechanically, let's take a step back and think about what a function is. Think back to Lesson 4: Expressions and Evaluation where we developed a mental model of evaluation in ClojureScript. Recall how an interior s-expression is evaluated and its results substituted into its outer expression:

```
(* (+ 5 3) 2)
;; => (* 8 2)
;; => 16
```

In Lesson 4, we took it for granted that an s-expression like (+ 5 3) evaluates to 8, but we did not consider how this happened. We need to expand that mental model of evaluation to account for what happens a function is called.

When we define a function, we declare a list of parameters. These are called the formal parameters of the function. The function body is free to refer to any of these formal parameters. When the function is called, the call is replaces with the body of the function where every instance of the formal parameters is replaced with the argument that was passed in - called the actual parameters. While this is a bit confusing to explain, a quick example should help clarify:

```
(defn hypotenuse [a b]                          ①
  (Math/sqrt
    (+ (* a a)
       (* b b))))


(str "the hypotenuse is: " (hypotenuse 3 4))    ②

(str "the hypotenuse is: " (Math/sqrt          ③
                  (+ (* 3 3)
                     (* 4 4))))

(str "the hypotenuse is: " 5)                   ④

"the hypotenuse is: 5"                          ⑤
```

① Define a function called `hypotenuse`
② Call the function we just defined
③ Replace the call to the function with the body from the function definition, substituting 3 in the place of `a` and 4 in the place of `b`
④ Evaluate the resulting expression
⑤ Continue evaluation until we have produced a final value

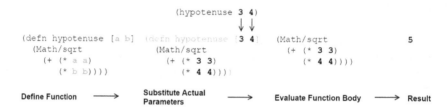

Figure 12.3: Parameter substitution

When we think about a function as a template for another expression, it fits nicely into our existing model of evaluation. Functions in ClojureScript are a simpler concept than in JavaScript because they do not have an implicit mutable context. In JavaScript, standard functions have a special `this` variable that can refer to some object that the function can read and mutate. Depending on how the function was defined, `this` may refer to different things, and even experienced developers sometimes get tripped up by `this`. ClojureScript functions - by contrast - are *pure* and do not carry around any additional state. It is this purity that makes them fit well into our model of expression evaluation.

Closures

Although ClojureScript functions do not have automatic access to some shared mutable state by default, there is one more detail that we have to account for when reasoning about how a function is evaluated. In ClojureScript, just like in JavaScript, functions have lexical scope, which means that they can reference any symbol that is visible at the site where the function is defined. When a function references a variable from its lexical scope, we say that it creates a *closure*. For example, we can reference any vars previously declared in the same namespace:

Listing 12.9: Lexical closures

```
(def http-codes                              ①
  {:ok 200
   :created 201
   :moved-permanently 301
```

```
  :found 302
  :bad-request 400
  :not-found 404
  :internal-server-error 500})

(defn make-response [status body]
  {:code (get http-codes status)                    ②
   :body body})
```

① Define a var in the current namespace
② Referencing this var inside our function creates a closure over it

Since ClojureScript has the concept of higher-order functions, a function that is returned from another function can also reference variables from the parent function's scope:

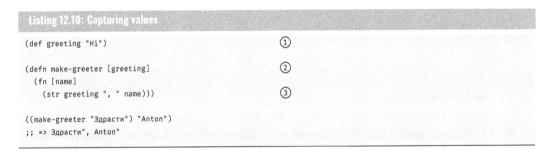

Listing 12.10: Capturing values

```
(def greeting "Hi")                               ①

(defn make-greeter [greeting]                     ②
  (fn [name]
    (str greeting ", " name)))                    ③

((make-greeter "Здрасти") "Anton")
;; => Здрасти", Anton"
```

① The symbol `greeting` will refer to a var with the value of `Hi` within this namespace
② Within this function, `greeting` will refer to whatever argument is passed in, not the namespace-level var
③ The inner function closes over the `greeting` from it's parent function's scope

In this example, the function returned from `make-greeter` creates a closure over `greeting`. If we were to call `(make-greeter "Howdy")`, the resulting function would always substitute `"Howdy"` for `greeter` whenever it was evaluated. Even though there was another value bound to the symbol `greeting` outside the `make-greeter` function, the inner function is not able to see it because there is another symbol with the same name *closer* to the function itself. We say that the namespace-level `greeting` is *shadowed* by the inner `greeting`. We will study closures in more detail in Lesson 21 and see how we need to modify our mental model of evaluation in order to accommodate them.

Functions as Abstraction

As we saw above, functions are ways to re-use expressions, but they are much more than that. They are the ClojureScript developer's primary means of abstraction. Functions hide the details of some transformation behind a name. Once we have abstracted an expression, we don't need to be concerned anymore with how it is implemented. As long as it meets our expectations, it should not matter to us anymore what happens under the hood. As a trivial example, lets look at several potential implementations for an `add` function.

Listing 12.11: Two versions of `add`

```
(defn add [x y]                          ①
  (+ x y))

(defn add [x y]                          ②
  (if (<= y 0)
    x
    (add (inc x) (dec y))))

(defn add [x y]                          ③
  47)

(add 17 23)                              ④
```

---

① A basic function to add two numbers
② Another function for adding. It's less efficient, but it works.
③ A very opinionated function for adding. Unfortunately, it is almost always wrong.
④ Call the `add` function. All we know is that it is supposed to add our numbers.

The real power comes when we move from specific, granular function to higher levels of abstraction. In ClojureScript, we often find ourselves starting a new project by creating many small functions that describe small details and processes in the problem domain then using these functions to define slightly less granular details and processes. This practice of "bottom-up" programming gives us the ability to focus on only the level of abstraction that we are interested in without caring about either the lower-level functions that it is composed of or the higher-level functions in which it serves as an implementation detail.

Quick Review

- Define a function using `my-inc` that returns the increment of a number. How would you define a function with the same name without using `defn`?
- What is the difference between the *formal parameters* and *actual parameters*
- What does *shadowing* mean in the context of a closure?

12.4   Recursion 101

As the last topic of this lesson, we will cover recursive functions. As we mentioned earlier, a recursive function is simply a function that can call itself. We made use of `loop/recur` in the last chapter to implement recursion within a function. Now let's see how to implement a recursive function using the classic factorial function.

Listing 12.12: Recursive factorial

```
(defn factorial [n]
  (if (<= n 1)
    n                                              ①
    (* n (factorial (dec n)))))                    ②
```

① Base case - do not call `factorial` again
② Recursive case, call `factorial` again

This example should be unsurprising to readers with prior JavaScript experience. Recursion works essentially the same in ClojureScript as it does in JavaScript: each recursive call grows the stack, so we need to take care not to overflow the stack. However, if our function is tail recursive - that is, if it calls itself as the very last step in its evaluation - then we can use the `recur` special form just as we did with `loop` in the last lesson. The only difference is that if it is not within a `loop`, `recur` will recursively call its containing function. Knowing this, we can write a tail-recursive version of `factorial` that will not grow the stack:

Listing 12.13: Tail-recursive factorial

```
(defn factorial
  ([n] (factorial n 1))
  ([n result]
   (if (<= n 1)
     result
     (recur (dec n) (* result n)))))
```

ClojureScript is able to optimize this recursive function into a simple loop, just as it did with `loop/recur` in the last lesson.

Quick Review

- If you are uncertain how recursion works, go back and read from "Recursion 101".

12.5   Summary

In this lesson, we took a fairly detailed look at functions in ClojureScript. We learned the difference between `fn` and `defn`, and we studied the various forms that `defn` can take. We considered the model of evaluation for functions and presented them as a means of extracting common expressions. Finally, we looked at recursive functions and saw how to use `recur` to optimize tail-recursive functions. While JavaScript and ClojureScript look at functions in a similar way, we made sure to point out the areas of difference so as to avoid confusion moving forward.

Lesson 13

Interacting With JavaScript Data

One of the advantages of ClojureScript is its excellent interoperability with JavaScript. When Clojure was first introduced, one of its primary goals was providing simple integration with existing Java code. ClojureScript continues in this spirit of valuing integration with its host platform. We will deal with JavaScript interoperability to a greater extent later, but at this point, we will concern ourselves with creating and manipulating JavaScript data structures.

In this lesson:

- Convert between ClojureScript and JavaScript data types
- Integrate ClojureScript code with an existing JavaScript codebase
- Understand the implications of using mutable JavaScript objects and arrays

---

13.1 Example: Integration With Legacy Code

Imagine that we have decided to slowly migrate a legacy JavaScript application to ClojureScript (an excellent choice). However, due to the size of the codebase, it is more practical to migrate one piece at a time. In the meantime, we need to interact with our legacy application, a classroom management application, from ClojureScript. We will need to read a list of scores from the legacy application, perform modifications in ClojureScript, and send the results back to the JavaScript application. Fortunately for us, ClojureScript has excellent interoperability with JavaScript, so let's learn how it's done!

13.2   Using Conversion Functions

When we are working with an existing JavaScript codebase or libraries, chances are that we
will be passing JavaScript data structures around, but we would like to treat them as ClojureScript data within our application. ClojureScript provides two handy functions for converting between JavaScript and ClojureScript data structures: js→clj for converting from
JavaScript and clj→js for converting to JavaScript. We can easily use these functions to
convert data to ClojureScript structures coming into our program and back to JavaScript
on the way out.

Let's try this out by opening up the REPL and the browser tab that it is connected to. Open
the dev tools and create an object called testScores that looks something like the following:

Listing 13.1: Creating a JS object

```
var testScores = [                                            ①
  { id: 1, score: 86, gradeLetter: "B" },                     ②
  { id: 2, score: 93, gradeLetter: "A" },
  { id: 3, score: 78, gradeLetter: "C" },
];
```

① The top-level structure is an array of objects
② The nested objects have id, score, and gradeLetter properties

This creates a global JavaScript variable called testScores, which we can access from the
REPL. ClojureScript creates a namespace (think a module for collecting functions and data)
called js that contains all of the global variables that are available within the browser. For
example, we can access the document object with js/document, the window object with js/window,
etc.

Figure 13.1: Sharing data between browser and REPL

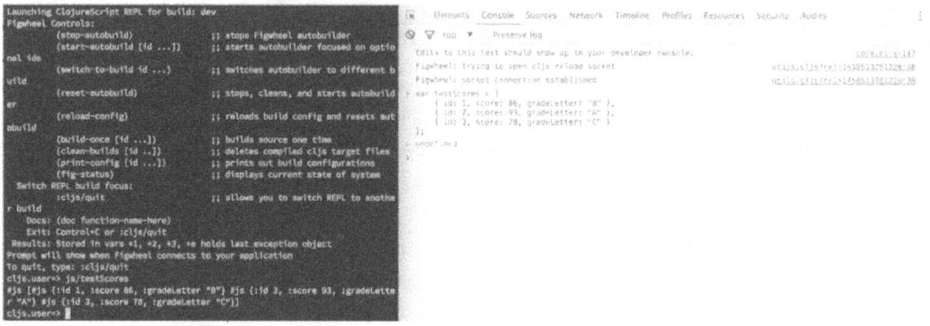

We can use the REPL to inspect this variable, convert it to a ClojureScript data structure, modify it and write a new version back out the the `testScores` variable.

Listing 13.2: Converting between JavaScript and ClojureScript data

```
cljs.user=> (def cljs-scores (js->clj js/testScores))      ①
#'cljs.user/cljs-scores

cljs.user=> cljs-scores
[{"id" 1, "score" 86, "gradeLetter" "B"}
 {"id" 2, "score" 93, "gradeLetter" "A"}
 {"id" 3, "score" 78, "gradeLetter" "C"}]

cljs.user=> (conj cljs-scores                              ②
                  {"id" 4, "score" 87, "gradeLetter" "B"})
[{"id" 1, "score" 86, "gradeLetter" "B"}
 {"id" 2, "score" 93, "gradeLetter" "A"}
 {"id" 3, "score" 78, "gradeLetter" "C"}
 {"id" 4, "score" 87, "gradeLetter" "B"}]

cljs.user=> cljs-scores
[{"id" 1, "score" 86, "gradeLetter" "B"}
 {"id" 2, "score" 93, "gradeLetter" "A"}
 {"id" 3, "score" 78, "gradeLetter" "C"}]

cljs.user=> (def updated-scores                            ③
              (conj cljs-scores {"id" 4, "score" 87, "gradeLetter" "B"}))
#'cljs.user/updated-scores

cljs.user=> (set! js/testScores (clj->js updated-scores))  ④
#js [#js {:id 1, :score 86, :gradeLetter "B"}
#js {:id 2, :score 93, :gradeLetter "A"}
#js {:id 3, :score 78, :gradeLetter "C"}
#js {:id 4, :score 87, :gradeLetter "B"}]
```

① Convert `testScores` to a ClojureScript value

② Create a modified value by appending a new score and verify that the value in the var `cljs-scores` was not changed

③ Bind the updated scores to the `updated-scores` var

④ Convert the updated scores back to a JavaScript object and update `testScores` to the new value

We can inspect the `testScores` variable in the browser to make sure that it has been changed to include the new score.

Quick Review

We still have a reference to the `js/testScores` variable.

Figure 13.2: Checking the updated scores

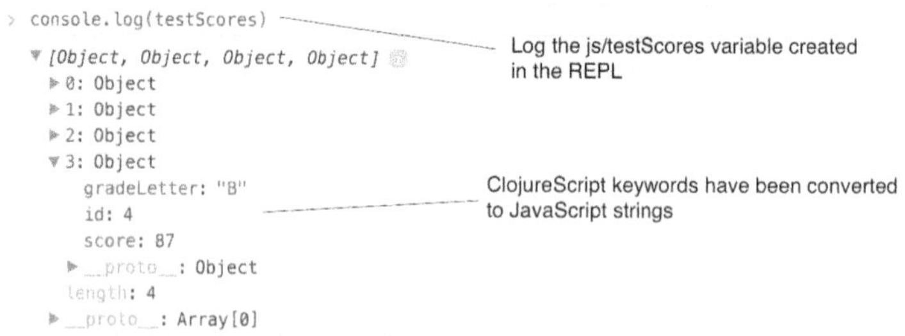

- What will happen if we change this variable in the browser's developer tools and print it out from ClojureScript?
- Will changing this JavaScript variable affect our `cljs-scores` variable?

Lossy Conversions

Since ClojureScript has richer data types than JavaScript, clj→js is a *lossy* operation. For instance, sets are converted to JS arrays, and keywords and symbols are converted to strings. This means that some ClojureScript value contained in the var, x, is not always equal to (js→clj (clj→js x)). For instance, if we have a set, #{``Lucy'' ``Ricky'' ``Fred'' ``Ethel''}, and we convert this to JavaScript, we will end up with an array: [``Ricky'', ``Fred'', ``Lucy'', ``Ethel''] (remember, sets are not ordered, so the order in which the elements appear when converted to an array is arbitrary). If we convert this array back to ClojureScript, we end up with the vector, [``Ricky'' ``Fred'' ``Lucy'' ``Ethel''], not the set that we started with, as we demonstrate below.

```
cljs.user=> (def characters #{"Lucy" "Ricky" "Fred" "Ethel"})
#'cljs.user/characters
cljs.user=> (def js-characters (clj->js characters))
#'cljs.user/js-characters
cljs.user=> js-characters
#js ["Ricky" "Fred" "Lucy" "Ethel"]
cljs.user=> (js->clj js-characters)
["Ricky" "Fred" "Lucy" "Ethel"]
cljs.user=> (= characters (js->clj js-characters))
false
```

You Try It

- Create a JavaScript object from the REPL and make it available as `window.myVar`.
- Create a JavaScript object in the dev tools called `jsObj` and modify it using the `set!` function in the ClojureScript REPL

13.3 Working with JavaScript Data Directly

Although it is very common to convert JavaScript data from the "outside world" to Clojure-Script data before working with it, it is also possible to create and modify JavaScript data directly from within ClojureScript. ClojureScript numbers, strings, and booleans are the same as their JavaScript counterparts, so they can be handled natively from ClojureScript.

Using Objects

Objects can be created either with the `js-obj` function or the literal syntax, `#js {}`.

```
Listing 13.3: Constructing JavaScript objects

cljs.user=> (js-obj "isJavaScript" true, "type" "object")   ①
#js {:isJavaScript true, :type "object"}

cljs.user=> #js {"isJavaScript" true, "type" "object"}      ②
#js {:isJavaScript true, :type "object"}
```

① Creating an object with the `js-obj` function
② Creating an object with the literal `#js {}` syntax

The `js-obj` function takes an even number of arguments, which expected to be pairs of key, value. The literal syntax looks like a ClojureScript map proceeded by `#js`. Both of these forms produce identical JavaScript objects, but the literal syntax is by far the most common.

We can get properties on JavaScript objects with the property access syntax: (`.-property object`), and we can use the `set!` function to update a property.

```
cljs.user=> (def js-hobbit #js {"name" "Bilbo Baggins", "age" 111})
#'cljs.user/js-hobbit
cljs.user=> (.-age js-hobbit)
111
```

A variant of the property access syntax supports accessing properties inside nested objects, similar to chaining property lookups on JavaScript objects. For instance, in JavaScript, we could do the following (if we were confident that all of the intermediate properties were valid):

Listing 13.4: Nested lookup in JavaScript

```
var settings = {                                              ①
  personal: {
    address: {
      street: "123 Rolling Hills Dr",
    },
  },
};

// Prints "123 Rolling Hills Dr"
console.log(settings.personal.address.street);               ②
```

① A nested JavaScript object
② Accessing a nested property

Using property access in ClojureScript accomplishes the same task. The syntax is slightly different from a normal property access: (`.. obj -propOne -propTwo`).

Listing 13.5: Nested lookup in ClojureScript

```
(println
  (.. settings -personal -address -street))
; Prints "123 Rolling Hills Dr"
```

In addition to letting us read properties on a potentially nested object, ClojureScript provides the `set!` function to mutate objects. This function takes a property access along with a new value to set, and it mutates the object at the specified property, returning the value that was supplied.

```
cljs.user=> (set! (.-name js-hobbit) "Frodo")               ①
"Frodo"

cljs.user=> (set! (.-age js-hobbit) 33)
33

cljs.user=> js-hobbit                                        ②
#js {:name "Frodo", :age 33}
```

① Setting two properties on the `js-hobbit` object
② `set!` mutates the object

Experiment

Since property access supports nested properties, it only makes sense that the the the `set!` function would support setting nested properties. Use the REPL to try to find the correct syntax for setting the following student's grade in her Physics class:

```
(def student #js {"locker" 212
                  "grades" {"Math" "A",
                            "Physics" "B",
                            "English" "A+"}})
```

Unlike the functions that we have seen that operate on ClojureScript data, `set!` actually modifies the object in-place. This is because we are working with mutable JavaScript data.

Using Arrays

Just like there is a function and a literal syntax for creating JavaScript objects, we can use the `array` function or the `#js []` literal for creating JavaScript arrays.

> **Listing 13.6: Creating JavaScript arrays**
>
> ```
> cljs.user=> (array "foo" "bar" "baz")
> #js ["foo" "bar" "baz"]
>
> cljs.user=> #js [1 3 5 7 11]
> #js [1 3 5 7 11]
> ```

For array access, we can use the `aget` and `aset` functions. `aget` takes a JavaScript array and an index into that array and returns the element at that index. `aset` has an additional parameter, which is the value to set at the specified index. Like `set!`, `aset` mutates the array in place.

> **Listing 13.7: Getting and setting array elements**
>
> ```
> cljs.user=> (def primes #js [1 3 5 7 11])           ①
> #'cljs.user/primes
>
> cljs.user=> (aget primes 2)                         ②
> 5
>
> cljs.user=> (aset primes 5 13)                      ③
> 13
>
> cljs.user=> primes                                  ④
> #js [1 3 5 7 11 13]
> ```

① Bind a var to a JavaScript array
② Get the element at index 2
③ Get the element at index 5 to 13
④ `aset` has mutated the array

We can also access the JavaScript array methods by using, `(.functionName array args*)`. This is the standard syntax for calling a method on a JavaScript object, which we will explain in much more detail later.

Listing 13.8: Using JavaScript array methods

```
cljs.user=> (.indexOf primes 11)                    ;; <1>
4

cljs.user=> (.pop primes)                           ;; <2>
13

cljs.user=> primes
#js [1 3 5 7 11]
```

① Call the `indexOf` method on `primes` - equivalent to `primes.indexOf(11)` in JavaScript
② Call the `pop` method - equivalent to `primes.pop()` in JavaScript

Quick Review

- Use the JavaScript `Array.prototype.push` function to add a value to the end of this array: `#js ["first", "second"]`
- Use the JavaScript `Array.prototype.pop` function to remove the value that you just added in the previous exercise

Best Practice

λ

Although ClojureScript makes working with JavaScript objects and arrays simple, we should prefer to use ClojureScript data structures and only convert to and from JavaScript data at the "edges" of our program or when interacting with another library. The advantages that we get from immutable data - particularly the safeguard against all sorts of mutation-related bugs - are significant, so the more of our apps are immutable, the better.

You Try It

Create the following variable in your browser's dev tools:

```
var books = [
  {
    title: "A History of LISP",
    subjects: ["Common Lisp", "Scheme", "Clojure"],
  },
  {
    title: "All About Animals",
    subjects: ["Piranhas", "Tigers", "Butterflies"],
  },
];
```

- Write an expression that will retrieve the value, "Scheme":
- Write an expression that will have the side effect of changing the title of, "All About Animals" to "Dangerous Creatures".

Challenge

Write a ClojureScript function that will take a book represented as a ClojureScript map, convert it to a JavaScript object, append it to the `books` array, and return the number of elements in `books` after adding the new book.

Possible Solution:

```
(defn add-book [book]
  (let [js-book (clj->js book)]
    (.push js/books js-book)
    (.-length js/books)))
```

13.4 Summary

ClojureScript has a symbiotic relationship with JavaScript, and to effective use it, we must be comfortable interacting with the host language. In this lesson, we looked at how to work with JavaScript data. We used both the ClojureScript REPL and the browser's JavaScript dev tools to walk through the process of converting between ClojureScript and JavaScript data structures as well as directly modifying JavaScript objects and arrays. We are now able to:

- Create JavaScript objects from ClojureScript code
- Modify JavaScript objects and arrays
- Convert between ClojureScript's data structures and JavaScript objects and arrays

Lesson 14

Performing I/O

Web applications are all about interaction. Whether it is a form to gather simple input or animated charts, almost everything that we as web developers do is about either getting data from users or displaying data to them. Considering how important I/O is to every web application, we will look at it as our next "building block."

In this lesson:

- Get user input from a webpage
- Manipulate the DOM with Google Closure libraries

Over the next couple of lessons, we will build an app that can convert temperatures between Fahrenheit and Celsius. It would probably be less than exciting if the app only converted a predefined temperature from one measurement system to the other. In order to do anything useful, we will need to interact with the user. Combining what we learn about I/O with our newfound knowledge of variables, control structures, and functions will help us build this temperature converter.

First, let's use clj-new to create a new project that uses the Figwheel template and start a REPL:

```
$ clj -X:new :template figwheel-main :name learn-cljs/doing-io :args '["+deps"]'
$ cd doing-io
$ clj -A:fig:build
```

147

Now we can go to our a browser and start learning about doing I/O the ClojureScript way.

14.1   Manipulating The DOM

Since ClojureScript has the entirety of the native JavaScript DOM libraries at its disposal, there is nothing preventing us from using these to manipulate the DOM directly. However, we have access to the entire Google Closure Library, we will opt to use that instead, since it smooths over browser quirks and provides a nicer event system than raw JavaScript. For applications that need only support recent browsers (and thus, modern versions of JavaScript), this is not much of an issue, but for applications that need to support legacy browsers, a higher-level DOM library is very nice to have.

First things first - we will create a DOM element in the REPL and append it to the body of the page. Our browser window will reflect these changes as we make them. The result will look like the following:

Figure 14.1: Dynamically creating a DOM element

In order to add an element to the DOM, we'll use Google Closure's DOM manipulation library to create an h1 element, set its text content, and append it to the end of the body. Let's walk through each of these steps in the REPL.

Listing 14.1: Creating a DOM element from the REPL

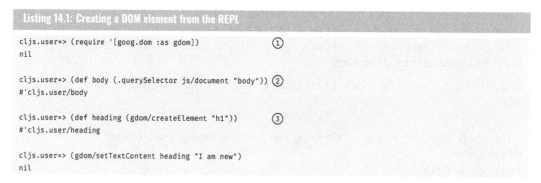

```
cljs.user=> (require '[goog.dom :as gdom])              ①
nil

cljs.user=> (def body (.querySelector js/document "body"))  ②
#'cljs.user/body

cljs.user=> (def heading (gdom/createElement "h1"))     ③
#'cljs.user/heading

cljs.user=> (gdom/setTextContent heading "I am new")
nil
```

```
cljs.user=> (gdom/appendChild body heading)          ④
nil
```

① Pull in the Google Closure Library that we need for DOM manipulation
② Use the native DOM library to get the HTMLElement for the `<body>` tag and bind it to the `body` var
③ Use Google Closure to create a new element and give it some content
④ Append the element to the body of our page

Since we are in unfamiliar territory, let's take a quick step back to look at precisely what is going on, expression by expression.

```
(require '[goog.dom :as gdom])
```

This expression loads all of the code in the `goog.dom` namespace. This namespace contains a number of useful functions for manipulating the DOM, and we will generally use this library instead of vanilla JavaScript due to the fact that the Closure Library normalizes many browser quirks. This `require` makes the functions in this namespace available under the alias, `gdom`. When calling code that we have imported from another namespace, we use the form, `(namespace/function args*)` Thus, we could call the `getDocument()` function in this namespace as `(gdom/getDocument)`.

```
(def body (.querySelector js/document "body"))
```

Next, we use native JavaScript code to get a reference to the `body` element. We do this by way of example to demonstrate that DOM elements that we obtain with raw JavaScript are fully compatible with the Google Closure Library.

```
(def heading (gdom/createElement "h1"))
```

Next, we create an `h1` element and bind it to the var, `heading`. At this point, the element is created but is not attached to the DOM.

```
(gdom/setTextContent heading "I am new")
```

Now we set the content of the detached `h1` node that we created. Now that we have created the element and set its content appropriately, we can append it to the document's body.

```
(gdom/appendChild body heading)
```

This will append the DOM node that we have created as `heading` to the document body, which we have bound to the `body` var. At this point, the DOM is modified, and the web browser will reflect the changes that we have made.

You Try It

- Using the example above as a reference, create a `p` tag with some content and append it to the body.
- Use the `goog.dom.removeNode()` function to remove both the `h1` and `p` tags. Hint: this function takes the node to remove as its only parameter.

Experiment

Now that we have created an element, let's take the next step and manipulate something that is already onscreen. Since we already have a var containing the `HTMLElement` of the `<h1>` tag that we created, let's change the style on it and add a class. According to the documentation for `goog.dom`[1], the `setProperties` function takes an element and a JavaScript object mapping properties to values and applies the properties to the DOM element.

```
cljs.user=> (gdom/setProperties heading #js {"style" "color:red;"
                                             "class" "big-title"})
nil
```

We used the JavaScript object literal syntax that we learned about in the last lesson to create a properties object. Then we called the `goog.dom.setProperties()` function with the element whose properties we wished to set and the properties object.

So far the process of manipulating the DOM is not dramatically different from what we would do in JavaScript, albeit the parenthesis are in different places, and we're using `def` instead of `var`. Most of the time, we will not be working at a "low level" like this, but we will use libraries like React to manage the DOM for us. However, we need to build a solid foundational understanding before we can fully take advantage of the higher-level technologies. Next, we will briefly talk about getting user input and handling events before putting it all together in a temperature conversion app.

14.2   Getting User Input

So far we have looked at the "O" side of "I/O", now we will turn to getting user input. For now, we will look at extracting values from form controls, since this is the most basic way to get data from users. As an exercise, we will use a text input on the page and copy the value from this input into another element. Instead of creating the entire DOM from scratch, let's modify the project's `index.html` with the structure that we want to work with. Be sure to reload your browser after updating this file, since Figwheel does not replace the entire HTML file on the fly.

---

[1]https://google.github.io/closure-library/api/

Listing 14.2: resources/public/index.html

```
<!DOCTYPE html>
<html>
<head>
  <meta charset="UTF-8">
  <meta name="viewport" content="width=device-width, initial-scale=1">
  <link href="css/style.css" rel="stylesheet" type="text/css">
</head>
<body>
  <div id="app">                                    ①
    <div class="form-control">
      <label for="user-input">What do you say?</label>
      <input id="user-input" type="text" />
    </div>

    <p>You said, "<span id="copy-target"></span>". How mighty interesting.</p>
  </div>
                                                    ②
  <script src="cljs-out/dev-main.js" type="text/javascript"></script>
</body>
</html>
```

① Populate the `app` div with markup we will use to test I/O
② Load the compiled ClojureScript

Now the process for getting the text from the `user-input` element is fairly straightforward. Once again, we will show the entire REPL session then walk through each interesting piece of it. The result will look like the following:

Figure 14.2: Getting user input

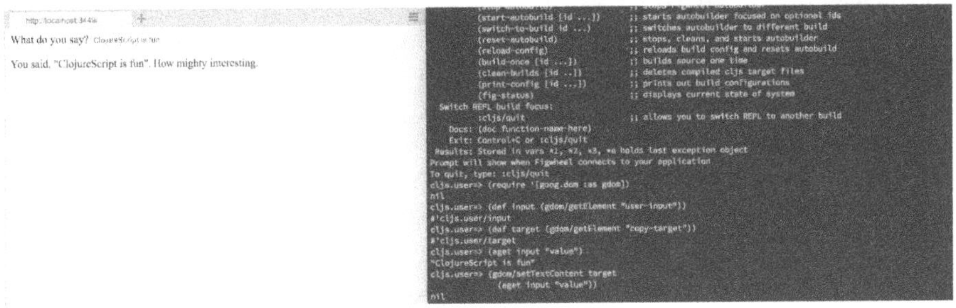

Listing 14.3: Reading the value of an input

```
cljs.user=> (require '[goog.dom :as gdom])
nil
```

```
cljs.user=> (def input (gdom/getElement "user-input"))
#'cljs.user/input

cljs.user=> (def target (gdom/getElement "copy-target"))
#'cljs.user/target

cljs.user=> (.-value input)                              ①
"ClojureScript is fun"

cljs.user=> (gdom/setTextContent target                  ②
             (.-value input))
nil
```

① `input` is a JavaScript object, so we can get its properties with property access syntax
② Get the value of the input and update the target in one expression

We have already discussed how `require` is used in this instance, so we will move on to the next expression:

```
(def input (gdom/getElement "user-input"))
```

Here, we use the `goog.dom.getElement()` function to retrieve the input element by id. We could have accomplished the same thing with native JavaScript as, `(.getElementById js/document "user-input")`, but `getElement` is more succinct. We do the same to get a reference to the target element where we will output the text that we receive from the user.

```
(gdom/setTextContent target
  (.-value input))
```

In this expression, we get the `value` property of the input element, which will contain whatever text the user has typed into it, and update the text content of the target node with this value. This code performs both the input (reading the input's `value`) and output (writing the text content of the `target`).

Since we will not spend much time with low-level DOM manipulation, we will not linger on this subject. If we ever find ourselves having to do write DOM manipulation code, the Google Closure Library has excellent documentation. Otherwise, do not be afraid to find a good ClojureScript DOM library and use it!

You Try It

- Include the dommy[2]https://github.com/plumatic/dommy) library and go through the DOM manipulation examples again using Dommy instead of Google Closure. You will

---

[2](

need to add *dommy* as a dependency to `deps.edn` and restart Figwheel in order to start using dommy. Is dommy easier to work with than goog.dom? Is there less boilerplate when working with a ClojureScript library directly?

14.3 Handling Events

Closely related to getting user inputs is the issue of handling events. We need triggers to tell us when something interesting has happened - the user clicked a button, changed the value of a text input, etc. Once again, we will use Google Closure libraries to create event handlers and bind them to the DOM. We will extend the example of copying the value from an input to another element, but this time, we will use an event to update the target element every time the user types in the input.

Listing 14.4: Using events to trigger updates

```
cljs.user=> (require '[goog.events :as gevents])
nil

cljs.user=> (defn update-target [evt]                    ①
               (gdom/setTextContent target
                 (.. evt -currentTarget -value)))
#'cljs.user/update-target

cljs.user=> (gevents/listen input                        ②
                   "keyup"
                   update-target)
#object[Object [object Object]]
```

① Define a callback function that will be called on every event
② Bind our event handler to the `keyup` event on the input

Once more, let's take a moment to walk through this code to make sure we can clearly grasp what is going on.

```
(defn update-target [evt]
  (gdom/setTextContent target
    (.. evt -currentTarget -value)))
```

Here we create an event handler function that we intend to call on every `keyup` event from the input. Notice that the inner portion of this code looks very similar to the code that we manually entered in the REPL. They both had the form, `(gdom/setTextContent target value)`. The difference here is that we are extracting the value from a JavaScript event rather than a DOM element directly.

```
(gevents/listen input "keyup" update-target)
```

Finally, we use the `goog.events.listen()` function to attach an event handler to the `input` element on the `keyup` event. Now when we type in the input, the target element should instantly be updated! We now have all of the pieces that we need to create the temperature conversion app in the next lesson.

Challenge

Using the `goog.dom` and `goog.events` libraries, write an app that does the following:

- Creates 2 password inputs (for password and password confirmation)
- Creates a status text
- Attaches listeners to the inputs so that the input values are compared every time a key is pressed
- Sets the status text to "Matches" when the inputs are the same and "Do not match" when they differ.

Hint:

- Don't forget to get the `app` node to attach the children onto.
- Bonus points if you do not disclose the typed text in the password fields

Possible Solution:

```
(ns passwords.core
  (:require [goog.dom :as gdom]
            [goog.events :as gevents]))

(defn values-same? [field-1 field-2]
  (= (aget field-1 "value")
     (aget field-2 "value")))

(defn handle-change [password confirmation status]
  (gdom/setTextContent status
                       (if (values-same? password confirmation)
                         "Matches"
                         "Do not match")))

(let [password (gdom/createElement "input")
      confirmation (gdom/createElement "input")
      status (gdom/createElement "p")
      app (gdom/getElement "app")]
  (gdom/setProperties password #js {"type" "password"})
  (gdom/setProperties confirmation #js {"type" "password"})
```

```
(gevents/listen password "keyup"
              #(handle-change password confirmation status))
(gevents/listen confirmation "keyup"
              #(handle-change password confirmation status))

(gdom/setTextContent app "")
(gdom/appendChild app password)
(gdom/appendChild app confirmation)
(gdom/appendChild app status))
```

14.4   Summary

In this lesson, we used both native JavaScript and Google Closure Library code to get user input from a webpage and manipulate the DOM. We also learned how to attach an event handler to an element so that we can evaluate a callback in response to some action that the user takes. Now that we have a way to interact with the user, we can begin creating much more useful apps. We should now know how to:

- Require and use Google Closure Library functions
- Create and manipulate DOM elements
- Retrieve user input from the DOM
- Attach event handlers to respond to user interactions

Lesson 15

Capstone 2 - Temperature Converter

Over the past few lessons, we have learned the basic concepts that we will need for practically any app that we write: variables for hanging on to values that we want to re-use, control structures for determining which code path should be taken, functions for defining re-usable behavior and calculations, and I/O for interacting with the user. While there is still much ground to cover, we can already begin to write useful apps.

In this lesson:

- Create the structure of an app declaratively in HTML
- Apply our knowledge of basic ClojureScript to create a widget-like app

---

In this lesson, we will build a simple app that will take the temperature and convert it from Celsius to Fahrenheit or vice-versa, depending on the value of a radio button that the user can toggle. For this app, we will need an input for the user to enter a temperature, a couple of radio buttons for them to select the unit of measure that they have entered, and a target to display the converted value. This is what the completed project looks like:

Figure 15.1: Complete temp converter app

First, we will create the Figwheel project:

```
$ clj -X:new :template figwheel-main :name learn-cljs/temp-converter :args '["+deps"]'
```

Again, since we will not be writing automated tests, remove the `"test"` entry from `:watch-dirs` in `dev.cljs.edn`.

15.1 Creating the Markup

In the last chapter, we manually built up the DOM, creating and appending elements in code. Besides being cumbersome to work with, this is not very idiomatic ClojureScript. Remember that we should favor *declarative* apps over *imperative* ones. This time, we will define our entire markup in HTML. Replace the `app` tag in the generated `index.html` with the following.

Listing 15.1: Temperature converter markup

```
<div id="app">
  <h1>Temp Converter</h1>

  <div class="user-input">
    <div class="unit-control">                                    ①
      <p>Convert from</p>
      <div class="radio-option">
        <input type="radio" id="unit-c" name="unit" value="c" checked="checked" />
        <label for="unit-c">Celsius</label>
      </div>
      <div class="radio-option">
```

```
    <input type="radio" id="unit-f" name="unit" value="f" />
    <label for="unit-f">Fahrenheit</label>
  </div>
</div>

<div class="temp-control">                              ②
  <label for="temp">Temperature:</label>
  <input type="number" id="temp" name="temp" />
</div>
</div>

<div class="converted-output">                         ③
  <h3>Converted Value</h3>

  <span id="temp-out">-</span>
  <span id="unit-out">F</span>
</div>
</div>
```

① Radio buttons used to switch between units
② Text input for the user to enter a temperature
③ Result display area

This markup defines all of the elements that we will use in our app, so we do not need to worry about creating any ad-hoc DOM elements in our code - we'll only deal with manipulating the elements that we have already defined. Notice that we have given each element that we will be interacting with a unique id attribute so that we can easily get a reference to them using the goog.dom/getElement function.

Quick Review

- What is the advantage of structuring an app declaratively?
- Before we write any ClojureScript code, list out the steps that are necessary to turn this static markup into an application

15.2 Code Walkthrough

Now we will write the ClojureScript code that will interact with the webpage we just created and handle the business logic of converting temperatures. To begin with, we will import the Google Closure libraries that we have been using over the past few lessons: goog.dom for DOM manipulation and goog.events for reacting to user input:

```
(ns learn-cljs.temp-converter
  (:require [goog.dom :as gdom]
            [goog.events :as gevents]))
```

ClojureScript is often written in a bottom-up fashion, in which we define the low-level operations in our domain first and develop more complex logic by combining the low-level operations. In this case, our domain is very simple, but we will still define the business logic of converting temperatures first:

```
(defn f->c [deg-f]
  (/ (- deg-f 32) 1.8))

(defn c->f [deg-c]
  (+ (* deg-c 1.8) 32))
```

Next, we want to get references to the important elements on the page. We will use Google Closure to find DOM elements on the page and bind each element to a var. This helps keeping the rest of the code clearer, and it helps with performance, since we do not have the overhead of searching the DOM every time we want to use one of these elements.

```
(def celsius-radio (gdom/getElement "unit-c"))
(def fahrenheit-radio (gdom/getElement "unit-f"))
(def temp-input (gdom/getElement "temp"))
(def output-target (gdom/getElement "temp-out"))
(def output-unit-target (gdom/getElement "unit-out"))
```

Next, we will create a few functions that we will use in our event handling code. As with any programming language, factoring each piece of logic into its own function is considered good practice.

```
(defn get-input-unit []
  (if (.-checked celsius-radio)
    :celsius
    :fahrenheit))

(defn get-input-temp []
  (js/parseInt (.-value temp-input)))

(defn set-output-temp [temp]
  (gdom/setTextContent output-target
                       (.toFixed temp 2)))
```

This code should look familiar, as we are dealing with the sort of DOM manipulation that we have been performing over the past few lessons. The `get-input-unit` and `get-input-temp` functions get the unit of measure and temperature to convert respectively, and the `set-output-temp` function updates the display element with the converted temperature.

We will also need a function that we will use as an event handler any time anything changes that will get the currently selected unit of measure and temperature and will update the results section with the converted temperature.

```
(defn update-output [_]
  (if (= :celsius (get-input-unit))
    (do (set-output-temp (c->f (get-input-temp)))
        (gdom/setTextContent output-unit-target "F"))
    (do (set-output-temp (f->c (get-input-temp)))
        (gdom/setTextContent output-unit-target "C"))))
```

This function is the core of our app. It handles each event and updates the UI accordingly. This function will be called with an event object as an argument, but we follow a common convention of using an underscore to name any parameter that we do not use. The other thing to note about this code is that it uses do to group several expressions together. do takes multiple expression, evaluates all of them in order, and it evaluates to the value of the last expression. Thus, the expression, (do x y z), would evaluate x then y then z, and the entire expression would have the same value as just z. This is useful if x and y have side effects (in our case, updating DOM elements), but we do not care what they evaluate to.

You Try It

- Add a button that will clear the temperature input

Finally, we will connect our logic to the UI by attaching the update-output function as an event handler whenever either radio button is clicked or the input is updated. This will ensure that any time the user changes anything that may affect the converted output, we recalculate the results.

```
(gevents/listen temp-input "keyup" update-output)
(gevents/listen celsius-radio "click" update-output)
(gevents/listen fahrenheit-radio "click" update-output)
```

There, in roughly 40 lines of code, we have a useful ClojureScript app! For the sake of completeness, the entire code is printed below:

Listing 15.2: learn_cljs/temp_converter.cljs

```
(ns learn-cljs.temp-converter
  (:require [goog.dom :as gdom]          ①
            [goog.events :as gevents]))

(defn f->c [deg-f]                       ②
  (/ (- deg-f 32) 1.8))

(defn c->f [deg-c]
```

```
   (+ (* deg-c 1.8) 32))

(def celsius-radio (gdom/getElement "unit-c"))          ③
(def fahrenheit-radio (gdom/getElement "unit-f"))
(def temp-input (gdom/getElement "temp"))
(def output-target (gdom/getElement "temp-out"))
(def output-unit-target (gdom/getElement "unit-out"))

(defn get-input-unit []                                 ④
  (if (.-checked celsius-radio)
    :celsius
    :fahrenheit))

(defn get-input-temp []
  (js/parseInt (.-value temp-input)))

(defn set-output-temp [temp]
  (gdom/setTextContent output-target
                       (.toFixed temp 2)))

(defn update-output [_]                                 ⑤
  (if (= :celsius (get-input-unit))
    (do (set-output-temp (c->f (get-input-temp)))
        (gdom/setTextContent output-unit-target "F"))
    (do (set-output-temp (f->c (get-input-temp)))
        (gdom/setTextContent output-unit-target "C"))))

(gevents/listen temp-input "keyup" update-output)       ⑥
(gevents/listen celsius-radio "click" update-output)
(gevents/listen fahrenheit-radio "click" update-output)
```

① Require the Google Closure modules needed for this app
② Define conversion functions
③ Store each element that we will use in a var
④ Helper functions
⑤ Event handling callback
⑥ Attach event handler to `keyup` event in the temperature input and the click event on each radio button

Challenge

This is a very simple app, and it could be extended quite easily. Here are a couple of options for new features that you can add:

- Allow the user to select Kelvin as well, and perform the appropriate conversions.

- Every time the code is reloaded, it will attach more event handlers. Use the initialization pattern discussed in Lesson 6 to ensure that the event handlers are attached only once.

15.3 Summary

We will continue to acquire new building blocks that we will be able to combine with what we have just learned to create more useful and interesting applications. By now, we have a good feel for how ClojureScript is structured, but so far we have not done much that showcases ClojureScript's advantages over JavaScript. That is about to change, as we begin to explore the areas that make ClojureScript unique. In the next lessons, we will look at the rich collection data types that make ClojureScript so productive.

Part IV

Working With Data

In this section, we will get to know one of the most distinguishing features of ClojureScript - its library of immutable collections and the functions that operate on them. First, we will survey the collections that ClojureScript offers as part of its standard library. Next, we will study the *sequence* abstraction that is one of the core abstractions of the language. Then we will devote an entire lesson to *reduce*, the most general and powerful function that operates on the sequence abstraction. We will finish this section by applying ClojureScript's collection types to real-world domain modeling. For the capstone, we will create a simple but functional contact book application.

- Lesson 16: Grokking Collections
- Lesson 17: Discovering Sequence Operations
- Lesson 18: Summarizing Data
- Lesson 19: Mastering Data With Maps and Vectors
- Lesson 20: Capstone 3 - Contact Book

Lesson 16

Grokking Collections

So far, we have been working with simple data types - strings, numbers, keywords, and the like. We saw a few collections when we took our survey of ClojureScript's syntax, but we glossed over exactly what they are and how to use them in real applications. As we might imagine, writing programs without any way to represent data that belongs together would be cumbersome at best. JavaScript has arrays for representing lists of things and objects for representing *associative* data - that is, data in which values are referred to by a specific string key, such as the `title` and `content` of a blog post. We are probably already familiar how these types of collections work from JavaScript or another language.

In this lesson:

- Using lists for managing ordered data
- Using maps for looking up values by a key
- Using sets for keeping data unique

Example: Contact Book

It should come as no surprise that collections are a core feature of ClojureScript - much more, in fact, than in most other languages. We deal with collections every day. Take the example of a contact book where we store details for friends and acquaintances. The

167

contact book itself is a collection of contact details, and each contact itself is a collection of personal information.

Figure 16.1: A contact book is a real-world collection

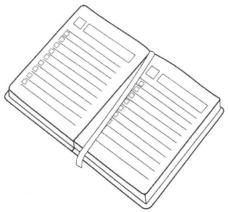

In JavaScript, we might model the contact book itself as a list and each individual contact as an object with the properties, name, address, etc. It would probably look something like the following:

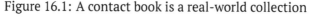

Listing 16.1: Modeling a contact book in JavaScript

```javascript
const contactBook = [                                          ①
    {
        name: "Phillip Jordan",
        address: "523 Sunny Hills Cir.",
        city: "Springfield",
        email: "phil.j@hotmail.com"
    },
    {                                                          ②
        name: "Clara Michaels",
        address: "4473 Point of the Pines",
        city: "Colorado Springs",
        email: null
    }
];
```

① Outer structure is an array for organizing a list of contacts
② Inner structure is an object for describing a contact by a specific set of properties

While we can effectively write programs using the arrays and objects that JavaScript provides, ClojureScript gives us more focused tools, and - more importantly - abstractions. In

JavaScript, we can sort or filter a list, and we can lookup a property on an object. They are different data types that have essentially different behaviors. In ClojureScript, there are multiple collection types that all conform to a specific collection protocol. For those familiar with the concept of an interface, all ClojureScript collections conform to a common interface. That means that any code that is designed to work with a collection can work with *any* collection, whether that is a vector, set, list, or map. We can then choose the specific collection type that we want to use based on its performance characteristics and have confidence that we can use the same familiar functions to operate on it. Not only that, but we can implement the collection protocol in our own code, and ClojureScript can operate on our own objects as if they were built into the language itself.

16.1   Defining Collections and Sequences

Let's take a brief step back to define what a collection is and to take a look at a closely related concept, the sequence. In ClojureScript, a collection is simply any data type that holds more than one thing. It is the opposite of a scalar, which represents only a single thing. Another way to think of a collection is as a container for other data. A sequence, on the other hand, is a linear collection that has a beginning and an end. All sequences are collections (because they are containers), but not all collections are sequences.

Figure 16.2: Collections and sequences

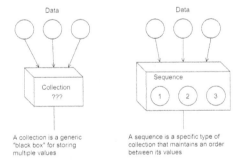

In order for ClojureScript to treat something as a collection, it only needs to be able to add something to it, and it does this by using the oddly named `conj` function (short for "conjoin"). How that something is added to the collection depends on the type of collection. For instance, items are added to the beginning of a list but to the end of a vector, and adding an item to a set only grows the set if the item does not already exist. We can see an example of the behavior of `conj` on different collections in the REPL.

Listing 16.2: Using `conj` with different collections

```
cljs.user=> (conj '(:lions :tigers) :bears)          ①
(:bears :lions :tigers)

cljs.user=> (conj [:lions :tigers] :bears)           ②
[:lions :tigers :bears]

cljs.user=> (conj #{:lions :tigers} :bears)          ③
#{:lions :tigers :bears}

cljs.user=> (conj #{:lions :tigers} :tigers)         ④
#{:lions :tigers}
```

① `conj` adds to the beginning of a list
② ...or the end of a vector
③ A set has no order, so the new element is simply added to it
④ Adding an element that is already in a set has no effect

Quick Review: Collections

- What is the only operation that we can be sure that *every* collection will support?
- Which collection type should we use to efficiently add to the beginning with `conj`?

16.2   Sequences

Sequences are a type of ClojureScript collection in which the elements exist in some linear fashion. Whereas collections need only support adding an element with `conj`, sequences must support 2 additional operations: `first` and `rest`. `first` should return the first item in the sequence, and `rest` should return another sequence with everything else. In the case that we have a singleton sequence - that is, a sequence with only one element - `rest` will evaluate to an empty sequence.

Figure 16.3: First and rest of a sequence

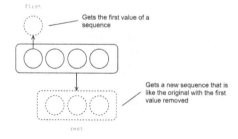

This sequence abstraction seems quite intuitive - as long as we can get the first bit of something an we can get another sequence with the remaining bits, we can traverse the entire sequence, taking the first bit off each time until nothing is left. Since the rest of a sequence is another sequence, we can take the first element of it until we finally get to the end. Keeping this in mind, we can create a function that performs some sort of aggregation over a sequence by repeatedly looping with the rest of a sequence until the sequence is empty. For example, to add all the numbers in a sequence, we could write the following function:

Listing 16.3: Traversing a sequence

```
(defn add-all [xs]
  (loop [sum 0                              ①
         nums xs]
    (if (empty? nums)                       ②
      sum
      (recur (+ sum (first nums))
             (rest nums)))))                ③
```

① Initialize the loop with a sum of 0 and all of the numbers that were given
② When no numbers remain, return the sum that has been accumulated
③ When there are still numbers left in the sequence, loop again with the old sum plus the first number in the sequence as the new sum and the rest of the numbers as the new nums

A visual will help us better understand what is going on here:

Figure 16.4: Traversing a sequence

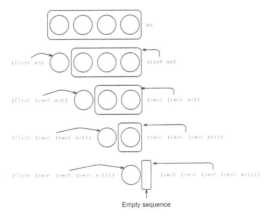

This process of repeatedly dividing a sequence between its first and rest illustrates a core concept in ClojureScript - sequence traversal. Thankfully, there is a rich library of functions that work with sequences, so we seldom have to write such tedious code as in the example above!

Extra Credit

- Look up the `reduce` function online. How could the add-all function be simplified using `reduce`?

Quick Review: Sequences

- In general, how would you get the *nth* element of a sequence using only the `first` and `rest` function?
- What is the `first` of an empty list?
- What is the `rest` of an empty list?

It's all about abstraction

Several JavaScript libraries - most notably *lodash* and *Ramda* - have similar functions that can get the first element and the rest of the elements from an array. The key difference between these libraries' sequence functions and ClojureScript's sequences is that sequences are an *abstraction* that are not intrinsically tied to any data type. If it looks like a sequence, then to ClojureScript, it is one. After getting used to programming to abstractions, JavaScript's data types start to feel a bit rigid like, well, concrete.

16.3   Using Lists for Sequential Data

Lists are one of the simplest data types in ClojureScript. They are sequences that can hold other objects of any type that can efficiently be accessed starting at the beginning and progressing linearly. Lists are most often used in two cases: first, when we have a collection of data that will always be accessed from beginning to end, and second, when we want to treat some data as a stack where the last item added is the first one to retrieve. Lists, however, are not efficient for random access (i.e. getting the *nth* element in the sequence).

data types!listsThere are two ways to create a list in ClojureScript. The first is with the `list` function, and the second is using the literal syntax, `'()`. As collections, lists support adding elements with `conj`; and as sequences, they support `first` and `rest`.

Listing 16.4: Working with lists

```
cljs.user=> (list 4 8 15 16 23 42)                    ①
(4 8 15 16 23 42)

cljs.user=> '(4 8 15 16 23 42)                        ②
(4 8 15 16 23 42)

cljs.user=> (conj '(:west :north :north) :south)      ③
(:south :west :north :north)

cljs.user=> (first '("Tom" "Dick" "Harry"))           ④
"Tom"

cljs.user=> (rest '("Tom" "Dick" "Harry"))
("Dick" "Harry")
```

① Creating a list with the `list` function
② Creating a list with the literal syntax
③ Prepending to a list with `conj`
④ Treating a list as a sequence with `first` and `rest`

16.4 Using Vectors for Indexed Data

While lists are useful in some applications, vectors are much more widely used in practice. Think of vectors as the (immutable) ClojureScript counterpart of JavaScript's array. They are a very versatile collection that can be traversed sequentially like a list or accessed by 0-based index. Unlike a list, `conj` adds elements to the *end* of a vector. For collections where we may want to get a specific element or extract a specific slice, a vector is usually the best choice.

Listing 16.5: Working with vectors

```
cljs.user=> (conj ["Moe" "Larry"] "Curly")            ①
["Moe" "Larry" "Curly"]

cljs.user=> (first ["Athos" "Porthos" "Aramis"])
"Athos"

cljs.user=> (rest ["Athos" "Porthos" "Aramis"])       ②
("Porthos" "Aramis")

cljs.user=> (nth ["Athos" "Porthos" "Aramis"] 1)      ③
"Porthos"

cljs.user=> (["Athos" "Porthos" "Aramis"] 1)          ④
"Porthos"
```

① `conj` adds to the end of a vector
② `rest` always returns a sequence
③ `nth` looks up a specific element by index
④ Vectors themselves are functions that can look up an element when given an index as an argument

We discovered a couple of interesting properties of vectors and sequences in the REPL session above. First, we see that when we applied the `rest` function to a vector, we did not get a vector back. Instead, what we got looked like a list but is in fact a generic sequence that acts much like a list. Since vectors are optimized for indexed access, ClojureScript performs some coercion whenever we use them as sequences. While this makes little difference most of the time, it is good to be aware of. Second, we see that in ClojureScript, vectors are functions that expect as their argument the index of an element to look up. That is why we could evaluate, (`["Athos" "Porthos" "Aramis"] 1`). Interestingly, almost everything in ClojureScript can be used as a function - vectors, maps, keywords, and symbols can all be used as functions (although if we do not give them the arguments that they require, we may get unexpected results).

We will be working with vectors a great deal, since their performance characteristics are appropriate in many real-world scenarios.

16.5   Using Maps for Associative Data

Maps are an incredibly useful collection that allow us to map keys to arbitrary values. They are the ClojureScript analog of JavaScript's object, but they are much simpler. Whereas JavaScript objects can have functions attached to them with complex rules (and some might say dark magic) surrounding what `this` refers to, maps are simply data. There is nothing preventing the use of a function as a value in the map, but that does not create any binding between the function and the map.

We can think of a map as a post office. Anyone who has a mailbox is assigned a specific number that they can use to find their mail. When the post office receives mail for a specific customer, they put that mail in the box that is associated with that customer. Essentially, the post office maintains an association between a box number and the mail belonging to a single customer. Likewise, maps maintain an association between some identifying *key* and some arbitrary *value*.

Maps can be created either with the literal syntax, {}, or with the `hash-map` function.

Listing 16.6: Creating maps

```
cljs.user=> {:type "talk"                          ①
             :title "Simple Made Easy"
             :author "Rick Hickey"}
```

```
{:type "talk", :title "Simple Made Easy", :author "Rick Hickey"}

cljs.user=> (hash-map :foo "bar", :baz "quux")                    ②
{:baz "quux", :foo "bar"}
```

① The common way to create a map is to alternate keys and values inside curly braces
② Maps can also be created with the `hash-map` function, which takes alternating keys and values

When using maps as a collection with `conj` or as a sequence with `first` and `rest`, the behavior may not be intuitive. ClojureScript allows us to treat a map as a sequence of `[key, value]` pairs, so when we want to add a map entry with `conj`, we append it as a vector containing a key and a value.

```
cljs.user=> (conj {:x 10 :y 12} [:z 7])
{:x 10, :y 12, :z 7}
```

Similarly, if we take the `first` of a map, we will get some map entry as a `[key, value]` pair, and if we take the `rest`, we will get a sequence of such pairs. Knowing about this behavior will help us in the next lesson when we discuss the common functions used to operate on sequences.

```
cljs.user=> (first {:x 10, :y 12, :z 7})
[:x 10]

cljs.user=> (rest {:x 10, :y 12, :z 7})
([:y 12] [:z 7])
```

One other advantage of ClojureScript maps over JavaScript objects is that any value may be used as the key - not just strings. For instance, if we were creating a Battleship-like game, we could use a vector of grid coordinates as keys.

```
cljs.user=> {[:b 3] :miss, [:a 7] :hit}
{[:b 3] :miss, [:a 7] :hit}
```

While we can use any value as a key, keywords are most commonly used because of their convenient syntax and because they also act as functions that can look up the map entry associated with themselves in a map. This is an extremely common idiom in ClojureScript and one that will be used extensively throughout this book. Additionally, maps may also be used as functions (surprise!) that can look up the value associated with the key given as the argument.

```
cljs.user=> (def fido {:breed "Boxer" :color "brown" :hungry? true})
#'cljs.user/fido
```

```
cljs.user=> (get fido :breed)
"Boxer"

cljs.user=> (:color fido)
"brown"

cljs.user=> (fido :hungry?)
true
```

We have seen that there are quite a few usage patterns for dealing with maps. This is by
no means a comprehensive reference, and we will continue to see more ways to work with
maps in later lessons.

You Try It

- What happens when you try to `conj` an element onto a map when that map already has a value for the key of the new element, e.g. `(conj {:flavor "Mint"} [:flavor`
  `"Chocolate"])`?
- As we just saw, ClojureScript treats a map as a collection of `[key value]` pairs. Knowing
  this, how might we add an entry to the following map such that we set a `:price` of `12.99`?

```
(conj {:title "Kneuter Valve", :part-num 5523} ...)
```

16.6   Using Sets for Unique Data

A set in ClojureScript resembles a mathematical set, which can contain any number of
elements, but they must be unique. Sets are often used for de-duplicating data in some
other collection or for checking whether a piece of data is contained in the set.

Listing 16.7: Working with sets

```
cljs.user=> (def badges
                  #{:quick-study :night-owl :neat-freak})    ①
#'cljs.user/badges

cljs.user=> (contains? badges :night-owl)                    ②
true

cljs.user=> (conj badges :quick-study)                       ③
#{:quick-study :neat-freak :night-owl}

cljs.user=> (conj badges :clojurian)                         ④
#{:quick-study :neat-freak :night-owl :clojurian}
```

```
cljs.user=> (first badges)                          ⑤
:quick-study
```

① Creating a set using the literal syntax, #{ ... }
② `contains?` is often used with sets and checks for membership
③ `conj` is a no-op if the element is already a member of the set
④ `conj` adds a new member if it is unique
⑤ We can treat a set as a sequence, although the order of elements is arbitrary

While sets are not used as often as vectors and maps, they are incredibly useful when dealing with unique values.

Quick Review

- Which collection should be used to represent each of the following: a product on an e-commerce site, a news feed, tags attached to a blog post?
- Using the Clojure(Script) documentation, find:
  - Additional functions that can be used with maps
  - Additional functions that can be used with sets
- Explain in your own words the difference between a collection and a sequence.

16.7 Summary

This was a long lesson, but a crucial one in our understanding of ClojureScript. One of the key features of the language is its rich collection library, but in order to wield this library effectively, we must first have a grasp on the collections available to us. We have learned:

- How the collection library is based around two abstract types - the collection and the sequence
- How sequence functions are built on top of the `first` and `rest` functions
- What data structures are built into ClojureScript and how they are used

Over the next few lessons, we will apply the collection library to some common UI programming problems, culminating in a contact book application.

Lesson 17

Discovering Sequence Operations

Programming is all about abstractions. The entire field of software engineering is devoted to making programs and systems that are better for human beings to reason about and maintain. The key to making clear and accurate systems is found in the concept of abstraction, which is identifying patterns that recur often and generalizing them to something that is more widely applicable. We humans are quite adept at abstracting concepts. In fact, it is one of the first skills that we learn in childhood. Imagine a toddler who calls every fruit that they see, "apple", because they are familiar with an apple and have identified a number of similarities between it and other fruits. Eventually, this child will learn that there is a whole class of distinct but similar objects called "fruit", each of which has its own unique properties yet shares many other properties with every other thing that we call fruit. The idea of abstraction in programming is very similar: we see a number of different constructs that appear similar in many ways, yet each of which are distinct from the rest, and we must determine how to appropriately generalize the properties that each construct shares in common.

In this lesson:

- Apply a transformation to every element in a sequence
- Efficiently convert between sequence types
- Filter sequences to only specific elements

Example: Calculating Sales Tax

Imagine that we are writing an e-commerce shopping cart app. One of the requirements is that we display the sales tax for each item in the cart as well as a summary section with the total price and the total sales tax. We will learn to apply a couple of ClojureScript's sequence operations to solve this problem.

Figure 17.1: A shopping cart

Shopping Cart

Item	Price	Sales Tax
Silicone Pancake Mold	$10.49	$0.83
Smal Pour-Over Coffee Maker	$18.96	$1.50
Digital Kitchen Scale	$24.95	$1.97
TOTAL	**$54.50**	**$4.30**

17.1 The Sequence Abstraction

As we have seen in the previous lesson, ClojureScript has identified collections as an important general abstraction. The collection abstraction had the single operation, conj, for "adding" an item into the collection. The important point to remember is that each specific collection type defines what it means for an item to be added to it, and adding to a list, a vector, a set, or a map, could have a different effect in each case. This is where the power behind abstraction comes into play - we can write code in a general way, using abstract operations like conj with the confidence that it will work regardless of the concrete data type that we work with. While collections are the most general abstraction in ClojureScript, *sequences* are a narrower, more focused abstraction. Sequences allow us to think about data that can be considered linearly, which will be perfect for the products in this shopping cart example.

Sequences are a core abstraction in many of the domains that we as web developer work in. Whether it is a feed of blog posts, an email inbox, or a series of financial transactions, most applications have one or more sequences of data at their core. When we approach these types of programs from an object-oriented approach, we usually think first about the individual objects in the system and what behaviors they support. For instance, in the case of an email program, we might be inclined to start by creating a Message object with messages like markRead() or getLabels(). Once we have modeled these objects, we might build some sort of collection object to put them in, or we may just use an array and iterate over it. The ClojureScript way is a little different (and simpler). Instead of focusing on the individual behaviors of each granular object, we begin by thinking about the collective properties such as, "Which messages are read?", or "How many messages are in the inbox?"

Let's take a step back and consider how we can think about the shopping cart problem in terms of sequences. First, we can model the cart as a vector of line items where each line item is a map with a :name and :price key.

```
Listing 17.1: Modeling a shopping cart

cljs.user=> (def cart [{:name "Silicone Pancake Mold" :price 10.49}
                        {:name "Small Pour-Over Coffee Maker" :price 18.96}
                        {:name "Digital Kitchen Scale" :price 24.95}])
#'cljs.user/cart
```

There are two properties that we need to know about this sequence. First, we need to know how to calculate sales tax for each item in the sequence, and second, we need to know how to sum all of the prices and all of the sales taxes. The general problems here are applying some operation to each element in a sequence and summarizing values from across a sequence into a single value. We can solve these problems with the functions map and reduce, respectively.

17.2 Transforming With Map

The map function takes a sequence and returns a new sequence in which every element corresponds to an element in the original sequence with some function applied to it. For instance, we can map the function inc - which gets the increment of an integer - over a list of numbers to get a new sequence in which each element is the increment of the corresponding number in the original sequence.

```
cljs.user=> (map inc '(100 200 300))
(101 201 301)
```

When we mapped the inc function over the list, (100 200 300), the result was a new list, (101, 201, 301). Each number in this new list is the increment of each element in the original list. You can imagine map as walking over a sequence, and as it comes to each element, it takes that element, passes it through a function, and puts the result into a new sequence. In this case, it applied inc to 100 and put the result, 101 into the new sequence. It did the same with the second and third elements, transforming 200 to 201 and 300 to 301. Finally, the call to map returned the list of all of the transformed numbers.

Figure 17.2: A concrete map example

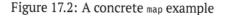

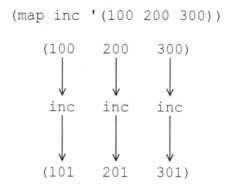

In general, map takes some function, f, and some sequence and returns a new sequence whose elements are the result of applying f to each element in the original sequence. Keep in mind that map returns a *new sequence*, so the original sequence is not touched. When the problem that we are working with involves any sort of a transformation of a sequence, map is usually the first tool that we should turn to. Many of the times that we would use a for loop in another language, we can use map in ClojureScript.

Figure 17.3: A general map example

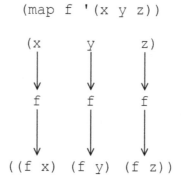

Quick Review

Take a look at the following code snippet:

```
(def samples [[8 12 4]
              [9 3 3 6]
              [11 4]])
```

```
(def result-1 (map first samples))

(def result-2 (map dec result-1))
```

- What is the value of `result-1`?
- What is the value of `result-2`?
- What is the value of `samples`?
- How would you get a collection with the length of each vector inside `samples`?

Adding Sales Tax With Map

Coming back to our initial example of adding sales tax to a shopping cart, we will use `map` to create a new cart where each item is like an item in the original cart, but with the addition of a `:sales-tax` key. If we were using JavaScript, this would be an obvious case for a for loop, similar to the code below:

Listing 17.2: Adding sales tax imperatively with JavaScript

```javascript
const taxRate = 0.079;
const cart = [                                          ①
    { name: "Silicone Pancake Mold", price: 10.49 },
    { name: "Small Pour-Over Coffee Maker", price: 18.96 },
    { name: "Digital Kitchen Scale", price: 24.95 },
];

for (let item of cart) {                                ②
    item.salesTax = item.price * taxRate;
}
```

① Define a cart as a list of products with a `name` and `price`
② Loop over every product in the cart, adding a new `salesTax` property

This code should feel very familiar for JavaScript programmers, as it just loops over an array and updates each element in-place. We updated the `cart` array in-place, which may have had an unintended consequence in some other part of the code that uses this array or any of the individual objects that it contains. What looked like a simple and innocuous piece of code could actually be the source of subtle bugs down the road.

We can use `map` to write a solution in ClojureScript (or JavaScript) that - in addition to being more concise - is simpler and less error-prone. Remember that `map` takes two arguments: a function to apply to each individual element, and a sequence. We already have a simple model of a shopping cart that we will use, so all that we need is a function to apply to each cart item that will produce a new item with sales tax added. Mapping this function over our shopping cart then becomes a one-liner.

```
Listing 17.3: Adding sales tax with ClojureScript

cljs.user=> (def tax-rate 0.079)
#'cljs.user/tax-rate

cljs.user=> (defn add-sales-tax [cart-item]              ①
              (let [{:keys [price]} cart-item]
                (assoc cart-item :sales-tax (* price tax-rate))))
#'cljs.user/add-sales-tax

cljs.user=> (add-sales-tax {:name "Medium T-Shirt"      ②
                            :price 10.00})
{:name "Medium T-Shirt", :price 10, :sales-tax 0.79}

cljs.user=> (map add-sales-tax cart)                    ③
({:name "Silicone Pancake Mold", :price 10.49, :sales-tax 0.8287100000000001}
 {:name "Small Pour-Over Coffee Maker", :price 8.96, :sales-tax 0.70784}
 {:name "Digital Kitchen Scale", :price 24.95, :sales-tax 1.97105})
```

① Define a function that transforms an item without sales tax into an item with sales tax

② Test this function on a single item

③ Map this transformation over the entire cart to get a new cart with sales tax added

The meat of this code is in the add-sales-tax function, which takes a single cart item and returns an item with sales tax. One of the most important aspects of creating maintainable code is choosing good names, so we use a let expression to name the price of the item passed in simply price. On the next line, we use the assoc function to create a new map that is like cart-item but with the addition of one more entry whose key is :sales-tax and whose value is (* price tax-rate). assoc is an incredibly useful utility function that allows us to add or update a specific entry in an *associative* collection - that is, a collection that has the concept of *keys* that are associated with a *value*, most commonly maps. We pass assoc a collection (in this case, cart-item), the key that we wish to set, and the value to set it to, and the result is a new collection with the appropriate entry added or updated.

Next, we test this function on a single cart item to ensure that it works as expected. This test could be copied almost verbatim into a unit test suite to protect against regressions, but we will save that for another lesson. Finally, we get the result that we want with one simple expression: (map add-sales-tax cart). This expression reads almost like English, "Map the 'sales-tax' function over the 'cart' sequence." There are no array indexes to maintain, no possibility of off-by-1 errors, overwriting variables, or unintended consequences of mutating cart. The solution, like all ClojureScript strives to be, is simple and concise.

You Try It

Now that we have seen how map works, let's write some code to perform various transformations to the product list.

- Write a map expression that returns a sequence of only the names of the products (hint: the :name keyword acts as a function that looks up the :name key in a map.
- Write a discount function that takes a list of products and a percent amount to deduct from the price of each product and returns a sequence of discounted products. You can fill in this template as a starting point:

```
(defn discount [products pct-discount]
  (map (fn [product] ...) products))
```

17.3 Coercing Results With Into

There is one final "gotcha" that we need to be aware of with map and other sequence operations. As we can see in this example, cart is a vector, but the result of the call to map was something that looked like a list. That is no mistake - map, filter, and other sequence functions commonly accept any type of sequence as input but return a general data structure called a seq as a result. A seq is a general sequence type that behaves similarly to a list. When we build up a pipeline of functions to pass some sequence through, we generally don't care about what data type is produced at each step, since we rely on the sequence abstraction to treat a vector in the same way as a list and a list in the same way as a seq, etc. A common ClojureScript idiom is to use the into function to convert a seq back into the type that we want afterwards:

```
Listing 17.4: Coercing a seq

cljs.user=> (def my-vec ["Lions" "Tigers" "Bears" "Lions"])
#'cljs.user/my-vec

cljs.user=> (defn loud [word]
              (str word "!"))
#'cljs.user/loud

cljs.user=> (map loud my-vec)                      ①
("Lions!" "Tigers!" "Bears!" "Lions!")

cljs.user=> (into [] (map loud my-vec))            ②
["Lions!" "Tigers!" "Bears!" "Lions!"]

cljs.user=> (into '() (map loud my-vec))           ③
("Lions!" "Bears!" "Tigers!" "Lions!")
```

```
cljs.user=> (into #{} (map loud my-vec))              ④
#{"Lions!" "Tigers!" "Bears!"}
```

① Mapping yields a seq
② The seq can be put into a new vector
③ Putting the seq into a list reverses the elements
④ Putting the seq into a set de-duplicates it

`into` takes a destination collection and a source collection and *conjoins* every element in the destination collection to the source collection. It walks over the source sequence one element at a time, using the same semantics as the `conj` function to add each element to the destination sequence. Since `conj` adds to the end of a vector but the beginning of a list, this explains why the elements in the resulting list is reversed. This pattern of coercing sequences with `into` is extremely common in ClojureScript, and we will use it extensively in later lessons.

Quick Review

As we have just learned, `into` repeatedly applies `conj` to add each element from some sequence into a collection. We need to be familiar with how `conj` works with different collections in order to understand the results of into.

- Re-write the following expression as a series of calls to `conj`: `(into [] '(:a :b :c))`
- What is the result of `(conj (conj (conj '() 1) 2) 3)`
- What would change if we replaced the empty list, `'()` in the previous exercise with an empty vector, `[]`?

17.4   Refining With Filter

We can now transform one sequence into another with `map`. There are many problems that we can solve with just this one tool, but consider the case where we don't want to consider *every* element in a sequence - for instance, we are only interested in processing taxable items or users over the age of 21 or addresses in the state of Vermont. In these cases, `map` will not suffice, since map always produces a new sequence in which each element has a 1-to-1 correspondence to an element in the original sequence. This is where `filter` comes into play. Whereas we use map to transform a sequence in its entirety, we use filter to narrow down a sequence to only the elements that we are interested in.

The `filter` function is fairly straightforward and similar to JavaScript's `Array.prototype.filter()` function. It takes a function, `f`, and a sequence, `xs` and returns a new sequence of only the elements for which (`f x`) returns a truthy value. Again, this is one of those functions that is much easier to understand once we see it in action.

Listing 17.5: Filtering a sequence

```
cljs.user=> (filter even? '(1 2 3 4 5))          ①
(2 4)

cljs.user=> (defn longer-than-4? [s]             ②
              (> (count s) 4))
#'cljs.user/longer-than-4?

cljs.user=> (filter longer-than-4?               ③
               ["Life" "Liberty" "Pursuit" "of" "Happiness"])
("Liberty" "Pursuit" "Happiness")
```

① Filter a sequence with a standard library function
② Define a predicate (a function that returns a boolean) to use with filter
③ Filter using the function we just defined

We can think of `filter` as inspecting the original sequence and only allowing certain elements through to the new sequence. It is kind of like a bouncer who enforces certain rules to determine who has access. If any element does not meet the criteria, they're out! In the first example, we gave `filter` the criteria function (often called a *predicate*), `even?`, and a list of numbers. It checked each number in the list against the function `even?` and built up a new sequence from only the even numbers. This process is illustrated below:

Figure 17.4: Applying filter to a sequence

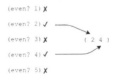

In the second example, we pass a function that we created to filter, but the process is exactly the same. The length of each string that we pass in is checked, and only words that exceed four characters are in the filtered sequence.

Finding Taxable Items With Filter

With this knowledge of how `filter` operates, it is simple to get only the taxable items from the shopping cart. First, we'll update our cart model to include a `:taxable?` key on each item.

```
cljs.user=> (def cart [{:name "Silicone Pancake Mold" :price 10.49 :taxable? false}
                        {:name "Small Pour-Over Coffee Maker" :price 18.96 :taxable? true}
                        {:name "Digital Kitchen Scale" :price 24.95 :taxable? true}])
#'cljs.user/cart
```

Now let's take a first pass at filtering the list to only the taxable items.

```
cljs.user=> (defn is-taxable? [item]
              (get item :taxable?))
#'cljs.user/is-taxable?

cljs.user=> (filter is-taxable? cart)
({:name "Small Pour-Over Coffee Maker", :price 18.96, :taxable? true}
 {:name "Digital Kitchen Scale", :price 24.95, :taxable? true})
```

Three lines of code (including the predicate function) to filter a sequence is not bad. Even better, there is no `for` loop in sight, which means that there is no room for off-by-one errors. This is pretty concise, but in ClojureScript, there is usually a way to make things more concise. Remember that keywords can be used as functions that look themselves up in a map. That means that if we call, (`:taxable? {:name "Small Pour-Over Coffee Maker" :price 18.96 :taxable? true})`, it will look up the `:taxable?` key in the map, `{:name "Small Pour-Over Coffee Maker" :price 18.96 :taxable? true}`, yielding `true`. This means that our `is-taxable?` function is redundant and can be replaced with just the keyword, `:taxable?`.

```
cljs.user=> (filter :taxable? cart)
({:name "Small Pour-Over Coffee Maker", :price 18.96, :taxable? true}
 {:name "Digital Kitchen Scale", :price 24.95, :taxable? true})
```

We just accomplished filtering the list with a 1-liner that is every bit as clear as the previous version and is far simpler than the JavaScript alternative. Now we can really start to appreciate the simplicity that is so highly prized in the ClojureScript community.

Challenge

Data manipulation is one of ClojureScript's strongest suits, but it does not serve much use until we somehow present it to the users of our system. Create a ClojureScript file that defines a shopping cart and renders a list of the name, price, and tax of every *taxable* product that it contains. One possible solution is below.

Listing 17.6: Rendering a shopping cart

```
(ns shopping-cart.core
  (:require [goog.dom :as gdom]))

(def tax-rate 0.079)
(def cart [{:name "Silicone Pancake Mold" :price 10.49 :taxable? false}
           {:name "Small Pour-Over Coffee Maker" :price 18.96 :taxable? true}
           {:name "Digital Kitchen Scale" :price 24.95 :taxable? true}])

(defn add-sales-tax [cart-item]
  (assoc cart-item
         :sales-tax (* (:price cart-item) tax-rate)))

(def taxable-cart
  (map add-sales-tax
       (filter :taxable? cart)))

(def item-list (gdom/createDom "ul" nil ""))

;; Helper function to generate the display text for a product
(defn display-item [item]
  (str (:name item)
       ": "
       (:price item)
       " (tax: "
       (.toFixed (:sales-tax item) 2)
       ")"))

;; Create the list of products
(doseq [item taxable-cart]
  (gdom/appendChild
    item-list
    (gdom/createDom "li" #js {} (display-item item))))

;; Clear the entire document and append the list
(gdom/removeChildren (.-body js/document))
(gdom/appendChild (.-body js/document) item-list)
```

17.5 Summary

In this lesson, we started to feel the power of programming using the high-level sequence abstraction. We learned that most of the places where we would use a `for` loop in JavaScript can be expressed more clearly and concisely with a sequence operation. Finally we put this knowledge to use in creating a shopping cart component that renders items in a cart with sales tax. The operations that we looked at in this lesson all took a sequence in and evaluated to a new sequence. In the next lesson, we will look at another useful class of problems that take a sequence in and evaluate to a scalar value.

Lesson 18

Summarizing Data

So far we have learned some useful operations that we can perform over sequences:

- `map` for transforming each element
- `filter` for selecting certain elements
- `into` for converting between collection types

There is a lot that we can do with just these few functions. In fact, we rarely need to use something like a `for` loop with these functions at our disposal. In the last lesson, we used these functions to calculate sales tax for items in a shopping cart and filter to only the taxable items. However, consider the scenario where we would like to get the total price of the cart or the average value of items in the cart. In this case, we cannot use map - we want a single value, and map always evaluates to another sequence the same size as the original. Filter is also obviously not what we are looking for. Is there some way to get "summary" data from out of a sequence without resorting to `for` loops? There are indeed other options, the most common of which is the `reduce` function.

In this lesson:

- Aggregating values over an entire sequence
- Writing reducing functions
- Simplifying recursive code with `reduce`

Exercise: Getting cart value

Let's take the same general shopping cart model from the last lesson and try to find the total value of every item in the cart. We will again consider an example of how we could do this imperatively in JavaScript. This time, we are going on a space journey and need to pick up a couple of supplies that we may need on the way:

Listing 18.1: Imperative shopping cart value

```javascript
const cart = [                                          ①
    { name: "Tachyon Emitter Array", price: 1099.45 },
    { name: "Dilithium Matrix", price: 2442.00 },
    { name: "Antimatter Chamber Sealant Rings (4)", price: 19.45 },
    { name: "Toothbrushes (2-pack)", price: 8.50 }
];

let total = 0;                                          ②
for (let item of cart) {
    total += item.price;
}

console.log(total.toFixed(2)); // "3569.40"
```

① Use the same cart data structure that we used in the previous lesson
② Calculate a running total with a `for` loop

The pattern here is easy to see: we have some value - in this case the variable, `total` that is updated for every element in the `cart` array. We see and use code like this on a daily basis, so it is not hard to figure out what is going on, but there is unnecessary complexity in the for loop. In ClojureScript, the pattern that we will use is a `reduce`.

```clojure
cljs.user=> (def cart                                   ①
              [{:name "Tachyon Emitter Array" :price 1099.45}
               {:name "Dilithium Matrix" :price 2442.00}
               {:name "Antimatter Chamber Sealant Rings (4)" :price 19.45}
               {:name "Toothbrushes (2-pack)" :price 8.50}])
#'cljs.user/cart

cljs.user=> (defn add-price [total item]                ②
              (+ total (:price item)))
#'cljs.user/add-price

cljs.user=> (def total (reduce add-price 0 cart))       ③
#'cljs.user/total

cljs.user=> (.toFixed total 2)
"3569.40"
```

1. Define the cart data structure
2. Create a reducing function that takes a running total and a new element and yields a new total
3. Apply this reducing function to the entire cart to extract the total

18.1 Understanding Reduce

While the workings of `map` and `filter` were evident just looking at some code that uses them, we need to dig a little deeper with `reduce`. Like `map` and `filter`, it takes a function and a sequence and returns *something*. However, `reduce` also takes an extra parameter, and the function that it takes looks a little different than the functions that we passed to `map` and `filter`. For one thing, this function takes two parameters instead of just one. It also does not always return a sequence. So then, how does `reduce` work?

Reduce commonly takes three parameters: an initial value, a reducing function, and a sequence. It first evaluates the reducing function with the initial value and the first element of the sequence as its arguments and takes the evaluated value and passes it into the reducing function again, along with the second item of the collection. It continues evaluating the reducing function for each element in the sequence, feeding the resulting value back into the next call. Finally, `reduce` itself evaluates to whatever the final call to the reducing function yields. This it quite a lot to wrap our heads around, so let's use a diagram to help us understand visually what is going on.

Figure 18.1: Reducing over a sequence

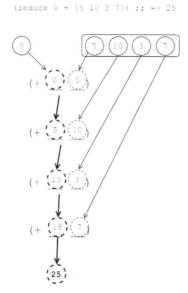

We can see that reduce keeps building up a value over each evaluation of the reducing function. On the first call, it added the initial value, 0 and the first element of the sequence, 5, to get 5. It then added this value and the next element in the sequence, 10, to get 15. It proceeded through the entire sequence in this manner and yielded the last value, 25, as the final result. Notice that we were able to take a function that does not know how to operate on a sequence (+) and somehow applied it to get the sum of all of the numbers in a sequence.

Imagine children packing snowballs for a snowball fight: they hold a little bit of snow in one hand and pack on more snow with their other hand. Every time they pack on more snow, the snowball grows larger and larger, until the snowball is to their liking. Reduce operates in a very similar way, "accumulating" more and more data with each pass. For this reason, the first parameter that is passed to the reducing function is often called an *accumulator* or a *memo*.

Quick Review

Given the following code:

```
;; Create a seq of words
(def words (clojure.string/split
            "it was the best of times it was the worst of times"
            #" "))
```

```
(defn count-words [counts word]
  (update-in counts [word] #(inc (or % 0))))

(def word-counts (reduce count-words {} words))
```

- What is the data type of `word-counts`?
- What is the value of `word-counts`?

Before trying this code out at the REPL, use a pencil and paper to write out the calls that will be made to the `count-words` function. If you need to look up documentation on a specific function that is unfamiliar, you can either call (`doc function-name`) from the REPL or look up the function on clojuredocs.org.

18.2 Reduce Use Cases

Reduce is the go-to tool for any case when:

- We need to accumulate state while walking over a sequence, and
- There is not an existing function in the standard library that does what we want

Imagine that our app tracks user events on a webpage for analytics purposes. We have a list of events that are modeled as a map with a the `:event` that the user performed and the `:timestamp` at which the event took place:

```
(def events [{:event :click, :timestamp 1463889739}
             {:event :typing, :timestamp 1463889745}
             {:event :click, :timestamp 1463889746}
             {:event :click, :timestamp 1463889753}])
```

Our task is to figure out the longest interval during which the user was idle. To do this, we need to keep track of the longest time between events that we have seen so far and the last timestamp that we have seen. Since there are multiple items that we want to keep track of, we can use a map as the accumulator:

```
(defn longest-idle-time [events]
  (:max-idle                                        ①
    (reduce (fn [{:keys [max-idle last-ts]} event]  ②
              (let [ts (:timestamp event)
                    idle-time (- ts last-ts)]
                {:max-idle (max max-idle idle-time)  ③
                 :last-ts ts}))
            {:max-idle 0
```

```
        :last-ts (:timestamp (first events))}          (4)
        events))))
```

---

① Since `reduce` will return a map, retrieve only a single value
② Define the reducing function inline
③ Return a map from the reducing function
④ Define the initial value as a map

In this case, we want to know the longest interval between events in seconds, but we also need to keep track of when the previous event occurred so that we can calculate the new interval time. Using a map as the accumulator allows us to keep track of as many pieces of state as we need, and as a final step we get only the specific value that we are interested in, discarding the intermediate results that we no longer need.

You Try It

- Write a function that returns how many times the user clicked something.
- Write a function that takes a sequence of events and tells us how many times the user double-clicked, where a double-click is defined as two clicks within the same timestamp. You may assume that the list of events is ordered by timestamp ascending.

18.3   Being More Concise

Reduce is a handy function that helps write clear and expressive code, but there are a couple things that we should keep in mind in order to write even more concise code. First, there is a two-argument version of reduce that we can use in quite a few circumstances:

```
(reduce reducing-fn vals)
```

In this case, we do not supply an initial value to pass to `reducing-fn`. It will instead be called initially with the first two elements in `vals`. This works very well in cases where we are doing something like summing numbers:

```
cljs.user=> (reduce + [6 7 8])
21

;; (+ 6 7)  => 13
;; (+ 13 8) => 21
```

Besides saving a few keystrokes, this 2-argument version of `reduce` is easier to read.

The second tip for making reduce more concise is to try to map or filter values before reducing them. Going back to the shopping list example, if we wanted to get the subtotal of the price of all taxable items, we *could* perform everything in a single `reduce`:

```
(reduce (fn [total item]
        (if (:taxable? item)
          (+ total (:price item))))
      0
      cart)
```

However, it is usually clearer to have transformation, filtering, and reducing done as separate steps:

```
(reduce +                            ①
        (map :price                  ②
             (filter :taxable? cart)))) ③
```

① Sum all values
② Of the prices
③ Of taxable items

With `map`, `filter`, and `reduce` split into their own separate steps, the intention of this code is crystal clear, and it is *simple*. Each concern is tightly encapsulated, and no piece of code is trying to do too much. Additionally, each piece is more re-usable than if we had put all of the logic in a single reducing function.

Challenge

Reduce is a much more general function than `map` or `filter` in fact, `map` and `filter` can both be implemented using `reduce`. Here is an implementation of `map`:

```
(defn my-map [xform vals]
  (reduce (fn [new-vals elem]
            (conj new-vals (xform elem)))
          '()
          (reverse vals)))
```

Following a similar pattern, implement your own version of `filter`, and call it `my-filter`.

18.4   Summary

Let's consider what we can now do with reduce:

- Keep a running total over a sequence
- Re-write much recursive code more succinctly
- Implement any sequence operation as a reduce

In this lesson, we covered the fundamental `reduce` function, and we applied it to the problem of summing the price of every item in a shopping cart. Because of its generality and its ability to simplify recursive code, `reduce` is quite common in ClojureScript code. Now that we know how to work with sequences, we will turn our attention to modeling a domain with ClojureScript collections.

Lesson 19

Mastering Data With Maps and Vectors

In this lesson, we will explore some of the features of ClojureScript that make it simple to work with data. ClojureScript places a strong emphasis on relying on generic collection types and the standard functions that operate on them rather than creating highly specialized functions that only work on a single type of object. The object-oriented approach, which most mainstream languages encourage, is to create objects that encapsulate both the data and behavior of a specific type of "thing". The practice that ClojureScript encourages, however, is to separate functions and data. Data is pure information, and functions are pure transformations of data.

In this lesson:

- Master the most common map functions: `assoc`, `dissoc`, `merge`, and `select-keys`
- Get and set deeply-nested values
- Use the constructor pattern for creating common objects

Figure 19.1: Functions and data

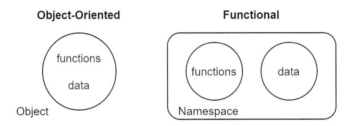

Example: Modeling a Domain

Say that we have been tasked with creating an analytics app. Before we get started, we want to model the type of objects that we will be working with. If we were using a statically typed language, we would probably start by writing type definitions. Even if we were working in JavaScript, we would likely define "classes" for the objects that we will be working with. As we define these objects, we would have to think about both the data that they contain and the operations that they support. For example, if we have a User and a ClickEvent, we might need the operation, User.prototype.clickEvent().

Figure 19.2: Analytics domain: users and their actions

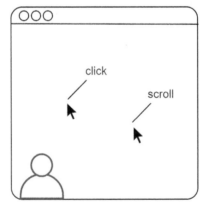

With ClojureScript, we will consider data and functions separately. This approach ends up being flexible, as we will see that most of the operations that we want to perform on the data are simple and re-usable. In fact, it is common to find that the exact operation that you need is already part of the standard library. Ultimately, the combination of the concision of code and the richness of the standard library means that we write fewer lines of code than we would in JavaScript, which leads to more robust and maintainable applications.

19.1 Domain Modeling with Maps and Vectors

We are now quite familiar with maps and vectors as well as some of the collection and sequence operations that can be used on them. Now we can put them in practice in a real domain: an analytics dashboard. The main concepts that we need to model are *user*, *session*, *page-view*, and *event*, and the relationships between these models are as follows:

- A user has one or more sessions
- A session has one or more page-views and may belong to a user or be anonymous
- A page-view has zero or more events

We now know enough to create some sample data. Let's start at the "bottom" with the simplest models and work our way up to the higher-level models. Since an *event* does not depend on any other model, it is a good place to start.

Modeling Events

An event is some action that the user performs while interacting with a web page. It could be a *click*, *scroll*, *field entry*, etc. Different events may have different properties associated with them, but they all have at least a type and a timestamp.

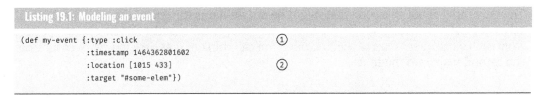

Listing 19.1: Modeling an event

```
(def my-event {:type :click                        ①
               :timestamp 1464362801602
               :location [1015 433]                ②
               :target "#some-elem"})
```

① Every event will have :type and :timestamp entries
② The remaining entries will be specific to the event type

When we think of data types like *event* in ClojureScript, we usually create at least a mental schema of the data type. There are libraries that we can use to enforce a schema on our data, most notably clojure.spec[1], but for now we will just enforce the "shape" of our data structures by convention. That is, we will ensure that whenever we create an event, we create it with a timestamp and a type. In fact, it is a common practice to define one or more functions for constructing the new data types that we create. Here is an example for how we might do this with *events*:

---

[1]https://clojure.org/about/spec

Listing 19.2: Using a constructor function

```
cljs.user=> (defn event [type]
              {:type type
               :timestamp (.now js/Date)})
#'cljs.user/event

cljs.user=> (event :click)
{:type :click, :timestamp 1464610050488}}]
```

This function simply abstracts the process of creating a new object that follows the convention that we have established for events. We should also create a constructor function for click events specifically:

```
cljs.user=> (defn click [location target]
              (merge (event :click)
                     {:location location, :target target}))
#'cljs.user/click

cljs.user=> (click [644 831] "#somewhere")
{:type :click,
 :timestamp 1464610282324,
 :location [644 831],
 :target "#somewhere"}
```

The only thing about this code that might be unfamiliar is the use of the `merge` function. It takes at least two maps and returns a new map that is the result of adding all properties from each subsequent map to the first one. You can think of it as `conj`-ing every entry from the second map onto the first.

Quick Review: Merge

- In the REPL, define 2 maps and merge them together
- Define 3 maps and merge them together, e.g. `(merge map-1 map-2 map-3)`
- Does `merge` mutate (change) any of the maps that we pass in?
- What is the result of the following expression?

```
(let [orig {:name "Cookie Monster" :food "Cookies!!"}
      overwrite {:profession "puppet" :food "Lasagne"}]
  (merge orig overwrite))
```

You Try It

- We are representing coordinates on a page with a 2-element vector containing, [x-position, y-position]. Define a function, location, that will create a location given two numbers, such that the following expressions will yield the same result:

```
;; Expression 1 - Define location inline
(click [644 831] ".link")


;; Expression 2 - Construct location with a function
(click (location 644 831) ".link")
```

A Word on Constructors

We have been talking about the concept of *constructors* in ClojureScript. Unlike JavaScript, constructors in ClojureScript are just plain functions that return data. There is no special treatment of constructor functions in the language - they are merely a convenience for us developers to easily create new data while consolidating the creation code in one place.

Modeling page-views

With events done, we can now model page-views. We will go ahead and define a constructor for page-views:

Listing 19.3: Modeling a page-view

```
cljs.user=> (defn page-view
              ([url] (page-view url (.now js/Date) []))      ①
              ([url loaded] (page-view url loaded []))
              ([url loaded events]
                {:url url
                 :loaded loaded
                 :events events}))

cljs.user=> (page-view "some.example.com/url")              ②
{:url "some.example.com/url",
 :loaded 1464612010514,
 :events []}

cljs.user=> (page-view "http://www.example.com"             ③
                       1464611888074
                       [(click [100 200] ".logo")])
{:url "http://www.example.com",
 :loaded 1464611888074,
```

```
:events [{:type :click,
          :timestamp 1464611951519,
          :location [100 200],
          :target ".logo"}]}
```

---

① Define `page-view` with 3 arities
② `page-view` can be called with just a URL
③ ...or with a URL, loaded timestamp, and vector of events

Just as we did with events, we created a constructor to manage the details of assembling a map that fits our definition of what a *page-view* is. One different aspect of this code is that we are using a multiple-arity function as the constructor and providing default values for the `loaded` and `events` values when they are not supplied. This is a common pattern in ClojureScript for dealing with default values for arguments.

Modeling Sessions

Moving up the hierarchy of our data model, we now come to the *Session*. Remember that a session represents one or more consecutive page-views from the same user. If a user leaves the site and comes back later, we would create a new session. So the session needs to have a collection of page-views as well as identifying information about the user's browser, location, etc.

```
Listing 19.4: Modeling a session

cljs.user=> (defn session
  ([start is-active? ip user-agent] (session start is-active? ip user-agent []))
  ([start is-active? ip user-agent page-views]
   {:start start
    :is-active? is-active?
    :ip ip
    :user-agent user-agent
    :page-views page-views}))

cljs.user=> (session 1464613203797 true "192.168.10.4" "Some UA")
{:start 1464613203797, :is-active? true, :ip "192.168.10.4", :user-agent "Some UA", :page-views []}
```

There is nothing new here. We are simply enriching our domain with more types that we will be able to use in an analytics application. The only piece that remains is the *User*.

You Try It

Now that we have walked through the definition of *events*, *page-views*, and *sessions*, you have all of the tools that you need to define a data type for users.

- Define the "shape" of a user. It should include at least the following: `:id`, `:name`, `:sessions`.
- Create a constructor function that can create a user with or without a collection of sessions
- For extra credit, create another function called `anonymous-user` that creates a user that has no id or name

We now have a fairly complete domain defined for our analytics application. Next, we'll explore how we can interact with it using primarily functions from ClojureScript's standard library. Below is a sample of what some complete data from our domain looks like at this point. It will be helpful to reference this data as we move on.

Listing 19.5: Sample data for an analytics domain

```
;; User
{:id 123
 :name "John Anon"
 :sessions [

   ;; Session
   {:start 1464379781618
    :is-active? true
    :ip 127.0.0.1
    :user-agent "some-user-agent"
    :page-views [

      ;; Pageview
      {:url "some-url"
       :loaded 1464379918936
       :events [

         ;; Event
         {:type :scroll
          :location [403 812]
          :distance 312
          :timestamp 1464380102036}

         ;; Event
         {:type :click
          :location [644 112]
          :target "a.link.about"
          :timestamp 1464380117760}]}]}]}
```

19.2 Working With Associative Data

Most of our analytics data is in the form of maps, which are simple key-value associations. As we have just seen, there is quite a lot of data that can be modeled using only maps, so it stands to reason that ClojureScript would provide good tools for operating on them. This is indeed the case. We will look at several functions that we will keep coming back to when we work with maps: `assoc`, `dissoc`, and `select-keys`. There are more function in the standard library that can be used on maps, but these are the most commonly used and deserve some explanation. The Clojure Cheatsheet[2] is an excellent reference for the functions that we will not be able to cover.

More or Less: Adding and Removing Elements

ClojureScript has a very helpful pair of functions for adding and removing map entries: `assoc` and `dissoc`. Unlike setting and deleting JavaScript object properties, `assoc` and `dissoc` do not touch the maps that we supply. Instead, they return new maps. By now, we should be familiar with the idea of working with immutable data, but it still takes some getting used to.

Adding Values With `assoc`

Let's consider the *session* model that we just created. It has identifying information about user's visit to our website. Our new requirement is to add a *duration* to every session once the user has logged out or left the site. In this case, we just need to add a new entry to the session map - let's call it `:duration`.

Figure 19.3: Associating data into a map

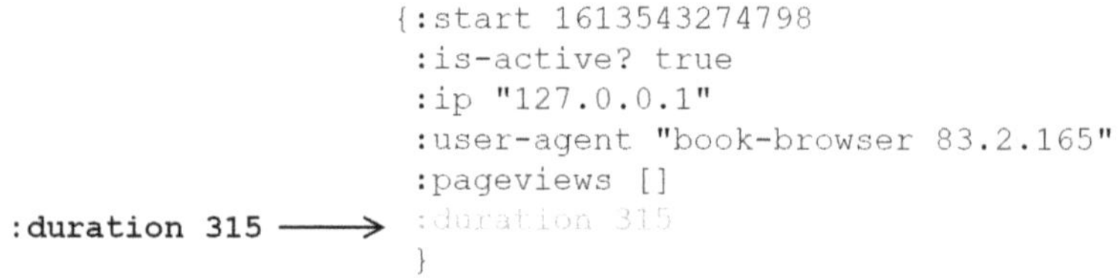

```
                          {:start 1613543274798
                           :is-active? true
                           :ip "127.0.0.1"
                           :user-agent "book-browser 83.2.165"
                           :pageviews []
      :duration 315 ———→   :duration 315
                           }
```

This is exactly the case that the `assoc` function solves: associating some key with a value inside a map. `assoc` takes a map and a key and value to associate into the map. It can also accept any additional number of keys and values as arguments, and it will associate all of the keys and values in the map.

Listing 19.6: Adding entries to a map

```
cljs.user=> (def trail {:name "Bear Creek Trail"
```

---

[2]http://clojure.org/api/cheatsheet

```
                           :distance 7.5})
#'cljs.user/trail

cljs.user=> (assoc trail :difficulty :moderate)          ①
{:name "Bear Creek Trail",
 :distance 7.5,
 :difficulty :moderate}

cljs.user=> (assoc trail                                 ②
                   :difficulty :moderate
                   :location "Colorado"
                   :max-elevation 12800)
{:name "Bear Creek Trail",
 :distance 7.5,
 :difficulty :moderate,
 :location "Colorado",
 :max-elevation 12800}
```

① Adding a single entry
② Adding multiple entries

With that, we can write a function that, given an end timestamp, will add a :duration entry
with the number of seconds in the session:

```
cljs.user=> (defn with-duration [session end-time]
              (let [duration-in-ms (- end-time (:start session))
                    duration-in-s (.floor Math (/ duration-in-ms 1000))]
                (assoc session :duration duration-in-s)))

cljs.user=> (def my-session
              (session (.now js/Date) true "127.0.0.1" "Some UA"))
#'cljs.user/my-session

;; Wait a few seconds

cljs.user=> (with-duration my-session (.now js/Date))
{:start 1464641029299,
 :is-active? true,
 :ip "127.0.0.1",
 :user-agent "Some UA",
 :page-views [],
 :duration 14}
```

Mini Review: assoc

- Is there a difference between (assoc some-map key val) and (conj some-map [key val])?
- Does assoc mutate (change) the map that is passed in?

Removing Values With `dissoc`

Now imagine that we have added a setting where users can request that we not track their IP or user agent, so we will need to remove this data from the map before we send it off to the server. This is exactly the functionality that `dissoc` gives us: it takes a map and any number of keys to remove from the map, and it returns a new map without the keys we specified. Let's create a function, `untrack`, that returns a session without these entries:

```
cljs.user=> (defn untrack [session]
              (dissoc session :ip :user-agent))
#'cljs.user/untrack

cljs.user=> (untrack my-session)
{:start 1464641029299, :is-active? true, :page-views []}
```

Mini Review: `dissoc`

- Use `dissoc` to remove the `:region` key from this map: `{:landmark "Uncompahgre", :region "San Juan Mountains"}`
- What happens when the map does not contain one or more of the keys that we pass to `dissoc`, e.g. `(dissoc {:temp 212} :color :material :mass)`?
- Update the `with-duration` function that we created earlier to remove the `:is-active?` key from the session.

Refining a Selection With `select-keys`

Another handy function to have in our toolbox when working with maps is `select-keys`. It takes a map and a collection of keys to retain, and it returns a new map with only the keys that were passed in. If we had some portion of the application that was only interested in when a session started, whether it was active, and its page-views, we could use `select-keys` to narrow down the data to only what we are interested in:

```
cljs.user=> (select-keys my-session [:start :is-active? :page-views])
{:start 1464641029299,
 :is-active? true,
 :page-views []}
```

You Try It

It is intuitive that ClojureScript considers maps to be associative. Interestingly, vectors are also associative collections that map an integer index to the element at that index:

```
cljs.user=> (associative? [])
true
```

- Define a vector with several elements at the REPL
- Use `get` to retrieve the element at a specific index
- Use `assoc` to update the element at a specific index
- Try using the `merge` and `dissoc`, functions on the vector. Do the results surprise you?

19.3 Working With Nested Data

In any but the simplest of programs, we will need to work with nested data at some point. The analytics application that we are considering in this chapter is a good example, since we have events nested inside page-views, which are in turn nested inside sessions, which themselves are nested inside users. Using only the functions we have seen so far would be intractable at best. We will now turn our attention to several functions that allow us to work with nested data.

Drilling Down With `get-in`

We have seen the `get` function a number of times for accessing a specific element in a map or a vector. It has a cousin, `get-in`, that is used for setting values that are nested deeper inside a data structure. Instead of supplying a single key for the value to get out, we supply a sequence of keys that will be looked up in turn. We can think of this sequence as a *path* to the data that we are interested in. It is like a road map for the computer to follow to locate the data to retrieve. For instance, to get the first page-view of the first session of some user, we could use something like the following:

```
(get-in user [:sessions 0 :page-views 0])
```

Getting Nested Data

This will first look up the `:sessions` key on the `user` that we passed in. Next, it will get the first session (at index 0), then it will get the `:page-views` key on this session. Finally, it will get the first of the page-views. Notice that the get-in is really just a convenience for repeated calls to `get`:

```
(get
  (get
    (get
      (get user :sessions)          ①
      0)                            ②
    :page-views)                    ③
  0)                               ④
```

① Get the user's sessions
② Get the first
③ Get the page-views
④ Get the first

This concept of a *path* is used commonly in ClojureScript to describe how to "get to" some specific piece of data. An analogy in the JavaScript world would be chained property access on some specific object:

Listing 19.7: Getting nested data with JavaScript

```
user.sessions[0].pageViews[0];
```

At first glance, the JavaScript version looks at least as clear as the ClojureScript version - in fact, perhaps a bit clearer. However, one key feature of get-in is that if at any point in the path the next property does not exist, the evaluation will stop, and the whole thing will evaluate to nil. A more accurate JavaScript translation would be the following[3]:

```
user &&                              ①
    user.sessions &&
    user.sessions[0] &&
    user.sessions[0].pageViews &&
    user.sessions[0].pageViews[0];   ②
```

① Check every intermediate step that may be undefined
② Only get the nested data if every step in the path to it is defined

Mini Review: get-in

- Fill in the blank to make this expression true

```
(= "second"
   (get-in {:tag "ul"
            :children [{:tag "li"
                        :id "first"}
                       {:tag "li"
                        :id "second"}]}
           ...)
```

- What does the following expression evaluate to?

```
(get-in {} [:does :not :exist])
```

---

[3]JavaScript's new optional chaining feature would simplify this expression as user ?. sessions?[0] ?. pageViews?[0]

Setting With `assoc-in`

Just as `get-in` is a variation of `get` that allows for nested data access, `assoc-in` is a variation of `assoc` that allows for the setting of nested data. Calling `assoc-in` is very similar to calling `assoc` - the difference is that instead of supplying a simple key, we pass in a path to the data that we want to set.

```
(assoc-in user
          [:sessions 0 :page-views]                     ①
          [(page-view "www.learn-cljs.com" 123456 [])]) ②
```

① Path to the data to update
② Value to associate

Mini Review: `assoc-in`

- What is the result of the following:

```
(assoc-in {:tag "ul"
           :children [{:tag "li"
                       :id "first"}
                      {:tag "li"
                       :id "second"}]}
          [:children 1 :class]
          "last-item")`
```

- What is the result of the following:

```
(assoc-in {} [:foo :bar :baz] "quux")
```

Updating With `update-in`

Now that we have seen how `get-in` and `assoc-in` work, it is time to complete our trio of functions for working with nested data with `update-in`. Like `assoc-in`, it takes a data structure and a path, but instead of taking a simple value to put into the data structure, it takes a function to apply to the existing item that it finds at the specified path. The entry at this path is then replaced with whatever the function returns. Let's consider a simple example:

```
cljs.user=> (update-in {:num 1} [:num] inc)
{:num 2}
```

In this case, we specified that we wanted to operate on the element located at the path `[:num]` and increment it. This yielded a new map in which the `:num` key is the increment of the `:num` key in the original map. In this simple example, we worked with flat data, but the principle is the same for nested data. Going back to the analytics example, let's say that we wanted to add 10 pixels to the x-coordinate of a click event. We could easily accomplish this with a single `update-in`:

```
(defn add-to-click-location [click-event]
  (update-in [:location 0] #(+ 10 %)))
```

When we start building single-page apps with Reagent, we will constantly be making use of `update-in`, so it is important to make sure that we are comfortable with how to use it.

Mini Review: `update-in`

- What is the result of `(update-in {} [:foo :bar] inc)`?
- Does update-in work with both maps and vectors? Why or why not?

19.4   Summary

We covered a lot of ground in this chapter, and we are now able to do quite a bit of data manipulation, including:

- Combining maps with `merge`
- Adding and removing single properties with `assoc` and `dissoc`
- Working with deeply nested data using `get-in`, `assoc-in`, and `update-in`

Between the sequence operations that we covered in the last lesson and the additional operations that we just learned, we can write quite intricate, data-driven programs. Next up, we'll put together all that we have learned about collections and sequences to build a contact list application that keeps its data in `localStorage`.

Lesson 20

Capstone 3 - Contact Book

Over the past few lessons, we have learned the core tools for working with data in Clojure-Script. First, we learned about the basic collection types - lists, vectors, maps, and sets - as well as the most common functions for working with these collections. Then we took a closer look at the important *sequence abstraction* that allows us to operate on all sorts of sequential data using a uniform interface. Next, we discovered the reduce function and the many cases in which it can be used to summarize a sequence of data. Last, we walked through the process of modeling a real- world analytics domain. With this knowledge in our possession, we are ready to build another capstone project. This time, we will take the example of a contact book that we mentioned back in Lesson 16, and we will build a complete implementation, *ClojureScript Contacts*.

In This Lesson:

- Create a complete ClojureScript application without any frameworks
- Build HTML out of plain ClojureScript data structures

ClojureScript Contacts

Jodie Whittaker	>
Peter Capaldi	>
Matt Smith	>
David Tenant	>
Christopher Eccleston	>

♟ Edit Contact   ✕ Cancel   💾 Save

First Name

George

Last Name

Dalek

Email

exterminator@evilrobots.com

Address
Street

624 Davros Dr.

City

Tardica

State

ZX

Postal Code

00000

Country

Skaro

While we will not be printing the code for this capstone in its entirety, the completed project code may be found at the book's GitHub project[1]. As we have done previously, we will create a new Figwheel project:

```
$ clj -X:new :template figwheel-main :name learn-cljs/contacts :args '["+deps"]'
$ cd contacts
$ clj -A:fig:build
```

20.1   Data Modeling

In this lesson, we will use the techniques and patterns from the previous chapter to model the data for our contact book. The goal will be to practice what we have learned rather than to introduce much new material. We will primarily model our data using maps and vectors, and we will implement the constructor function pattern for creating new contacts. We will also implement the operations that the UI will need to update the contact list using simple functions to transform our data. With that, let's dig in to the data model!

---

[1]https://github.com/kendru/learn-cljs/tree/master/code/lesson-20/contacts

Constructing Entities

Since a contact book represents an ordered list of contacts, we will need a data structure to represent that ordered list, and as we have already seen, a vector fits the bill nicely. We can define an empty contact list as an empty vector - no constructor function necessary:

```
(def contact-list [])
```

Since an empty vector is not terribly interesting, let's turn our attention to the contacts that it will hold. Each contact will need a first name, last name, email address, and a physical address, including city, state, and country. This can easily be accommodated with a nested map, such as the following:

```
{:first-name "Phillip"
 :last-name "Jordan"
 :email "phil.j@hotmail.com"
 :address {:street "523 Sunny Hills Cir."
           :city "Springfield"
           :state "MI"
           :postal "11111"
           :country "USA"}}
```

In order to construct a new contact, we will use a variation on the constructor pattern introduced in the last lesson. Instead of passing in each field individually, we will pass in a map that we expect to contain zero or more of the fields that make up a contact. You will recall from the last lesson that the `select-keys` function takes a map and a collection of keys that should be selected, and it returns a new map with only the selected keys copied. We can use this function to sanitize the input, ensuring that our contact contains only valid keys.

```
(defn make-contact [contact]
  (select-keys contact [:first-name :last-name :email :postal :address]))
```

Since the address itself is a map, let's factor out creation of an address to another function. We can then update the `make-contact` function to use this address constructor:

```
(defn make-address [address]
  (select-keys address [:street :city :state :country]))

(defn make-contact [contact]
  (let [clean-contact (select-keys contact [:first-name :last-name :email])]
    (if-let [address (:address contact)]
      (assoc clean-contact :address (make-address address))
      clean-contact)))
```

This new version of `make-contact` introduces one expression that we have not seen before: `if-let`. This macro works just like `if` except that it binds a name to the value being tested (just like `let` does). Unlike `let`, only a single binding may be provides. At compile time, this code will expand to something like the following[2]:

```
Listing 20.1: if-let transformation

(if (:address contact)
  (let [address (:address contact)]
    (assoc clean-contact :address (make-address address)))
  clean-contact)
```

We will soon make use of a similar macro, `when-let`. Like `if-let`, it allows a binding to be provided, and like `when`, it only handles the case when the bound value is non-nil.

However, we can make the `make-contact` function a bit more concise and easier to read using one of ClojureScript's *threading macros*, → (pronounced "thread first"). This macro allows us to take what would otherwise be a deeply nested expression and write it more sequentially. It takes a value and any number of function calls and injects the value as the first argument to each of these function calls. Seeing this transformation in action should make its functionality more intuitive:

```
Listing 20.2: Thread-first transformation

(-> val                                              ①
  (fn-1 :foo)                                        ②
  (fn-2 :bar :baz)                                   ③
  (fn-3))

(fn-3                                                ④
  (fn-2
    (fn-1 val :foo)
    :bar :baz))
```

① Start with `val` as the value to thread through the following expressions
② `fn-1` will be evaluated with the arguments, `val` and `:foo`
③ The result of the evaluation of `fn-1` will be threaded as the first argument to `fn-2`
④ The macro will rewrite into a nested expression that evaluates `fn-1` then `fn-2`, then `fn-3`

This macro is extremely common in ClojureScript code because of how it enhances the readability of our code. We can write code that looks sequential but is evaluated "inside-out". There are several additional threading macros in ClojureScript that we will not go into now, but we will explain their usage as we run into them.

---

[2]The actual implementation of the `if-let` macro is slightly more complex, but the effect is the same.

Figure 20.1: Thread first macro

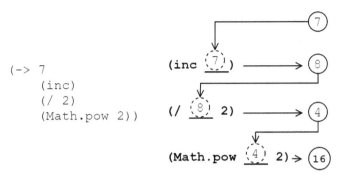

```
(-> 7
    (inc)
    (/ 2)
    (Math.pow 2))
```

With this macro, we can make our make-contact function even clearer:

```
(defn maybe-set-address [contact]                    ①
  (if (:address contact)
    (update contact :address make-address)
    contact))

(defn make-contact [contact]
  (-> contact                                        ②
      (select-keys [:first-name :last-name :email])
      (maybe-set-address)))
```

① Refactor the code that conditionally constructs an address
② Rewrite make-contact using the → macro

Quick Review

- Does if-let allow multiple bindings? For example, what would this code do?

```
(if-let [contact (find-by-id 123)
         address (:address contact)]
  (println "Address:" (format-address address)))
```

- How would the → macro rewrite the following expression?

```
(let [input {:password "s3cr3t"}]
  (-> input
      (assoc :password-digest (-> input :password digest))
      (dissoc :password)))
```

Defining State Transitions

In order for our UI to do anything other than display a static list of contacts that we define in code, we need to enable some interactions in the UI. Again, we are building our low-level domain logic before any UI code so that we can take advantage of the bottom-up programming style that ClojureScript encourages - composing small, granular functions into larger and more useful structures.

First, we want the user to be able to add a new contact to the contact list. We can assume that we will receive some sort of form data as input, which we can pass to our make-contact constructor, adding the resulting contact to our list. We will need to pass in the contact list and input data as arguments and produce a new contact list.

```
(defn add-contact [contact-list input]
  (conj contact-list
        (make-contact input)))
```

We can paste these function definitions into the REPL and then test them to make sure that they function as expected:

```
cljs.user=> (-> contact-list                                    ①
                (add-contact {:email "me@example.com"
                              :first-name "Me"
                              :address {:state "RI"}})
                (add-contact {:email "you@example.com"
                              :first-name "You"}))
[{:first-name "Me", :email "me@example.com"}
 {:first-name "You", :email "you@example.com"}]
```

Testing with the REPL

① Once again, the → macro makes our code easier to read and write

Next, we will need a way to remove a contact from the list. Since we are using a vector to hold our contacts, we can simply remove an element at a specific index:

Listing 20.3: Removing a contact

```
(defn remove-contact [contact-list idx]
  (vec                                                          ①
```

```
(concat                                         ②
  (subvec contact-list 0 idx)                   ③
  (subvec contact-list (inc idx)))))
```

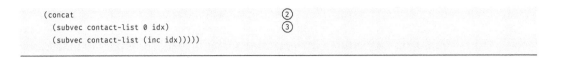

① vec converts a sequence into a vector
② concat returns a seq that contains all elements in the sequences passed to it in order
③ subvec returns a portion of the vector that it is given

Since there are a couple of new functions here that we have not seen yet, let's quickly look at what they do. Starting from the "inside" of this function, we have subvec. This function provides an efficient way to obtain a slice of some vector. It comes in a 2-arity and a 3-arity form: (subvec v start) and (subvec v start end). This function work similarly to JavaScript's Array.prototype.slice() function. It returns a new vector that starts at the start index of the original vector and contains all elements up to but not including the end index. If no end is provided, it will contain everything from start to the end of the original vector.

Next, we have concat. This function takes a number of sequences and creates a new lazy[3] seq that is the concatenation of all of the elements of its arguments. Because the result is a seq, we use the vec function to coerce the result back into a vector. Since much of ClojureScript's standard library operates on the sequence abstraction, we will find that we often need to convert the result back into a more specific type of collection.

Finally, when we update a contact, we want to replace the previous version. This can be done by using assoc to put the updated contact in the same index of contact-list that was occupied by the old version:

```
(defn replace-contact [contact-list idx input]
  (assoc contact-list idx (make-contact input)))
```

Quick Review

- We mentioned that vec converts a sequence into a vector. Given what we learned about the sequence abstraction, what will happen if you pass vec a map? What about a set?

20.2   Creating the UI

Now that we have defined all of the functions that we need to work with our data model, let's turn our attention to creating the application UI. In Section 5, we will learn how to

---

[3]Lazy evaluation was covered in Lesson 11.

create high-performance UIs using the Reagent framework, but for now, we will take naive approach of re-rendering the entire application whenever anything changes. Our application will have two main sections - a list of contacts that displays summary details about each contact and a larger pane for viewing/editing contact details.

We will use the hiccups[4] library to transform plain ClojureScript data structures into an HTML string. This allows us to represent the interface of our application as a ClojureScript data structure and have a very simple interface to the actual DOM of the page. In order to use this library, we need to add it to our dependencies in `deps.edn`:

Listing 20.4: deps.edn

```
:deps {;; ...Other dependencies
       hiccups/hiccups {:mvn/version "0.3.0"}}
```

Then, we need to import this library into our `core` namespace. Note that since we are using a macro from this library, the syntax is a little different:

Listing 20.5: learn_cljs/contacts.cljs

```
(ns learn-cljs.contacts
  (:require-macros [hiccups.core :as hiccups])
  (:require [hiccups.runtime]))
```

The translation between ClojureScript data structures and HTML is very simple:

1. HTML tags are represented by vectors whose first element is the tag name as a keyword
2. Attributes are represented by maps and should come immediately after the tag name. Omitting attributes is fine.
3. Any remaining elements in the vector are children of the outer element

For example, the following code renders a div containing a single anchor tag:

Listing 20.6: Rendering with hiccups

```
(hiccups/html                                            ①
  [:div                                                  ②
    [:a {:href "https://www.google.com"                  ③
         :class "external-link"}
        "Google"]])                                      ④
;; <div><a class="external-link" href="https://www.google.com">Google</a></div>
```

---

[4]https://github.com/teropa/hiccups

① The `html` macro renders hiccups data to an HTML string
② Create a `div`. We do not need to specify any attributes
③ Create an `a` element with an attributes map as a child of the outer `div`
④ The `a` only contains text

With this knowledge, we can start defining components for our various UI elements that produce a hiccups-compatible data structure. We can compose these functions together to create a data structure that represents the entire UI, and we'll pass this to another function that renders the whole structure to the page.

UI State

Let's take a quick step back and think about the additional state that we need for the UI. First, we need to have a flag indicating whether we are in editing mode. In editing mode, a form with contact details will be displayed in the right-hand pane. Also, we need to keep track of which contact has been selected for editing - in the case of a new contact that has not been saved yet, this property will be `nil` or omitted. Naturally, we also need the contacts on the application state. This leaves us with a pretty simple state model to support everything that we want in our UI:

```
(def initial-state
  {:contacts contact-list
   :selected nil
   :editing? false})
```

We will also define a `refresh!` function that is responsible for rendering the entire application and attaching event handlers every time our state changes. We must re-attach event handlers because we are replacing the DOM tree that contains our app, and our handlers remain attached to the DOM nodes that are discarded.

```
(defn attach-event-handlers! [state])              ①

(defn set-app-html! [html-str]
  (set! (.-innerHTML app-container) html-str))

(defn render-app! [state]
  (set-app-html!
    (hiccups/html
      [:div])))                                    ②

(defn refresh! [state]                             ③
  (render-app! state)
  (attach-event-handlers! state))

(refresh! initial-state)                           ④
```

① All event handlers that we need to attach will be attached in this function
② We will replace the empty div with our actual application HTML
③ `refresh!` will be called every time that we update the application state
④ We kick off the application with an initial `refresh!` to render the page from `initial-state`

Rendering Contacts

Let's start with the component that displays the contact summary in the list. We will be using the Bulma CSS framework to help with styling[5], so most of the markup that we are generating is for the purpose of styling the page. Additionally, we will be using the Microns[6] icon font, which uses `mu-ICON` class names.

Listing 20.7: Rendering a contact summary

```clojure
(defn format-name [contact]                                       ①
  (->> contact                                                    ②
       ((juxt :first-name :last-name))                            ③
       (str/join " ")))

(defn delete-icon [idx]
  [:span {:class "delete-icon"
          :data-idx idx}
   [:span {:class "mu mu-delete"}]])

(defn render-contact-list-item [idx contact selected?]
  [:div {:class (str "card contact-summary" (when selected? " selected"))
         :data-idx idx}                                           ④
   [:div {:class "card-content"}
    [:div {:class "level"}
     [:div {:class "level-left"}
      [:div {:class "level-item"}
       (delete-icon idx)
       (format-name contact)]]
     [:div {:class "level-right"}
      [:span {:class "mu mu-right"}]]]]])
```

① Extract the logic for a contact's display name into another function
② Use the →» (thread last) macro to pass a value through as the last argument to each subsequent function
③ The `juxt` function extracts the first and last name from the contact. It is described below
④ `idx` is needed so that we will be able to get the correct contact in our event handlers

---

[5]Bulma's styles can be found in `bulma.min.css` in the corresponding lesson of this book's GitHub repository.
[6]https://www.s-ings.com/projects/microns-icon-font/

Both of the things that we should note about this code occur in the format-name function. First, we use the —» macro to thread a value through several function calls. This works almost exactly like the → macro that we used earlier in this lesson with the exception that it feeds threads the value as the *last* argument to each subsequent function.

Second, the juxt function is a very interesting function that deserves a bit of an explanation. juxt takes a variable number of functions and returns a new function. This resulting function will call each of the original functions passed to juxt in turn using the arguments provided to it. The results are finally placed into a vector in the same order as the functions that were passed to juxt. For example, this code snippet will create a function that will get 2-element vector containing the minimum and maximum values from a collection:

```
(def minmax
  (juxt #(reduce Math/min %)
        #(reduce Math/max %)))

(minmax [48 393 12 14 -2 207])
;; [-2 393]
```

The reason for the extra set of parentheses in the call to juxt - ((juxt :first-name :last-name)) - is that we need to call the function *returned by* juxt rather than threading the contact into the call to juxt itself. Since keywords are functions that can look themselves up in maps, this expression will effectively create a vector with the first name and last name of the contact respectively.

```
((juxt :first-name :last-name) {:first-name "Bob" :last-name "Jones"})
;; ["Bob" "Jones"]
```

Adding Interactions

Let's now think about the interactions that we want to enable on the contact summary. When the row is clicked, we want to open up this contact's details for view/editing. We will attach an event handler to each list item that will set an :editing? flag on the app state and will set :selected to the index of the contact that was clicked (this is why we needed to pass idx into the rendering function and set the data-idx attribute on the row).

```
(defn on-open-contact [e state]
  (refresh!
    (let [idx (int (.. e -currentTarget -dataset -idx))]
      (assoc state :selected idx
                   :editing? true))))

(defn attach-event-handlers! [state]
  ;; ...
  (doseq [elem (array-seq (gdom/getElementsByClass "contact-summary"))]
    (gevents/listen elem "click"
```

```
(fn [e] (on-open-contact e state)))))
```

We should be familiar with the use of doseq to eagerly iterate over a sequence, but this is the first time we have seen array-seq. This function takes a JavaScript array and transforms it into a ClojureScript seq that can be used with any sequence operation - in this case, doseq.

Now that we can render a single contact list item, let's create the list that will display each list item:

```
(defn render-contact-list [state]
  (let [{:keys [:contacts :selected]} state]
    [:div {:class "contact-list column is-4 hero is-fullheight"}
     (map-indexed (fn [idx contact]
                    (render-contact-list-item idx contact (= idx selected)))
                  contacts)]))
```

This function is pretty straightforward: it renders a wrapper div with each contact list item, then it delegates to the render-contact-list-item function to render the summary for each contact in turn. There is a new function that we have not yet met, however: map-indexed. This function works just like map except that it calls the mapping function with the index of the element in the sequence as well as the element itself.

This pattern of building a UI by composing components is common in the JavaScript world as well, but in most ClojureScript applications, the method of composing UIs is function composition with pure functions that produce plain data structures.

Finally, we will briefly cover rendering the contact details form and adding/updating contacts without too much additional explanation. First, let's look at the function that renders the entire app HTML:

```
(defn render-app! [state]
  (set-app-html!
   (hiccups/html
     [:div {:class "app-main"}
       [:div {:class "navbar has-shadow"}
         [:div {:class "container"}
           [:div {:class "navbar-brand"}
             [:span {:class "navbar-item"}
               "ClojureScript Contacts"]]]]
       [:div {:class "columns"}
         (render-contact-list state)
         [:div {:class "contact-details column is-8"}
           (section-header (:editing? state))
           [:div {:class "hero is-fullheight"}
             (if (:editing? state)
               (render-contact-details (get-in state [:contacts (:selected state)] {}))
               [:p {:class "notice"} "No contact selected"])]]]]))))
```

We have already seen the `render-contact-list` function, but we still need to define `page-header`, which will display the buttons for adding or saving a contact, and `render-contact-details`, which will render the edit form. Let's start with `render-contact-details`:

Listing 20.8: Rendering contact details

```
(defn form-field                                        ①
  ([id value label] (form-field id value label "text"))
  ([id value label type]
   [:div {:class "field"}
    [:label {:class "label"} label]
    [:div {:class "control"}
     [:input {:id id
              :value value
              :type type
              :class "input"}]]]))

(defn render-contact-details [contact]
  (let [address (get contact :address {})]        ②
    [:div {:id "contact-form" :class "contact-form"}
     (form-field "input-first-name" (:first-name contact) "First Name")
     (form-field "input-last-name" (:last-name contact) "Last Name")
     (form-field "input-email" (:email contact) "Email" "email")
     [:fieldset
      [:legend "Address"]
      (form-field "input-street" (:street address) "Street")
      (form-field "input-city" (:city address) "City")
      (form-field "input-state" (:state address) "State")
      (form-field "input-postal" (:postal address) "Postal Code")
      (form-field "input-country" (:country address) "Country")]]))
```

① Since we will be rendering multiple form fields, we will extract the code for a field into its own function

② The address may or may not be present, so we provide an empty map as a default

Now let's look at the code for processing the form and either adding or updating a contact:

```
(defn get-field-value [id]
  (let [value (.-value (gdom/getElement id))]
    (when (not (empty? value)) value)))

(defn get-contact-form-data []
  {:first-name (get-field-value "input-first-name")
   :last-name (get-field-value "input-last-name")
   :email (get-field-value "input-email")
   :address {:street (get-field-value "input-street")
             :city (get-field-value "input-city")
             :state (get-field-value "input-state")
             :postal (get-field-value "input-postal")
             :country (get-field-value "input-country")}})
```

```
(defn on-save-contact [state]
  (refresh!
    (let [contact (get-contact-form-data)
          idx (:selected state)
          state (dissoc state :selected :editing?)]        ①
      (if idx
        (update state :contacts                            ②
                replace-contact idx contact)
        (update state :contacts
                add-contact contact)))))
```

① `state` within the `let` will refer to this updated state
② Use our domain functions to update the contact list within our app state

Before moving on, let's take a look at the use of `update` to transform our application state. `update` takes an indexed collection (a map or vector), a key to update, and a transformation function. This function is variadic, and any additional arguments after the transformation function that will be passed to the transformation function following the value to transform. For instance, the call, `(update state :contacts replace-contact idx contact)`, will call `replace-contact` with the contacts list followed by `idx` and `contact`.

Now, we will finally implement the page header with its actions to create and save contacts:

```
(defn action-button [id text icon-class]
  [:button {:id id
            :class "button is-primary is-light"}
    [:span {:class (str "mu " icon-class)}]
    (str " " text)])

(def save-button (action-button "save-contact" "Save" "mu-file"))
(def cancel-button (action-button "cancel-edit" "Cancel" "mu-cancel"))
(def add-button (action-button "add-contact" "Add" "mu-plus"))

(defn section-header [editing?]
  [:div {:class "section-header"}
    [:div {:class "level"}
      [:div {:class "level-left"}
        [:div {:class "level-item"}
          [:h1 {:class "subtitle"}
            [:span {:class "mu mu-user"}]
            "Edit Contact"]]]
      [:div {:class "level-right"}
        (if editing?
          [:div {:class "buttons"} cancel-button save-button]
          add-button)]]])

(defn on-add-contact [state]
  (refresh! (-> state
```

```
                (assoc :editing? true)
                (dissoc :selected))))

(defn replace-contact [contact-list idx input]
  (assoc contact-list idx (make-contact input)))

(defn on-save-contact [state]
  (refresh!
    (let [contact (get-contact-form-data)
          idx (:selected state)
          state (dissoc state :selected :editing?)]
      (if idx
        (update state :contacts replace-contact idx contact)
        (update state :contacts add-contact contact)))))

(defn on-cancel-edit [state]
  (refresh! (dissoc state :selected :editing?)))

(defn attach-event-handlers! [state]
  ;; ...
  (when-let [add-button (gdom/getElement "add-contact")]
    (gevents/listen add-button "click"
      (fn [_] (on-add-contact state))))

  (when-let [save-button (gdom/getElement "save-contact")]
    (gevents/listen save-button "click"
      (fn [_] (on-save-contact state))))

  (when-let [cancel-button (gdom/getElement "cancel-edit")]
    (gevents/listen cancel-button "click"
      (fn [_] (on-cancel-edit state))))))
```

By now, this sort of code should be no problem to read and understand. In the interest of space, we will not reprint the entire application code, but it can be found at the book's GitHub project.

You Try It

- Allow contacts to have phone numbers. Each phone number will need a :type and :number. This will require updates to the models, components, and event handlers.

20.3 Summary

While this application is not a shining example of modern web development (don't worry - we will get to that in Section 5), it showed us how to build a data-driven application using the techniques that we have been learning in this section. While this is not a large application, is is a non-trivial project that should have helped us get more familiar with transforming data using ClojureScript. Still, much of our ClojureScript code still looks a lot like vanilla JavaScript with a funky syntax. In the next section, we will start to dig in to writing more natural, idiomatic ClojureScript.

Part V

Idiomatic ClojureScript

ClojureScript is more than just an alien syntax for writing JavaScript. It is a well-designed language with its own idioms and best practices. In the first three sections, we approached ClojureScript in a way that made it as familiar as possible to JavaScript programmers. However, in order to become as effective as possible with the language, we need to learn how to write idiomatic ClojureScript. First, we will consider learn how to write pure, well-factored functional programs that operate on immutable data. Next, we'll finally learn how to deal with state that changes over time, which will be a critical component to most of the applications that we build. Then, we will learn about namespaces - the unit of modularity - and how to effectively lay out a larger project. After learning about program structure, we will look at our options for dealing with when things go wrong. Finally, we will learn the basic of working with ClojureScript's default concurrency model and the core.async library that implements this model. The capstone will lean on all of these concepts to create a group chat application.

- Lesson 21: Functional Programming Concepts
- Lesson 22: Managing State
- Lesson 23: Namespaces and Program Structure
- Lesson 24: Handling Exceptions and Errors
- Lesson 25: Intro to core.async
- Lesson 26: Capstone 4 - Group Chat

Lesson 21

Functional Programming Concepts

ClojureScript sits at the intersection of functional programming and pragmatism. In this lesson, we will take a deeper look at what it means to be a functional language. As we shall see, functional programming is about much more than simply being able to use functions as values. At its core, the more important concepts are composability, functional purity, and immutability. Composability means that we build larger modules and systems out of small, reusable pieces. The concept of functional purity means that our functions do not have side effects like mutating global state, modifying the web page, etc. Immutability means that instead of modifying variables in-place, we produce new, transformed values. These three concepts together make for effective functional programming, and by the end of this lesson, we will have a better understanding of what it means to write functional code in ClojureScript.

In this lesson:

- Apply bottom-up design by composing small functions into larger ones
- Make programs easier to reason about with functional purity
- Learn the key role that immutability plays in functional programming

21.1 Composing Behavior from Small Pieces

In imperative programming, we often keep some sort of mutable state and write functions that operate on this state. The key insights introduced by object-oriented programing is that programs are easier to reason about when we encapsulate our mutable state with the methods that are allowed to operate on that state into an object. Clean object-oriented code is factored into methods that have only a single responsibility. While this may sound good on the surface, it often ends up being both more and less restrictive than we desire. It is more restrictive than we would like because it is difficult to share similar logic between multiple objects without introducing significant complexity. It is less restrictive than we would like because any of these methods may change the state of the object to which they belong such that the future behavior of any method on the object may be altered in a way that the caller does not anticipate.

Like object-oriented programming, functional programmingfunctional programming encourages writing functions that do one thing, but it does not suffer from the two deficiencies stated above. Instead, functions may operate on any data without having to be encapsulated into an object, which leads to simpler code with less duplication. Additionally, pure functions by definition do not modify any state, and their behavior cannot be affected by any mutable state, so their behavior is well-defined in all cases.

When our data is modeled using common data structures (primarily maps and lists), and we do not rely on shared mutable state, something very interesting occurs: we can compose a handful of functions in many, many ways. In fact, we can often create our programs without doing much outside of composing functions from the standard library. At this point, we must include the quote that must make an appearance in every good text on functional programming to further this point:

> *It is better to have 100 functions operate on one data structure than to have 10 functions operate on 10 data structures.*

> Alan Perlis,

What Perlis means is that when we have 100 functions that operate on the same common data type or abstraction, we can compose them to do many more than 100 things. However, if we go the object-oriented route and tie methods to specific classes of objects, then the ways in which we compose behavior is much more limited.

As we will be building a group chat application at the end of this section, let's consider a component that displays a user's "badge", which is essentially their nickname and their current online status.

Figure 21.1: User status badge

We can break this component down into a couple of small composable pieces. First, let's write functions that will get a user's nickname as well as a function that wraps any hiccup-like structure that we give it in a `strong` tag to make it bold.

```
(def alan-p {:first-name "Alan"                    ①
             :last-name "Perlis"
             :online? false})

(defn nickname [entity]                            ②
  (or (:nickname entity)
      (->> entity
           ((juxt :first-name :last-name))
           (s/join " "))))

(defn bold [child]                                 ③
  [:strong child])

(bold (nickname alan-p))
;; => [:strong "Alan Perlis"]
```

① Define sample data
② Extract a user's nickname
③ Make some DOM bold

Next, since we know that we will want to add classes to certain elements for styling purposes, we can create a function to add a class to any hiccup-like tag.

```
(defn concat-strings [s1 s2]
  (s/trim (str s1 " " s2)))

(defn with-class [dom class-name]
  (if (map? (second dom))
    (update-in dom [1 :class] concat-strings class-name)
    (let [[tag & children] dom]
      (vec (concat [tag {:class class-name}]
                   children)))))
```

Since we are using plain data structures to represent the DOM, this function can be written in terms of data manipulation functions from the standard library. In fact, it does not refer to anything specific to hiccup at all! Now we can write a function that adds an "online" or "offline" class to the user badge based on the value of the user's `online?` flag:

```
(defn with-status [dom entity]
  (with-class dom
    (if (:online? entity) "online" "offline")))
```

Note that even though we are inspecting the `online?` property of a user, there is nothing preventing us from using this function on entities that we want to add in the future, such as chatbots. Finally, we can define a `user-status` component almost purely in terms of these small building blocks that we just created:

```
(defn user-status [user]
  [:div {:class "user-status"}
   ((juxt
     (comp bold nickname)                                         ①
     (partial with-status                                        ②
              [:span {:class "status-indicator"}]))
    user)])
```

① `comp` creates a new function that *composes* others together
② `partial` creates a function that already has some arguments supplied

We first saw `juxt` in the last lesson, but there are two more functions in this example that are used very commonly in ClojureScript and are incredibly useful in combining smaller functions into larger applications: `comp` and `partial`. `comp` performs function composition, similar to mathematical function composition:

Figure 21.2: Mathematical function composition

$$(f \circ g)(x) = (f(g(x)))$$

As in mathematics, composing functions f and g creates a function that when applied to some argument, x, evaluates `(g x)` and then passes that result as the argument to f, as in the following example.

Listing 21.1: Function composition in ClojureScript

```
(= ((comp f g) x)
   (f (g x)))
```

We can think of `comp` as similar to the → macro applied in reverse, except that rather than evaluating the entire pipeline of functions, it produces a new function that will evaluate the pipeline with any input that we give it. In the case of our user status component, we use `(comp bold nickname)` to create a function that will take a user and return a bolded version of that user's nickname. We can think of the new function as a pipeline that connects each function from right to left.

Figure 21.3: comp function pipeline

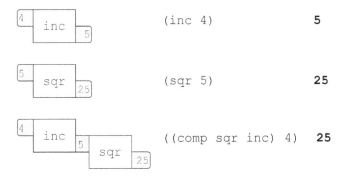

The other new function that we used is partial. While partial is not directly related to function composition, it does give us the ability to take a general function and create a more specified version of it by supplying one or more of its parameters. The canonical example of partial application is the addition function: (add x y). We can use partial to supply the x argument, creating a new function that only takes y and adds the x that we already supplied:

```
(defn add [x y]                          ①
  (+ x y))

(def add-5 (partial add 5))              ②

(add-5 10)
;; 15
```

① Define our own add function that only has 2 parameters
② Create a partially applied version

In this example, partial generates a new function that will call add with 5 plus any other argument that we give it. The call to partial is functionally equivalent to the following definition:

```
(def add-5
  (fn [y]
    (add 5 y)))
```

This trivial example of building a user status component out of small, composable functions that operate on simple data should illustrate the power of function composition to create an extensible, reusable codebase.

21.2 Writing Pure Functions

Side effects are essential in every useful program. A program with no side effects could not modify the DOM, make API requests, save data to localStorage, or any of the other things that we typically want to do in a web application. Why, then, do we talk about writing code without side effects as a good thing? The purely functional programming model does not allow side effects, but all functional programming languages provide at least some facility for side effects. For instance, Haskell provides the I/O monad for performing impure I/O operations behind an otherwise pure functional API. ClojureScript is even more practical though, allowing us to write side-effecting code as needed. If we were not careful, we could end up writing code that has all of the same pitfalls as most JavaScript code in the wild. Since the language itself is not going to prevent us from writing code riddled with side effects, we need to intentionally constrain ourselves to write *mostly* pure applications. Thankfully, ClojureScript makes that sort of constraint easy.

Figure 21.4: Keeping a purely functional core

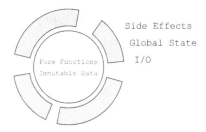

While we need side effects, we should strive to segregate functions that perform side effects from those that can be pure. The pure functions can then be easily tested and reasoned about. For instance, let's take a look at the code that we wrote for the temperature converter app in Lesson 15:

```
(defn update-output [_]
  (if (= :celsius (get-input-uom))
    (do (set-output-temp (c->f (get-input-temp)))
        (gdom/setTextContent output-unit-target "F"))
    (do (set-output-temp (f->c (get-input-temp)))
        (gdom/setTextContent output-unit-target "C"))))
```

While this code gets the job done, it is not especially clean or elegant because it both performs a conversion and does I/O. In order to test this code, we need to run it on a page where all of the elements exist, and in order to test it, we would have to manually set the input fields, call the function, then assert on the content of the output element. Instead, we could refactor this into several pure functions: a pure function to get the label, a pure function to perform the conversion, and an impure function that reads from and mutates the DOM.

```
(defn target-label-for-input-unit [unit]          ①
  (case unit
    :fahrenheit "F"
    :celsius "C"))

(defn convert [unit temp]                         ②
  (if (= :celsius unit)
    (c->f temp)
    (f->c temp)))

(defn update-output [_]                           ③
  (let [unit (get-input-unit)
        input-temp (get-input-temp)
        output-temp (convert unit input-temp)
        output-label (target-label-for-input-unit unit)]
    (set-output-temp output-temp)
    (gdom/setTextContent output-unit-target output-label)))
```

① Extracted code for getting the converted unit label from the input unit
② Extracted code for converting a temperature from one unit to the other
③ The impure code now only orchestrates the UI logic

Not only is the pure functional core of our code easier to test, it is also more resilient to changes that we may want to make to the UI and user experience application. If we wanted to change the way that the UI works, we would only need to replace the `update-output` function, not any of the conversion logic.

Referential Transparency

A function is said to be *referentially transparent* if it fits in the pure substitution model of evaluation that we have discussed. That is, a call to a function can always be replaced with the value to which it evaluates without having any other effect. This implies that the function does not rely on any state other than its parameters, and it does not mutate any external state. It also implies that whenever a function is called with the same input values, it always produces the same return value. However, since not every function can be referentially transparent in a real application, we apply the same strategy of keeping our business logic pure and referentially transparent while moving referentially opaque code to the "edges" of the application. A common need in many web apps is to take the current time into consideration for some computation. For instance, this code will generate a greeting appropriate to the time of day:

```
(defn get-time-of-day-greeting-impure []
  (condp >= (.getHours (Date.))
    11 "Good morning"
    15 "Good day"
    "Good evening"))
```

The problem with this code is that its output will change when given the same input (in this case, no input) depending on what time of day it is called. Getting the current time of day is intrinsically not referentially transparent, but we can use the technique that we applied earlier to separate side-effecting functions from a functionally pure core of business logic:

```
(defn get-current-hour []                              ①
  (.getHours (js/Date.)))

(defn get-time-of-day-greeting [hour]                  ②
  (condp >= hour
    11 "Good morning"
    15 "Good day"
    "Good evening"))

(get-time-of-day-greeting (get-current-hour))
;; "Good day"
```

① Factor out the function that is not referentially transparent
② Ensure that the output of our business logic is solely dependent on its formal parameters

This is a fairly trivial example, but any code that relies on external state - whether it is the time of day, the result of an API call, the (Math.random) random number generator, or anything other than its explicit parameters - breaks the functional paradigm and is more difficult to test and evolve as requirements change.

21.3   Immutable Data

We have just walked through the process of refactoring code that mutates the DOM into an impure wrapper around a functional core. However, there is another type of side effect that we must avoid if we want to write functional code: data mutation. In JavaScript, the two built-in collection data structures - objects and arrays - are mutable, meaning they can be modified in-place. All of the object-oriented features in JavaScript rely on mutability. For example, it is very common to see code that makes directly manipulates an object, such as the following:

```
const blog = {
  title: 'Object-Oriented JavaScript',
  tags: ['JavaScript', 'OOP'],
  rating: 4
};

blog.tags.push('mutability');
blog.rating++;
blog.title += ' considered harmful';
blog.isChanged = true;
```

In ClojureScript, instead of modifying an object, we create copies of the original object with modifications. While this sounds inefficient, ClojureScript uses data structures that are constructed in such a way that similar objects can often share much of their structure in the same memory locations. As we will see, these immutable data structures actually enable highly-optimized user interfaces and can even speed up an application. Working with immutable data structures takes a mind shift but is every bit as easy as working with mutable data, as we can see below.

```
(def blog {:title "Functional ClojureScript"
            :tags ["ClojureScript" "FP"]
            :rating 4})

(def new-blog
  (-> blog                                      ①
      (update-in [:tags] conj "immutability")
      (update-in [:rating] inc)
      (update-in [:title] #(str % " for fun and profit"))
      (assoc :new? true)))

new-blog                                        ②
; {:title "Functional ClojureScript for fun and profit",
; :tags ["ClojureScript" "FP" "immutability"], :rating 5, :new? true}
blog
; {:title "Functional ClojureScript", :tags ["ClojureScript" "FP"], :rating 4}
```

① Build up a series of transformations using the → macro
② Inspect both the original `blog` and transformed `new-blog` maps

In this example, we see that the original `blog` variable is untouched. We stack a series of modifications on top of the `blog` map and save the modified map as `new-blog`. The key take-away here is that none of the `update-in` or `assoc` functions touched `blog` - they returned a new object that was similar to the one passed in but with some modification. Immutable data is key to functional programming because it gives us the assurance that our programs are repeatable and deterministic (at least the parts that need to be). When we allow data to be mutated as it is passed around, complexity skyrockets. When we allow mutable data, we need to keep track of a potentially enormous number of variables in our heads to debug a single computation.

> **Use Immutable Data**
>
> The author once worked on a team responsible for a very large JavaScript application. That team discovered that unexpected mutation was the cause of so many defects that they started keeping a tally of every hour spent finding and fixing bugs that were due to mutable data. The team switched to the Immutable.js library when their tallies no longer fit on the whiteboard.
>
>

21.4   Functional Design Patterns

Design patterns have gotten something of a bad reputation over the past decade or so, and in many cases, the criticism has been well-deserved. Most of the "Gang of Four"[1] design patterns were discovered as workarounds for a lack of flexibility in the object-oriented languages at the time. In fact, Peter Norvig, a major player in the Lisp and AI communities, found that 16 out of the 23 design patterns presented in the Gang of Four book are either unnecessary in Lisp or arise through natural use of the language.[2] Still, the goal of design patterns is to create a common vocabulary around describing problems that occur often in software development and present a template for an often-used solution. Even in a dynamic functional language like ClojureScript, there is some merit to defining problem and solution sets that occur often, so in this section, we will describe several: constructor, closure, strategy, and middleware.

---

[1]*Design Patterns: Elements of Reusable Object-Oriented Software* by Erich Gamma, John Vlissides, Richard Helm, and Ralph Johnson

[2]Design Patterns in Dynamic Languages: http://www.norvig.com/design-patterns/

Constructor

This should be a familiar pattern, as we already covered it in Lesson 19 and revisited it in Lesson 20. The idea here is to abstract the creation of some data structure behind a function in order to assign a name to that data structure and to make it easier to change the structure in the future. Since we have already been using this pattern for a couple of lessons, we need not belabor an explanation here.

Closure

Like JavaScript, ClojureScript has the concept of lexical closures. That is, a function can refer to any variables that were visible in the scope in which the function was defined. This allows us to retain (immutable) state in our functions. This allows us to do things like define a DOM element at the top level of a namespace and refer to it within a function defined in that same namespace:

```
(def user-notes (gdom/getElement "notes"))

(defn get-notes []
  (.-value user-notes))
```

This is a pretty trivial use of a closure. Their real power shines when used in conjunction with higher-order functions. Recall how at the beginning of this chapter we defined an `add` function that simple adds 2 numbers together. We then used partial application to generate a function that always adds 5 to its argument. It would be much more flexible, however, if we defined a `make-adder` function that accepts a number and returns an adding function that always adds *that* number to its argument. Because of closures, we can do this:

```
(defn make-adder [x]
  (fn [y]
    (add x y)))

((make-adder 1) 5)   ;; 6
((make-adder 2) 5)   ;; 7
((make-adder 10) 5)  ;; 15
```

Note that the function we return from `make-adder` can reference any arguments passed into is parent function by name. Closures require us to tweak the mental model of evaluation that we introduced back in Lesson 4 and extended in Lesson 12, since we can no longer assume that we can simply replace a function call by the function's definition with all formal parameters replaced by actual parameters. If we did that in the `make-adder` case, we would end up with the following:

```
((make-adder 1) 10)
```

```
((fn [y]
  (add x y)) 10)
```

This would be a big problem because we would "lose" knowledge of the 1 that we passed into make-adder and would leave the symbol x that is not bound to any value. Let's introduce the concept of an *environment*, which is simply a mapping of symbols to vars that were visible where the function was defined, and update our model of evaluation to say that when we evaluate a function, we replace all symbols within the function definition with the formal parameter of the same name *or the value found for the corresponding name in the environment* if no matching formal parameter is found.

Figure 21.5: Environment for a closure

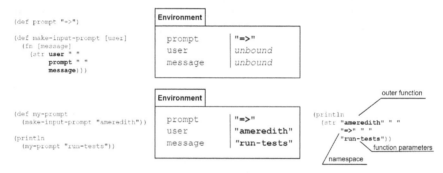

Using this simple principle, we can use closures to emulate objects from the OOP world. Consider that we have a constructor that takes some initial state for an object, and we return a map of functions that can either update this state, returning a new object, or query the state, returning some value.

Listing 21.2: Purely functional objects

```
(defn make-mailbox
  ([] (make-mailbox {:messages []                    ①
                     :next-id 1}))
  ([state]
   {:deliver!                                        ②
    (fn [msg]
      (make-mailbox
        (-> state
            (update :messages conj
              (assoc msg :read? false
                         :id (:next-id state)))
            (update :next-id inc))))

    :next-unread                                     ③
    (fn []
```

```
        (when-let [msg (->> (:messages state)
                            (filter (comp not :read?))
                            (first))]
          (dissoc msg :read?)))

        :read!
        (fn [id]
          (make-mailbox
            (update state :messages
              (fn [messages]
                (map #(if (= id (:id %)) (assoc % :read? true) %)
                     messages)))))}))

(defn call [obj method & args]
  (apply (get obj method) args))                        ④

(defn test-mailbox []
  (loop [mbox (-> (make-mailbox)
                  (call :deliver! {:subject "Objects are Cool"})
                  (call :deliver! {:subject "Closures Rule"}))]
    (when-let [next-message (call mbox :next-unread)]
      (println "Got message" next-message)
      (recur
        (call mbox :read! (:id next-message)))))
  (println "Read all messages!"))
;; Got message {:subject "Objects are Cool", :id 1}
;; Got message {:subject "Closures Rule", :id 2}
;; Read all messages!
```

① Provide a no-arg constructor for convenience
② By convention, methods ending in ! will update the object state and return a new object
③ Methods not ending in ! will not update the object but will return a value instead
④ `apply` calls a function with a collection of arguments

You Try It

- Add a few more methods to the mailbox "object":

    - `:all-messages` - returns all messages in the mailbox
    - `:unread-messages` - returns all unread messages in the mailbox
    - `:mark-all-read!` - mutates the state by marking every message as read

Strategy

As in object-oriented programming, the strategy pattern is a way to separate the implementation of an algorithm from higher-level code. This pattern is so natural in functional languages that it barely qualifies as a pattern. Let's take an example from the standard library: `filter`. This function filters (surprise, surprise!) a sequence, but it does not specify the criteria by which each element should be tested for inclusion. That criteria is dictated by the function passed to `filter`, which specifies the concrete *strategy* for determining which elements should be included in the new sequence.

```
(let [xs [0 1 2 3 4 5 6 7 8 9]]
  (println (filter even? xs))
  (println (filter odd? xs)))
;; (0 2 4 6 8)
;; (1 3 5 7 9)
```

Middleware

The final pattern that we will consider is the middleware pattern. This pattern allows us to declare "hooks" in a request/response cycle that can transform the request on the way in, the response on the way out, or both. It can even be used to short-circuit a request.

Imagine that we need to make a call to some API, but we want to be able to validate the request before it is sent. We could add the validation logic directly to the function that performs the API request, but this is less than ideal for two reasons: first, it couples validation logic to API logic, and second, it makes our app less testable by combining both pure and impure business logic in the same function. No problem, let's add separate validation function:

```
(defn handler [req]
  (println "Calling API with" req)
  {:data "is fake"})

(defn validate-request [req]
  (cond
    (nil? (:id req)) {:error "id must be present"}
    (nil? (:count req)) {:error "count must be present"}
    (< (:count req) 1) {:error "count must be positive"}))

;; Client code
(if-let [validation-error (validate-request req)]
  validation-error
  (handler req))
```

This works well for a while, but now we need to add logging around each request that goes out and its response. We could add more logic to our client code, such as the following:

```
(do
  (println "Request" req)
  (let [res (if-let [validation-error (validate-request req)]
              validation-error
              (handler req))]
    (println "Response" res)
    res))
```

Even with 2 hooks that we want to add to the request/response, the code is starting to get unwieldy. With the middleware pattern, we can extract each hook into a function that "wraps" the handler function. A middleware is simply a function that takes a handler and returns a new handler. If we think of a `handler` in general as any function from Request → Response, then a middleware is a function from (Request → Response) → (Request → Response). One nice feature of middleware is that since they have the same input and output types, they can be combined in any order using ordinary function composition!

Figure 21.6: Middleware pattern

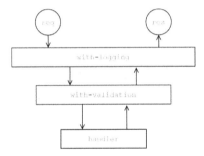

Returning to the wrapped API handler example above, writing the validation and logging as middleware would look something like the following:

```
(defn with-validation [handler]
  (fn [req]
    (if-let [error (validate-request req)]
      error
      (handler req))))

(defn with-logging [handler]
  (fn [req]
    (println "Request" req)
    (let [res (handler req)]
      (println "Response" res)
      res)))

(let [wrap-handler (comp with-logging with-validation)
      handler (wrap-handler handler)]
  ; Example invalid request
```

```
(handler {})
;; Request {}
;; Response {:error id must be present}

; Example valid request
(handler {:id 123, :count 12})
;; Request {:id 123, :count 12}
;; Calling API with {:id 123, :count 12}
;; Response {:response is fake}
)
```

Quick Review

- Why can middleware be composed using ordinary function composition?
- Does the order in which middleware are composed matter? What would have happened if we defined `wrap-handler` as `(comp with-validation with-logging)`?

21.5 Summary

In this lesson, we looked briefly at three cornerstones of functional programming: minimizing and segregating the side effects, using immutable data, and keeping our business logic referentially transparent. When we these ideas, we naturally write programs that take a piece of data, pass it through a number of transformations, and the result is the output of the program. In reality, most programs are made up of many pure data pipelines that are glued together with impure code that interacts with the DOM, but if we follow the functional programming concepts that we have learned in this lesson, we will end up with a clean functional core of business logic that is primarily concerned with data transformation. Over the next few lessons, we will learn more language features and techniques that will enable us to be effective practitioners of functional programming.

Lesson 22

Managing State

This lesson has been a long time coming, and it is a critical one. By this point, we have seen that it is possible to write whole applications without using any mutable data, but for most cases, it is inconvenient to say the least. As we learned in the last lesson, ClojureScript encourages writing programs as a purely functional core surrounded by side-effecting code, and this incudes code that updates state. Being a pragmatic language, ClojureScript gives us several constructs for dealing with values that change over time.

In this lesson:

- Use atoms to manage values that change over time
- Observe and react to changes in state
- Use transients for high-performance mutations

22.1 Atoms

As we have seen many times, ClojureScript encourages us to write programs primarily as pure functions that transform immutable values. We have also seen that this can be somewhat cumbersome. Following the philosophy of pragmatism over purity, ClojureScript provides a convenient tool for representing state that changes over time: the *atom*. Atoms are containers that can hold a single immutable value at any point in time. However, the value that they refer to can be swapped out with another value. Moreover, our code can observe whenever these state swaps occur. This gives us a convenient way to deal with state that changes over time.

Unlike JavaScript, ClojureScript separates the ideas of identity and state[1]. An *identity* is a reference to a logical entity. That entity may change over time, but it still retains its identity in the same way that a river retains its identity even though it has different water flowing through it over the course of time. An identity may be associated with various values over the course of time, and these values are its *state*. Atoms are the state containers that we use in CloureScript to represent identities.

Figure 22.1: A river has many states over time

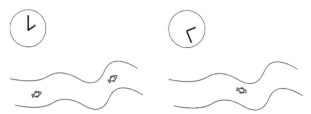

Updating state with swap!

The most trivial example of an identity that we can learn from is the lowly counter. A counter is an identity whose state is a number that increases over time. We can wrap any Clojure value in an atom just by calling `(atom v)` where v is the value that becomes the atom's initial state:

```
(def counter (atom 0))
```

Since an atom provides a reference to some value at any point in time, we can *dereference* it - that is, get the immutable value to which it refers - by using the `deref` macro or its shorthand form, @.

Listing 22.1: Dereferencing an atom

```
counter                                              ①
;; => #object[cljs.core.Atom {:val 0}]

(deref counter)                                      ②
;; => 0

@counter                                             ③
;; => 0
```

---

[1] See https://clojure.org/about/state for a discussion on identity and state.

① The atom itself is an object that wraps a value
② Atoms can be dereferenced with `deref`
③ Prefixing an atom's name with `@` is sugar for calling `deref`

Of course to be able to do anything useful with an atom we have to be able to update it's state, and we will use the `swap!` function to do this. `swap!` takes an atom and a transformation. That function will be given the atom's current state and should return its new state. `swap!` itself will return the atom's new state. Any additional arguments to `swap!` are passed as additional arguments to the transformation function. For our simple counter, we can use `inc` to increment it and `+` to add more than 1 at a time.

```
(swap! counter inc)

@counter
;; => 1

(swap! counter + 9)

@counter
;; => 10
```

Atoms are ClojureScript's way of providing a very controlled mechanism for updating state. When we dereference an atom, we still get an immutable value, and even if the atom's state is updated, the value that we received does not change:

```
(def creature
  (atom {:type "water"
         :life 50
         :abilities ["swimming" "speed"]}))

(def base-creature @creature)                          ①

(swap! creature update :abilities conj "night vision")

@creature                                              ②
;; => {:type "water"
;;     :life 50
;;     :abilities ["swimming" "speed" "night vision"]}

base-creature                                          ③
;; => {:type "water"
;;     :life 50
;;     :abilities ["swimming", "speed"]}
```

① Dereference the atom before we `swap!` in a new state
② After the `swap!`, the atom's state has changed
③ The initial state that we got is unchanged

We can also provide a function that acts as a validator that lets us define what sort of values are allowed in the atom using the `set-validator!` function[2]. The validator function takes what would be the new value of the atom. If it returns `false` (or throws an error), then our attempted update will fail and throw an error. For instance, to guarantee that we can never set a negative `:life` value on our creature, we could supply a validator to ensure this property:

```
(set-validator! creature
  (fn [c] (>= (:life c) 0)))

(swap! creature assoc :life 10) ;; Ok

(swap! creature assoc :life -1) ;; Throws error

(:life @creature) ;; 10
```

As we just observed, updating the atom's state in a way that makes the validator return false results in an exception being thrown and no update being made. Validators are not commonly used in ClojureScript, but like pre- and post-conditions for functions, they can be a useful tool during development.

Quick Review

- What value does `swap!` return?
- How does a validator function indicate whether a state should be allowed or not?

Replacing state with `reset!`

While `swap!` is useful for transforming the state of an atom, sometimes we just want to update the atom's entire state at once. Using ClojureScript's standard library, this is not a difficult task: `(swap! counter (constantly 0))`. `constantly` returns a function that always returns a specific value every time it is called, so in this case, it returns a function that will always return 0, given any argument, which will effectively reset the counter state to 0. However, this code is not as cleat as it could be, which is why ClojureScript also provides the `reset!` function. This function simply takes the atom and a value, which it sets as the atom's new state. Like `swap!`, it returns the new state:

```
(reset! counter 0)

@counter
;; => 0
```

---

[2]Alternatively, a validator may be supplied when the atom is created by passing a map as a second argument to `atom` where the `:validator` key points to the validator function: `(atom init-val {:validator validator-fn})`

The reset! function is useful especially when we have some known initial state that we want to revert to, but otherwise, swap! is more commonly used in practice.

Observing Change with Watches

One of the most useful features of atoms is the ability to be notified whenever their state changes. This is accomplished with the add-watch function. This function takes 3 arguments: the atom to watch, a keyword that uniquely identifies the watcher, and a watch function. The watch function itself takes the keyword that was passed to add-watch, the atom itself, the atom's old state, and its new state. In most cases, the old and new state are the only things that we are interested in. To get our feet wet, let's implement a simple counter with buttons that can be used to add or subtract from its value.

Figure 22.2: Watching a counter atom

Listing 22.2: Counter component

```
(defonce app-state (atom 0))                          ①

(def app-container (gdom/getElement "app"))

(defn render [state]                                  ②
  (set! (.-innerHTML app-container)
      (hiccups/html
        [:div
          [:p "Counter: " [:strong state]]
          [:button {:id "up"} "+"]
          [:button {:id "down"} "-"]])))

(defonce is-initialized?
  (do
    (gevents/listen (gdom/getElement "app") "click"
      (fn [e]
        (condp = (aget e "target" "id")
          "up"   (swap! app-state inc)
          "down" (swap! app-state dec))))

    (add-watch app-state :counter-observer           ③
      (fn [key atom old-val new-val]
        (render new-val)))

    (render @app-state)
```

```
    true))
```

① Create an `atom` to hold the counter state
② Render takes the current state
③ Add a watch function that re-renders the component whenever state changes

In this example, we use `add-watch` to observe changes to the state of the `app-state` atom. There is a related function, `remove-watch`, that can de-register the watch function. It takes the atom that is being observed and the keyword identifying the watcher to remove. If we wanted to remove the watcher in the example above, we could call this function like so:

```
(remove-watch app-state :counter-observer)
```

Challenge

Take the Contact Book app from Lesson 20 and refactor it to keep the state in an atom.

22.2   Transients

While atoms are the defacto tool for managing state that changes over time, transients come in handy when we need to introduce mutability for the sake of performance. If we need to perform many transformations in a row on a single data structure, ClojureScript's immutable data structures are not the most performant. Every time we perform a transformation of an immutable data structure, we create garbage that JavaScript's garbage collector will need to clean up. In cases like this, transients can be very useful.

A transient version of any vector, set, or map may be created with the `transient` function:

```
(transient {})
;; #object[cljs.core.TransientArrayMap]
```

The API for working with transients is similar to the standard collection API, but the transformation functions all have a `!` appended, e.g. `assoc!`, `conj!`. The read API, however, is identical to that of immutable collections. A transient collection may be converted back to its persistent counterpart using the `persistent!` function:

```
(-> {}
    transient                              ①
    (assoc! :speed 12.3)
    (assoc! :position [44, 29])
    persistent!)                           ②
```

① Convert map to a transient
② Convert transient map back to a persistent (immutable) structure

Transients are not commonly used and should only be considered as a performance optimization when we have proven that a portion of code is too slow.

22.3 Using State Wisely

ClojureScript's state management - particularly atoms - give us great power to more naturally and intuitively model things that change over time, but with that power comes the potential of introducing anti-patterns. If we follow a couple of simple guidelines, we can ensure that our code remains clear and maintainable.

Guideline #1: Pass atoms explicitly

In order to keep a function testable and easy to reason about, we should always explicitly pass in any atom(s) on which it operates as arguments rather than operating on a global atom from its scope:

```
;; Don't do this
(def state (atom {:counter 0}))                      ①
(defn increment-counter []
  (swap! state update :counter inc))

;; OK
(defn increment-counter [state]                      ②
  (swap! state update :counter inc))
```

① Increment a global counter atom
② Increment a counter atom passed in as a parameter

While neither function is pure (they both have the side effect of mutating state), the second option is more testable and reusable because we can pass in any atom that we wish. We do not need to implicitly depend on the current global state.

Guideline #2: Prefer fewer atoms

In general, an application should have fewer atoms with more data rather than a separate atom for every piece of state. It is simpler to think about transitioning our entire app state one step at a time rather than synchronizing separate pieces of state:

```
;; Don't do this
(def account-a (atom 100))                          ①
(def account-b (atom 100))
(swap! account-a - 25)
(swap! account-b + 25)

;; OK
(def accounts (atom {:a 100                          ②
                     :b 100}))
(swap! accounts
  (fn [accounts]
    (-> accounts
        (update :a - 25)
        (update :b + 25))))
```

① Represent each piece of state as a separate atom
② Represent our "world" as an atom

While the second version is a bit more verbose, it has the advantage of creating cohesion
between different steps that are all part of a "transaction", and it allows us to create complex state transitions without relying on many separate inputs. As we will see in the next
section, this is also a common pattern when using the Reagent framework.

22.4   Summary

In this lesson, we were introduced to the critical feature of managing state that changes
over time. As we have seen, we *can* create complete applications without resorting to mutability, adding just a small amount of controlled mutability can make our code dramatically
simpler. We spent most of our time looking at how to use atoms to work with mutable state
and how to observe and react to those state changes. We also looked briefly at transients
- mutable version of ClojureScripts collections - and learned that while they are good for
optimizing performance, they are not good general state containers. Finally, we looked at
a couple of guidelines for constraining our use of mutable state that help make our applications maintainable and testable.

Lesson 23

Namespaces and Program Structure

In ClojureScript, the unit of modularity is the namespace. A namespace is simply a logical grouping of functions and data that can be required and used by another namespace. External libraries expose modules as namespaces that we can require in our code, and we can (and should) break our code into multiple modules as well. In this lesson, we'll learn how to declare and require modules as well as how to use them to create clean architectural boundaries in our programs.

In this lesson:

- Organize functions and data into namespaces
- Architect a logical and intuitive project structure
- Work with namespaces at the REPL

23.1 Namespace Declarations

In each of the ClojureScript files that we have written so far, clj-new has kindly generated a namespace declaration at the top of the file for us. We have used the (:require ...) form to pull in third-party libraries, but we have judiciously avoided diving in to what exactly is happening here. That is about to change.

For the purpose of exploring namespaces in this lesson, let's create a new Figwheel project:

```
$ clj -X:new :template figwheel-main :name learn-cljs/import-fns :args '["+deps"]'
$ cd import-fns
```

If we look at the file that was generated in `src/learn_cljs/import_fns.cljs`, we see the following declaration at the top of the file:

```
(ns learn-cljs.import-fns
  (:require
    [goog.dom :as gdom]))
```

The ClojureScript compiler will turn this declaration into a Google Closure Compiler module declaration, which will ultimately be compiled into a JavaScript object containing all of the functions and vars that we define in this namespace. From this bare-bones declaration, we can note a couple of things:

1. We declare the name of the namespace as `learn-cljs.import-fns`. This name must follow the naming convention discussed in Lesson 5.
2. There is a skeleton `(:require ... )` form that we can use to require code from other namespaces into this one.

Using Require

Since declaring a name is fairly self-explanatory, we will focus on the second item - requiring code from other namespaces. The `:require` form in the `ns` declaration is by far the most common way to require code from another file - including third party libraries - to make it available in our code[1]. Let's look at the various forms of `:require`, using the project that we created above. We will again build on the example of a text-based adventure game, specifically displaying a player's inventory:

```
(ns learn-cljs.import-fns
  (:require learn-cljs.import-fns.ui              ①
            [learn-cljs.import-fns.format         ②
             :refer [pluralize]]
            [learn-cljs.import-fns.inventory      ③
             :as inventory]
            [goog.dom :refer [getElement]         ④
                      :rename {getElement get-element}]))

(defn item-description [i item]
  (let [qty (inventory/item-qty i item)
        label (if (> qty 1) (pluralize item) item)]
    (str qty " " label)))
```

---

[1]There is another form, `(:use [namespace :only [var1 var2]])` that works just like `(:require [namespace :refer [var1 var2]])`. It used to be used heavily in Clojure before `:refer` was available inside `(:require)`, but it has all but fallen out of use.

```
(let [i (-> (inventory/make-inventory)
            (inventory/add-items "Laser Catapult" 1)
            (inventory/add-items "Antimatter Scrubber" 5))]
  (learn-cljs.import-fns.ui/render-list (get-element "app")
    (map (partial item-description i)
         (inventory/list-items i))))
```

---

① Require the entire `learn-cljs.import-fns.ui` namespace
② Require a single function from the `learn-cljs.import-fns.format` namespace
③ Require the `learn-cljs.import-fns.inventory` namespace with the alias `inventory`
④ Require a single function from the Google Closure Library namespace, renaming that function

This snippet illustrates all of the common ways of requiring code into a namespace. After the `:require` keyword, we can include any number of *libspecs*. The libspec may be either a fully-qualified namespace or a vector containing the namespace and some optional modifiers. This syntax is interpreted by the `ns` special form to pull in vars from other namespaces according to the exact form of the libspec.

Form 1: Simple Namespace

In the first form, we simply use the name of a namespace that we would like to require: `learn-cljs.import-fns.ui`. We can then refer to any public var within this namespace by using the full namespace followed by `/` and the name of the var, e.g. `learn-cljs.import-fns.ui/render-list`.

Form 2: Refer

In the second case, we follow the namespace by `:refer [pluralize]`. `:refer` will make every var that is listed in the vector that follows available without any prefix. Thus, we can write `(pluralize item)` instead of `(learn-cljs.import-fns.format/pluralize item)`. Any function in the `learn-cljs.import-fns.format` namespace can still be called using the fully-qualified syntax.

Form 3: Aliased Namespace

In the third case, we alias the namespace that we require using `:as`. This works similar to the first case in that we are able to refer to any public var in the namespace. However, we can use the symbol that we specified after `:as` instead of the full namespace. Thus, `learn-cljs.import-fns.inventory/make-inventory` becomes `inventory/make-inventory`. The use of

:as can be very useful when requiring from namespaces with very verbose names. In general, we should also prefer :as to :refer, since it makes it clear where a var that we reference comes from without needing to look back at the namespace declaration.

Form 4: Aliased Vars

Finally, in the fourth case, we rename a specific var that we referred. Here, we alias the getElement function from the Google Closure Library's goog.dom module in order to give it a more idiomatic kebab-case name. In practice, renaming is used more often to prevent a name collision. For example, we may want to import functions called mark-inactive from both my-app.users and my-app.customers namespaces. We can use :rename to import them as mark-user-inactive and mark-customer-inactive.

Require Form	Description	Function Usage
my.namespace	require entire namespace	my.namespace/compute
my.namespace :refer [compute other-fn]	require specific functions and refer to them unqualified	compute
my.namespace :as mine	require namespace with alias	mine/compute
my.namespace :refer [compute] :rename {compute calculate}	require namespace with specific vars aliased	calculate

Forms of Require

> **:refer-clojure**
>
> There is a form, :refer-clojure that allows us to rename a var from the ClojureScript standard library (or exclude it altogether) in the event that we want to define a var in our namespace with the same name. (:refer-clojure :rename {str string}) will alias the str function as string, so that we are free to reuse the str name without generating any warnings. Similarly, we can exclude the str function altogether with, (:refer-clojure :exclude [str]). That said, we should usually be giving things names that are descriptive enough that they do not conflict with anything in the standard library.

Importing Google Closure Library Classes

In the case that we are importing a class constructor from the Google Closure Library, there is one form that we should be aware of in addition to :require - that is :import. This form

exists only for bringing a class constructor from a Google Closure module into our namespace in the same way that the :refer keyword in a libspec lets us bring in a var from another
namespace. Like :require, :import expects to be followed by a number of import specs. The
most common form is a vector with the namespace from which to import classes followed
by the unqualified constructor names to import from that namespace:

```
(ns my-ns
  (:import [goog.math Coordinate Rect]))

(.contains (Rect. 10 50 5 5)
           (Coordinate. 12 50))
```

The thing to remember about :import is that it is *only* used for requiring classes (including
enums) from Google Closure modules - never for including a ClojureScript namespace or a
(non-constructor) function from a Google Closure module.

Requiring Macros

One of ClojureScript's most powerful features is its macro support. However, the way in
which macros are implemented presents a bit of a quirk in the way that we have to require
them. A macro has access to the ClojureScript code that is "inside" its call site as raw
data (lists, vectors, symbols, etc.), and it can manipulate this code as data structure before
returning the code that actually gets compiled to JavaScript. The tricky thing is that since
the ClojureScript compiler is written in Clojure, the macros themselves are *Clojure* code
that generates *ClojureScript* code. We will learn more about macros in a later lesson, but
for now the important thing to remember is that since macros are Clojure code, we need to
go about requiring them another way. That way is the :require-macros form:

```
(:require-macros [macro-ns :as macros])
```

This form functions very much like :require with the exception that it works with importing
macros from Clojure namespaces rather than vars from ClojureScript namespaces.

Figure 23.1: Macro compilation

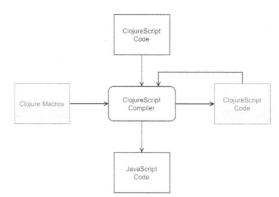

23.2   Grouping Related Functions

Now that we have discussed the mechanics of declaring a namespace and requiring other code that we would like to use, let's take a step back and look at how to organize our namespaces. One of the features of ClojureScript that can be both liberating and frustrating is that it is not opinionated about how namespaces are structured. We can put as little or as much into a namespace as we would like, and as long as we do not create circular dependencies, all is well. Some of the insights from object-oriented programming can also help us here: high cohesion and low coupling.

High cohesion means that if two pieces of code are closely related in purpose, they should be close in the architecture of the program - usually in the same namespace. Low coupling is the other side of the same coin: if two pieces of code are unrelated, they should be distant from each other in the architecture of the program. Unlike OOP practitioners, we extend this principle to data as well. Since hiding data is not a goal of functional programming, we tend to group functions and the data that they operate on into the same namespace and expose both freely.

Let's return to the adventure game inventory code by way of example. In the `import-fns.core` namespace, we require the `learn-cljs.import-fns.inventory` and `import-fns.ui` namespaces as well as `pluralize` from `learn-cljs.import-fns.format`. These files contain the business and presentation logic for this little app. First, we will look at `learn-cljs.import-fns.inventory`:

Listing 23.1: learn_cljs/import_fns/inventory.cljs

```
(ns learn-cljs.import-fns.inventory)                        ①

(defn make-inventory []                                     ②
  {:items {}})
```

```
(defn- add-quantity [inventory-item qty]          ③
  (update-in inventory-item [:qty]
    (fn [current-qty] (+ current-qty qty))))

(defn add-items
  ([inventory item] (add-items inventory item 1))
  ([inventory item qty]
   (update-in inventory [:items item]
     (fnil add-quantity
       {:item item :qty 0}
       qty))))

(defn list-items [inventory]
  (keys (:items inventory)))

(defn item-qty [inventory item]
  (get-in inventory [:items item :qty] 0))
```

① All functions in this file will be part of the `import-fns.inventory` namespace
② Declare a public function named `make-inventory`
③ Use `defn-` to declare a private function

As the name suggests, this namespace contains all of the code relating to creating and managing an inventory. It has no formatting or display logic. We expose `make-inventory` for constructing a new inventory, `add-items` for adding some quantity of a specific item, `list-items` for getting the distinct items in the inventory, and `item-qty` for getting the quantity of a particular item. We make the `add-quantity` function private by declaring it with `defn-` because it exists solely as an implementation detail of `add-items` and serves little value outside this context. Next, let's look at the `learn-cljs.import-fns.format` namespace:

Listing 23.2: learn_cljs/import_fns/format.cljs

```
(ns learn-cljs.import-fns.format
  (:require [clojure.string :as s]))

(defn ends-with-any? [word suffixes]
  (some (fn [suffix]
          (s/ends-with? word suffix))
        suffixes)))

(defn replace-suffix [word old-suffix new-suffix]
  (let [prefix-len (- (count word)
                      (count old-suffix))
        prefix (.substring word 0 prefix-len)]
    (str prefix new-suffix)))

(defn pluralize [word]
  (cond
```

```
(ends-with-any? word ["s" "sh" "ch" "x" "z"])
(str word "es")

(s/ends-with? word "f")
(replace-suffix word "f" "ves")

(s/ends-with? word "fe")
(replace-suffix word "fe" "ves")

(re-find #"[^aeiou]y$" word)
(replace-suffix word "y" "ies")

:else (str word "s")))
```

Again, this namespace contains all of the string formatting functions that we need for the app. Even though we only require pluralize in our main namespace, we make all of the functions public since they all contain reusable logic. Additionally, when we expose every function, we make it possible to test every function in isolation. Note that all of these function are general functions that will work with any string. If we had code that was specific to inventories, we would put it in the inventory namespace. So what should we do if we have a set of functions that are formatting functions specific to inventories? One common practice is to create a new namespace called something like learn-cljs.import-fns.format-inventory, and this namespace could require functions and data from both formatting and inventory namespaces to perform its specialized work. When we do not have to squeeze the architecture of our code into a class hierarchy, it gives us a great deal of flexibility. Finally, for the sake of completeness, let's look at the learn-cljs.import-fns.ui namespace:

Listing 23.3: learn_cljs/import_fns/ui.cljs

```
(ns learn-cljs.import-fns.ui
  (:require [goog.dom :as gdom]))

(defn append-list-item [list text]
  (gdom/appendChild list
    (let [li (gdom/createElement "li")]
      (gdom/setTextContent li text)
      li)))

(defn render-list [elem items]
  (let [ul (gdom/createElement "ul")]
    (doseq [item items]
      (append-list-item ul item))
    (gdom/removeChildren elem)
    (gdom/appendChild elem ul)))
```

There is not much that is novel to note about this namespace, except that its API is formed around rendering text rather than an inventory specifically. The "glue code" that ties inventories and rendering together is all in our core namespace.

Avoiding "Hidden" OOP

One thing that many new ClojureScript developers will realize is that with atoms and namespaces that can contain private variables, we can easily emulate stateful objects. This is true - we can define a private var to hold our object state within an atom, then we can use public functions to define the API and private functions as implementation details. However, as soon as we introduce hidden state, we lose the benefits of functional purity and referential transparency in terms of both testability and reasonability.

23.3 Namespaces and the REPL

Before moving on, let's look briefly at how to interact with namespaces from the REPL. When we used `:require` or `:import` in the namespace declaration, the `ns` special form used these directives to determine what code to make available within our namespace. There are macros that act as analogs to these directives - `require` and `import` - which we can run from the REPL to expose code to our REPL session:

```
dev:cljs.user=> (require '[learn-cljs.import-fns.format :as fmt] :reload)
nil
dev:cljs.user=> (fmt/pluralize "burrito")
"burritos"
```

The primary difference is that we must quote the vector that we pass to `require` - otherwise, the REPL would try to resolve the `import-fns.format` and `fmt` symbols to vars that are bound in our current namespace. Quoting the vector (i.e. using `'[]` instead of `[]`) causes ClojureScript to interpret each symbol in it as a literal symbol rather than attempting to resolve them. An additional difference is that we can add the `:reload` keyword after the require spec to cause the REPL to reevaluate the namespace in order to pick up on any changes that were made to the file since we last required it.

By default, when we start up a REPL, it operates inside a namespace called `cljs.user`. Anything that we `def` (or `defn`) will be defined inside this namespace for the duration of the REPL session. If we would like to operate inside another namespace, we can use the `in-ns` special form to instruct the REPL to operate within another namespace instead:

```
dev:cljs.user=> (in-ns 'import-fns.format)

dev:import-fns.format=> (replace-suffix "programmer" "er" "ing")
"programming"
```

Using `in-ns` can simplify our workflow when we are practicing REPL-driven development. We can start writing our code for a namespace in the REPL then copy all of our definitions to the file when we are satisfied with how they work.

23.4   Summary

In this lesson, we learned what namespaces are as well as how to declare a namespace with its dependencies using `:require` and `:import`. We also looked at how to think about organizing our code into namespaces using the principles of high cohesion and low coupling. Finally, we looked at how to interact with namespaces from the REPL so that we can effectively navigate and test our code.

Lesson 24

Handling Exceptions and Errors

We would like to think of programming as an idealized discipline where we write our programs declaratively and the computer converts them into pure computational models that can churn away until the heat death of the universe. In practice, bad things will happen, and they will happen much sooner than the heat death of the universe. Networks fail, we divide by zero, we miss a corner case that generates input in the "wrong" shape. All of these are exceptional conditions that we need to be aware of and somehow handle when they occur. Welcome to the domain of exceptions!

In this lesson:

- Handle exceptional conditions with try/catch
- Add metadata to errors
- Handle exceptions as values
- Use conditions for more flexible error handling

24.1 Handling Exceptions with try/catch

Handling exceptions in ClojureScript is more similar to than it is different from handling them in JavaScript. ClojureScript provides a special form called `try` that compiles down to a `try/catch` construct in JavaScript. The basic usage should look familiar to any JavaScript programmer:

265

Listing 24.1: Catching exceptions

```
(try
  (do-stuff 42)
  (call-api {:id 17})                               ①
  true                                              ②
  (catch js/Error e                                 ③
    (println "An error occurred:" e)
    false)
  (finally
    (do-cleanup)))                                  ④
```

① Multiple expressions can occur inside the body of `try`
② `try` is an expression and returns a value
③ `catch` is always used with the class of the value that should be caught
④ If a `finally` clause is present, it is called for side effects

While `try/catch` behaves almost exactly like its JavaScript counterpart, there are a few differences that are worth noting:

First, `try` is an expression rather than a statement. When all of the expressions inside the body of the try succeed, then the `try` itself evaluates to the value of its body's final expression. When any expression throws an exception that is caught, the `try` evaluates to the value of the final expression in the `catch` block. Just like in JavaScript, a `finally` clause may optionally be specified. If it is, it will be run purely for side effects after the body and potentially the `catch` clause are evaluated. Only the value of the body of the `try` (on success) or the body of the `catch` (on failure) will be returned - the value of `finally` is discarded.

Second, the constructor of the exception to catch must be specified, and if the value thrown is not of that constructor's type ,the `catch` clause is not evaluated, causing the exception to be re-thrown. This requirement arises from ClojureScript's roots in Clojure, which runs on the Java Virtual Machine and whose `try/catch` form mimics that of Java. In order to maintain more syntactic consistency with Clojure, ClojureScript follows the same syntax. In practice, `js/Error` is almost always used as the value of the error type. However, since JavaScript lets us throw any value - not just an `Error` - there are times when we need to catch some other value. In lieu of the constructor of the error, we may use the keyword `:default` to catch a value of any type - including ClojureScript values:

```
dev:cljs.user=> (try
        #_=>    (throw {:type :custom-error
        #_=>            :message "Something unpleasant occurred"})
        #_=>    (catch :default e
        #_=>      (println "Caught value:" e)))
Caught value: {:type :custom-error, :message Something unpleasant occurred}
nil
```

Quick Review

- What is the value of each of the following expressions?

```
;; 1
(try
  :success
  (catch :default _
    :failure))

;; 2
(* 2
  (try
    (throw (js/Error.))
    4
    (catch :default _
      6)
    (finally 8)))

;; 3
(try
  (try
    (throw "a string")
    (catch js/Error e
      "Inner"))
  (catch :default e
    "Outer")))
```

Conveying Information

Sometimes it is desirable to convey extra information when we throw an error. For instance, if we are loading a string from `localStorage`, parsing it, then using it to construct a domain object, there are at 3 steps that can fail, and we probably want to handle these failures differently - perhaps to determine what type of message to display to the user or whether to log the error to a service for later inspection. In this case, we can use `ex-info` to create a `ExceptionInfo` object, which is a subclass of the JavaScript `Error` type that ClojureScript defines. This function allows us to attach a message, a map of arbitrary metadata, and an optional field describing the cause of the exception. For example:

Listing 24.2: Creating an ExceptionInfo error

```
(ex-info "A parse error occurred"                    ①
         {:line 17 :char 8 :last-token "for"}        ②
         :unexpected-end-of-string)                  ③
```

① Error message

② Metadata
③ Cause (optional)

When we catch an `ExceptionInfo`, we can use the `ex-message`, `ex-data` and `ex-cause` functions to extract the extra information back out. Going back to the example of parsing a string in `localStorage` and hydrating a domain model from it, we can detect the type of error and handle it differently depending on where the error occurred.

Listing 24.3: Using ExceptionInfo

```clojure
(def required-attrs [:id :email])
(def allowed-attrs [:id :email :first-name :last-name])

(defn make-user [user-data]
  (cond
    (not (every? #(contains? user-data %) required-attrs))
    (throw (ex-info "Missing required attributes"
                    {:required required-attrs
                     :found (keys user-data)}
                    :validation-failed))
    (not (every? #(some (set allowed-attrs) %) (keys user-data)))
    (throw (ex-info "Found disallowed attributes"
                    {:allowed allowed-attrs
                     :found (keys user-data)}
                    :validation-failed))
    :else (assoc user-data :type :user)))

(defn hydrate-user []
  (let [serialized-user (try
                          (.getItem js/localStorage "current-user")
                          (catch js/Error _
                            (throw (ex-info "Could not load data from localStorage"
                                            {}
                                            :local-storage-unsupported))))
        user-data (try
                    (.parse js/JSON serialized-user)
                    (catch js/Error _
                      (throw (ex-info "Could not parse user data"
                                      {:string serialized-user}
                                      :parse-failed))))]
    (-> user-data
        (js->clj :keywordize-keys true)
        make-user)))

(try
  (hydrate-user)
  (catch ExceptionInfo e
    (case (ex-cause e)
      :local-storage-unsupported
      (display-error (str "Local storage not supported: "
                                              (ex-message e)))

      :parse-failed
```

```
(do (display-error "Could not load user data from browser")
    (log-error {:type :user-parse-failed
                :source (:string (ex-data e))}))
:validation-failed
(do (display-error "There was an error in your submission. Please correct it before continuing.")
    (update-field-errors (ex-data e)))
;; Re-throw an unknown error
(throw e))))
```

Using this pattern, we can provide more information along with an exception that can be used by the handling code in order to dispatch different business logic. In JavaScript, we can achieve a similar result by sub-classing `Error` and including `instanceof` checks in our error handling logic. ClojureScript is simply a bit more opinionated, and it provides the tools to do this out of the box.

24.2   Functional Alternatives to Exceptions

While handling errors with try/catch should be familiar to every JavaScript developer, it runs against the grain of pure functional programming, of which we have already seen the benefits. When exceptions can be thrown, a function is no longer a mapping of input to output. It additionally becomes a mechanism for signaling control flow: when a function throws an exception, it does not return a value to its caller, and the code that ultimately receives the value thrown is not necessarily the immediate caller. We can always use the pattern that we learned in Lesson 21 to segregate our exception-handling code from our core business logic. This is usually possible, and it is often the simplest option. However, there are more functional ways to handle exceptional conditions, and we will look at two of those: treating errors as values, and using condition systems.

Figure 24.1: Control flow for `try/catch`

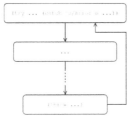

Errors as Values

The simplest and most functionally pure option for writing code to deal with exceptional conditions is to simply return any error that may occur. In this case, a function that may fail will return a *wrapper* value that can contain either a success value or an error. There are many ways to represent a wrapper value, but a simple option is as a 2-element vector that either has :ok in the first position and a normal value in the second position or has :error in the first position and an error value in the second position. It is trivial to create a few functions that define this "error" type and work with its values:

Listing 24.4: Defining an error type

```
(ns errors.err
    (:refer-clojure :exclude [map]))

(defn ok [val]
  [:ok val])

(defn error [val]
  [:error val])

(defn is-ok? [err]
  (= :ok (first err)))

(def is-error? (complement is-ok?))

(def unwrap second)

(defn unwrap-or [on-error err]
  (if (is-ok? err)
    (unwrap err)
    (on-error (unwrap err))))

(defn map [f err]
  (if (is-ok? err)
    (-> err unwrap f ok)
    err))

(defn flat-map [f err]
  (if (is-ok? err)
    (-> err unwrap f)
    err))
```

With these few functions, we can construct and transform values that have this "error type" wrapper.[1]

```
(defn div [x y]                                    ①
  (if (zero? y)
    (error "Cannot divide by zero")
    (ok (/ x y))))

(unwrap (div 27 9))                                ②

(unwrap (div 27 0))                                ③
```

---

[1]Yes, this is just the Error monad.

```
(map #(+ % 12)
     (div 27 9))                                    ④

(unwrap
 (flat-map                                          ⑤
  #(div % 2)
  (div 27 9)))
```

① Define a division function that can fail if asked to divide by 0
② A success value, `[:ok 3]`
③ An error value, `[:error "Cannot divide by zero"]`
④ `map` will transform a success value inside an error type
⑤ `flat-map` will take a success value inside an error type and return the result of passing this to another error-type producing function.

When we write code in this style, we can end up with functions that all include the same boilerplate. For example, every function that handles an error returned by another function that it calls will look like the following:

Listing 24.5: Handling an error

```
(defn get-results-and-handle-error []
  (unwrap-or
   (fn [err]                                        ①
    (display-err err)
    [])
   (get-results)))                                  ②
```

① The callback will be called when `get-results` fails, and its value will be returned from `get-results-and-handle-error`
② `get-results` may fail

On the other hand, when we have a function that should propagate an error when one of the functions that it calls fails, our function will look like this:

Listing 24.6: Propagating an error

```
(defn transform-results-and-propagate-error []
  (map
   #(transform-results %)                           ①
   (get-results)))
```

(1) `transform-results` will be called with results only when `get-results` succeeds

The downside to this approach is that we need always be mindful of which functions may fail and deal with their results as wrapped results. In the end, we have more boilerplate for handling errors, but our control flow is explicit, and our functions remain free of side effects. Sometimes the trade-off will be worthwhile, but other times we are better served by a judicious use of exception handling code at the boundaries of our application. There are several excellent libraries that help minimize the boilerplate associated with this error-as-value approach, such as Adam Bard's failjure[2].

Figure 24.2: Control flow for errors as values

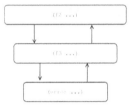

Conditions and Restarts

Given the long history of the Lisp family of programming languages, we should briefly mention the concept of *conditions*, which were popularized in Common Lisp.[3] The basic idea behind a condition system is that there are pieces of code that can have different outcomes that are beyond our control. For example, we cannot parse malformed input, a browser may have disabled a certain feature that we wish to use, etc. Additionally, the code that encounters these special conditions is not necessarily the code that we want deciding what to do as a result. However, *control should not be passed arbitrarily far up the call stack when some condition is encountered.* A popular library for working with conditions in ClojureScript is special[4].

Condition systems let us *signal* a condition, which may be *handled* by a function that was registered to handle that specific type of condition. Finally, this handler can optionally invoke a *restart*, which returns control to the location where the condition was signaled. Additionally, the lower-level function that signaled the condition may offer multiple restarts, and it is up to the handler to choose which restart to invoke.

In order to see how this works, let's return to the example of parsing a string in `localStorage` to hydrate a domain model. We end up with low-level code that we call from higher-level

---

[2]https://github.com/adambard/failjure
[3]As much as anything can be said to have been *popularized* by Common Lisp
[4]https://github.com/clojureman/special

code. That low-level code that gets data from `localStorage` should not be in charge of deciding what is the appropriate course of action - otherwise, it gets coupled to the higher-level logic of the program and is no longer reusable. Using the *special* library, our code might look like this:

Listing 24.7: Handling conditions

```
(defn get-localstorage [key]
  (try
    (.getItem js/localStorage key)
    (catch js/Error _
      (condition :localstorage-unsupported nil))))     ①

(defn get-parsed-data [key]
  (let [serialized (get-localstorage key)]
    (try
      (if-let [parsed (js->clj
                        (.parse js/JSON serialized)
                        :keywordize-keys true)]
        parsed
        (condition :no-data key
          :normally {}))                                ②
      (catch js/Error _
        (condition :parse-error {:key key :string serialized}
          :normally {}
          :reparse #(get-parsed-data %))))))            ③

(defn handle-parse-error [{:keys [key]}]
  (if (= key "current-user")
    (condition :reparse "currUser")                     ④
    (do (display-error "Cannot parse")
      (initialize-user))))

(defn hydrate-user []
  (let [managed-fn (manage get-parsed-data             ⑤
                      :localstorage-unsupported (fn [_] ⑥
                                                  (display-error "Unsupported")
                                                  "{}")
                      :parse-error handle-parse-error)
                      :no-data (fn [_]
                                 (initialize-user)))]
    (managed-fn "current-user")))
```

① Signal the `:localstorage-unsupported` condition with `nil`
② Provide a default value if the condition is not managed
③ Provide a "restart" that allows us to proceed with specific behavior
④ Trigger the `:reparse` restart
⑤ Create a managed version of the `get-parsed-data` function with handlers for each condition type

⑥ Declare a handler as the condition keyword followed by a function of the condition value to the desired value

This example is fairly dense, so let's unpack it a bit. First, there are two functions that we use as part of the condition system: `condition` and `manage`. `condition` signals a condition of a specific type along with a value. For example, when there is an error parsing user data, we signal the condition of type `:parse-error` with the value, `{:key key :string serialized}`. `manage` creates a version of the function that provides handlers for each condition that may be signaled, whether in the function that was called directly or in any functions that it eventually calls arbitrarily deep in the call stack. The handlers are given the value of the signaled condition and may either return a value that is used at the location where the condition was signaled, or they can signal a new condition.

This second option is how "restarts" are accomplished: when we signal a `condition`, we can provide restart handlers as well. The `:normally` handler is called automatically if no handler is provided higher in the call stack. Any other restart can be selected by raising the corresponding restart condition in uor handler function. In the example above, we provide a `:reparse` restart that attempts to parse data from another key from `localStorage`. We signal this restart in the `handle-parse-error` function: `(condition :reparse "currUser")`. This ability to provide code in the lower-level functions that can be dispatched based on higher-level logic is what makes conditions so powerful.

Figure 24.3: Control flow for conditions

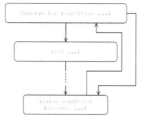

Quick Review

- What is the result of the following code?

```
(let [f (fn [s]
          (if (= 0 (mod (count s) 2))
            (condition :even-length s
              :normally "EVEN"
              :shout (.toUpperCase s))
            (str "You said: " s)))
      managed (manage f
                :even-length (fn [s]
```

```
                                  (if (= "loud" s)
                                    (condition :shout)
                                    (str s "!"))))]

  [(managed "test")
   (managed "foo")
   (managed "loud")])
```

As we can see, conditions let us decouple the code that specifies the recovery strategy from the code that decides what recovery strategy to invoke. Like exceptions, conditions are not purely functional because they introduce control flow outside of the normal return value of a function. However, since a restart returns control to the function where the error occurred, they are closer to the functional end of the spectrum than are exceptions.

24.3 Summary

In this lesson, we learned how to use ClojureScript's version of try/catch to deal with exceptions that occur in our code or code that we call. We saw how to use ex-info to create error values that convey extra information that we can use in our error handling code. Finally, we looked at two ways to approach errors in a more functional programming-friendly way. We "wrapped" the return values of functions that could fail in a special error type, and we also used conditions to allow higher-level code to specify the strategy for handling an exceptional case in lower-level code.

Lesson 25

Intro to Core Async

Asynchronous programming lives at the heart of web development. Almost every app needs to communicate with an API backend, respond to user input, or perform some other I/O task without blocking the main thread. While it is entirely possible to use JavaScript's Promise API from ClojureScript, we have another paradigm for asynchronous programming at our disposal - the `core.async` library. This library implements the same concurrency model as the Go programming language, and it allows us to write code as sequential processes that may need to communicate with each other.

In this lesson:

- Learn about CSP, the concurrency model behind ClojureScript (and Go)
- Think of concurrent problems in terms of processes
- Use channels to communicate between processes

25.1 Overview of CSP

ClojureScript's library for concurrency is based on a mathematical process calculus (concurrency model) called Communicating Sequential Processes, which was described by Tony Hoare in 1978. The basic idea behind CSP is that there are a number of independent *processes* that each execute some ordered sequence of steps. These processes can communicate with each other by sending or receiving messages over *channels*. When a process wants to read a message from a channel, it blocks until a message is available, then it consumes the message and moves on. A process can also place a message on a channel either synchronously or asynchronously. By using communication over channels, multiple processes can *synchronize* such that one process waits for a specific input from another before proceeding.

In ClojureScript, the *core.async* library provides the functionality that we need to create these asynchronous workflows in the form of the `go` macro, which creates a new lightweight process, `chan`, which creates a channel, and the operators, `<!` (take), `>!` (put), and `alts!` (take from one of many channels). Using only these primitives, we can create very sophisticated asynchronous communication patterns. Before diving in with `core.async`, let's take a quick step back to talk about CSP.

In CSP, the fundamental object is the *process*. A process is simply an anonymous (unnamed) piece of code that can execute a number of steps in order, potentially with its own control flow. Code in a `process` always runs synchronously - that is, the process will not proceed on to the next step until the previous step completes. Each process is independent of every other process, and they all run concurrently (ClojureScript is is charge of scheduling what process should run when). Finally, even though communication is a cornerstone of CSP, processes do not necessarily *have* to communicate with any other processes.

Figure 25.1: Concurrent processes

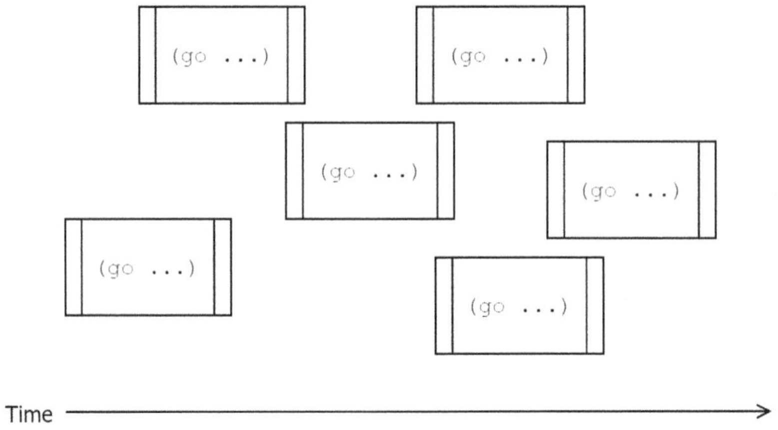

Moving on from processes, the next key object in CSP is the *channel*[1]. A channel is simply a conduit that can carry values from one process to another. By default, each channel can only convey a single value at once. That is, once a process sends a value on a channel, the

---

[1]The original formulation of CSP did not have channels. Instead, each processed had a unique name and passed messages to other processes directly. All notable implementations of CSP today use named channels to communicate between anonymous processes.

next process that tries to send on that channel will be parked until another process takes the value out of that channel. Additionally, trying to take a value from an empty channel will park the receiver until a value is put in. Channels can also be created with buffers that can hold up to some specified number of values that have not been taken out of the channel. Additionally, these buffers can either park producers when they fill up (which is the default behavior), or they can silently discard any new values (via `dropping-buffer`) or push out the oldest value in the buffer (via `sliding-buffer`).

Parking or Blocking?

We mention that processes can *park* when trying to read from an empty channel or write to a full channel. From the perspective of the process, it is *blocked* and cannot make any progress until the state of the channel changes. However, from the perspective of the ClojureScript runtime, other processes can continue running, and the *parked* process can eventually be *resumed* if the state of the channel changes. We avoid using the language of blocking, since ClojureScript runs in the single-threaded context of JavaScript, and parking a process does not block that thread.

Figure 25.2: Synchronization with channels

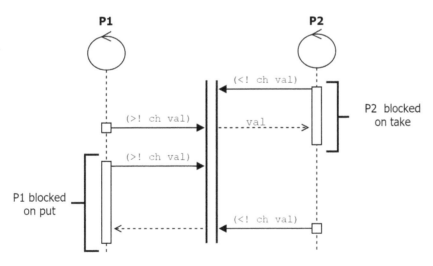

With this understanding of how processes and channels work, we are ready to dig in to an example. Let's say that we are building an SQL query editor, and whenever the user is focused in the query input and presses keystrokeCtrl + keystrokeEnter, we send off the query to a server and wait for a response. We will have one process that watches keystrokes, and another process that coordinates user input and performing a server request when necessary.

Since `core.async` is exposed as an official library rather than part of the core library, we need to add a dependency to `deps.edn` for any project in which we would like to use it:

Listing 25.1: deps.edn

```
:deps {;; Other deps}
       org.clojure/core.async {:mvn/version "1.3.610"}}
```

25.2   Go Blocks as Lightweight Processes

In ClojureScript, we create a process using the `go` macro containing the block of code to execute. A simple `go` block could look like the following:

```
(go (println "Hello Processes!"))
```

This will asynchronously print, `Hello Processes!` to the console, similar to the following JavaScript code:

```
setTimeout(() => console.log("Hello Processes!"), 0);
```

We can create as many of these go blocks as we would like, and they will all run independently of each other. The interesting part comes when we introduce channels into a `go` block. In the next example, we read values from one channel and forward the ones that satisfy a predicate onto another channel. This is essentially a channel filter operation:

Listing 25.2: A filtering process

```
(go (loop []
     (let [val (<! in-ch)]                    ①
       (when (pred? val)                      ②
         (>! out-ch val)))                    ③
     (recur)))
```

① Read a value from `in-ch`
② Test the value with `pred?`
③ Write the value to `out-ch`

This example illustrates a common paradigm in `core.async`: we create go blocks that infinitely loop, performing the same task over and over. Just like JavaScript has its global event loop that will execute our code and callbacks, we can create mini event loops that are concerned only with a very small piece of functionality. In fact, this infinitely-looping process pattern is so common that `core.async` provides a `go-loop` macro that combines a `go` block with a `loop`. Using this macro, our code becomes:

```
(go-loop []
  (let [val (<! in-ch)]
    (when (pred? val)
      (>! out-ch val)))
  (recur))
```

To illustrate how each process runs independently, we can make use of the `timeout` function provided by the `core.async` library. This function returns a channel that closes after a specified timeout (in milliseconds). Let's create 2 processes that each log to the console on a given interval:

```
(go-loop []
  (<! (timeout 100))
  (println "Hello from process 1")
  (recur))

(go-loop []
  (<! (timeout 250))
  (println "Hello from process 2")
  (recur))
```

Quick Review

- True or false? Each go block always runs to completion before any other go blocks are run.
- What is the more concise way of writing `(go (loop [] ... (recur)))`?

25.3 Communicating Over Channels

Returning to the example of the SQL query editor, we could spawn a process to listen to keyboard input and emit events for all "key chords" consisting of one or more modifier keys (Ctrl, Alt, Shift, etc.) plus another key. For this, we will need to listen for `keydown` and `keyup` events and place them on channels. When we detect a chord, we place the results on another channel:

Listing 25.3: Detecting key chords

```
(def keydown-ch (chan))                              ①
(gevent/listen js/document "keydown"
```

```
   #(put! keydown-ch (.-key %)))

(def keyup-ch (chan))                                          ②
(gevent/listen js/document "keyup"
   #(put! keyup-ch (.-key %)))

(def is-modifier? #{"Control" "Meta" "Alt" "Shift"})

(def chord-ch (chan))
(go-loop [modifiers []                                         ③
          pressed nil]
  (when (and (seq modifiers) pressed)                          ④
    (>! chord-ch (conj modifiers pressed)))
  (let [[key ch] (alts! [keydown-ch keyup-ch])]               ⑤
    (condp = ch
      keydown-ch (if (is-modifier? key)                        ⑥
                   (recur (conj modifiers key) pressed)
                   (recur modifiers key))
      keyup-ch (if (is-modifier? key)
                 (recur (filterv #(not= % key) modifiers)
                        pressed)
                 (recur modifiers nil)))))
```

① Put the key for all `keydown` events on a channel
② Put the key for all `keyup` events on a channel
③ Keep track of any modifiers keys held down as well as the last other key pressed
④ If we have any modifiers as well as a pressed key, send the chord on the `chord-ch` chan-nel
⑤ Wait for values of either `keydown-ch` or `keyup-ch` channels
⑥ Add the key that was pressed or remove the key that was released and recur

Sending Values Asynchronously

In addition to using a `go-loop` that maintains state on each recursive pass, we encounter a couple of new pieces of `core.async` here. The first is the `put!` function. This function puts a value on a channel asynchronously. The normal put and take operators (`>!` and `<!` respectively) are only designed to be run inside a go block. One option that we have is to spin up a new go block every time that we want to put a value onto a channel. For instance, the `keydown` listener could have been written as follows:

```
(gevent/listen js/document "keydown"
   #(go (>! keydown-ch (.-key %))))
```

However, this incurs some additional overhead that we may not want every time that a key is pressed. The `put!` function is a much cheaper option in this case. Remember that using `>!`

will park the process, but when we are not in a go block, we do not want to wait for a channel to be ready before proceeding. We want to be able to send a value off asynchronously, knowing that it will be received by the channel when it is ready. This is exactly what put! does. Like >!, it takes a channel and a value to put on that channel. Additionally, we can supply a callback as a third argument, which will be called when the value is delivered to the channel.

Alternating Between Channels

As we mentioned in out introduction to CSP above, there is one additional function that we often use to consume values from more than one channel: alts!. Like >! and <!, alts! can only be called from within a go block. It takes a vector of channels to "listen to" and parks until it receives a value from any of them. Upon receiving a value, it evaluates to a vector whose first element is the value received and whose second element is the channel from which the value came. By checking the channel that we get from alts!, we can determine where the value came from and decide what to do with it.

One common use case is to implement a timeout by alternating between a channel that we expect to eventually deliver a value and a timeout channel that will close after a certain amount of time:

```
(go
  (let [[val ch] (alts! long-task-ch (timeout 5000))]
    (if (= ch long-task-ch)
      (println "Task completed!" val)
      (println "Oh oh! Task timed out!"))))
```

Adding Communication

So far, we have only a single process that is reading from and writing to channels. Let's change that with another process that submits the query to a mocked server and updates the results area:

Listing 25.4: Making a mock request

```
(defn mock-request [query]                          ①
  (let [ch (chan)]
    (js/setTimeout
      #(put! ch (str "Results for: " in))
      (* 2000 (js/Math.random)))                    ②
    ch))

(go-loop []
  (let [chord (<! chord-ch)]                         ③
    (when (and (= chord ["Control" "r"])
```

```
            (= js/document.activeElement query-input))
    (set! (.-innerText results-display) "Loading...")
    (set! (.-innerText results-display)
      (<! (mock-request (.-value query-input)))))))        ④
  (recur)))
```

① Simulate making a request to a server, returning a channel that will eventually get
   results
② Wait for a random interval between 0 and 2 seconds to simulate latency
③ Wait for key chords
④ Perform a request and wait for the results before updating `results-display`

Here we spin up another process that repeatedly takes key chords from the `chord-ch` channel,
and checks to see if we have the correct chord and whether the query input is focused. If
both of these conditions are met, then we simulate making a server request, and when the
results come back, we update the results area. One thing to note is that `(set! (.-innerText
results-display) (<! (mock-request (.-value query-input))))` will halt its evaluation until we
can take a value from the channel returned by `(mock-request (.-value query-input))`. Internally, the `go` macro rewrites our code into a state machine, but all that we need to know is
that whenever we need to park a process until a value is ready, any code that depends on
that value will be deferred until after the value is delivered.

Quick Review

- Describe the difference between `>!` and `put!`
- How could we change the previous go block to time out a request after 1500 milliseconds?

25.4   Channels as Values

As we saw in the `mock-request` function, we can create channels anywhere in our code. We
can pass them as arguments to functions or return them from functions. Although the
serve the special purpose of facilitating communication between processes, they are just
regular ClojureScript values.

It is a common idiom to return a channel from a function that produces some result asynchronously. Whereas in JavaScript, we would usually return a Promise (or write the function as `async`), we often return a channel when we intend for a function to be called from
within a go block. Author and Clojure instructor Eric Normand suggests naming functions

that return channels with a < prefix.[2] Following this convention, our `mock-request` function would become `<mock-request`. This makes it easy to visually distinguish functions that return channels from other functions. Remember, however, that a function that returns a channel is less general than one that accepts a callback because when we return a channel, we dictate that any value eventually produced by that function must be consumed in a go block. For this reason, we should usually prefer writing functions that take callbacks if we do not know how we will eventually want to call them.

In addition to channels that simply create a channel that they will eventually put a value into, we can create some interesting higher-order channel functions. For instance, we can create a channel that merges values from any number of other channels:

```
(defn merge-ch [& channels]
  (let [out (chan)]
    (go-loop []
      (>! out (first (alts! channels)))
      (recur))
    out))
```

At the beginning of the lesson, we already saw another useful higher-order channel function that filters the values in a channel to only ones that satisfy a predicate. Let's look at one more example - a function that synchronizes 2 channels such that it waits for one value in each channel then produces a pair of `[chan-1-val chan-2-val]`:

```
(defn synchronize-ch [chan-1 chan-2]
  (let [out (chan)]
    (go-loop []
      (>! out [(<! chan-1) (<! chan-2)])
      (recur))
    out))
```

With very simple functions, we can easily create very sophisticated asynchronous systems. Most importantly, because channels are values, we can create functions that manipulate channels in such a way that we abstract the communication patterns out of our business logic.

25.5 Summary

In this lesson, we learned about the Communicating Sequential Processes concurrency model and `core.async`, its ClojureScript implementation. After learning about the core concepts of CSP, we explored how go blocks create lightweight processes that run concurrently and can *park* when waiting to write to or read from a channel that is not ready. We talked

---

[2]Eric Normand's style guide for core.async can be found at https://purelyfunctional.tv/mini-guide/core-async-code-style/

about how channels help us communicate between processes and synchronize their state. Finally, we saw that the fact that channels are plain ClojureScript values makes it possible for us to manipulate the communication structure of our processes separately from our business logic. While `core.async` has the same expressive power as Promises and `async/await` in JavaScript, it presents a very useful way of thinking about concurrency that lends itself to SPAs, which often have multiple sequential interactions that all need to be handled concurrently.

Lesson 26

Capstone 4 - Group Chat

Congratulations! At this point, we have learned enough ClojureScript to write pretty much any sort of app that we would like. Sure, over the coming chapters, we will pick up some tools and techniques that will make us more productive, but nothing is stopping us from writing complete, production-quality apps with what we have learned so far. For this capstone, we will be writing a realtime group chat application - similar to a very slimmed-down version of Slack. You can connect to a live instance of this application at https://chat.learn-cljs.com/.

In This Lesson:

- Design a non-trivial application in terms of state, events, and components
- Interact with a WebSocket API
- Learn some principles for refactoring

Figure 26.1: Screenshot of ClojureScript Chat

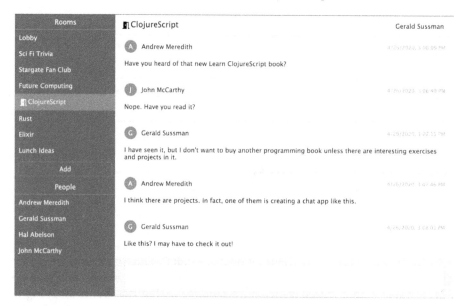

26.1   Thinking About Interactions

There are many ways to start building an application, and no one way is necessarily best. However, for ClojureScript, a natural place to start is by thinking about the state and how we want the user to interact with that state. At a high level, we will have 2 types of data that we want to keep track of: *application data* and *UI state*. Application data is any data that we receive from the server that powers the application UI state, on the other hand, is made up of pieces of data that are never persisted but are useful for determining what state various components are in.

Application Data

For our chat application, we will keep a vector of `rooms` that we can join, a vector of `people` that we can enter into conversations with, and a vector of `messages` that we can read in the current room or conversation. We will also want to keep track of the current user for a couple of reasons: first, we will display the user's name in the upper right-hand corner of the screen, and second, if there is no user, we will display a modal so that the user can sign up or sign in.

Listing 26.1: learn_clj/chat/state.cljs

```
(ns learn-cljs.chat.state)

(def initial-state                              ①
  {:rooms []
   :people []
   :messages []
   :current-user nil})

(defonce app-state (atom initial-state))        ②
```

① Define the initial application state as an immutable map
② Define the app state as an atom whose starting value is the same as `initial-state`

We will next add functions to transform the application data such that our UI components can easily consume it. We will also provide functions that transition the app state as well. In the interest of writing pure and testable code wherever possible, our functions that update the app state will take in an immutable `state` and return a new state (rather than mutating the `app-state` atom directly). These functions will be invoked when we receive a response from the API.

```
;; Application data queries
(defn room-by-id [state id]
  (->> state
       :rooms
       (filter #(= id (:id %)))
       first))

(defn person-by-username [state username]
  (->> state
       :people
       (filter #(= username (:username %)))
       first))

;; Application data transition functions
(defn received-people-list [state people]
  (assoc state :people people))

(defn person-joined [state person]
  (let [username (:username person)
        is-joined-user? #(= username (:username %))]
    (update state :people
      (fn [people]
        (if (some is-joined-user? people)
          (map
            (fn [user]
              (if (is-joined-user? user)
                (assoc user :online? true)
                user))
            people)
```

```
          (conj people person))))))

(defn person-left [state username]
  (update state :people
    (fn [people]
      (map #(if (= username (:username %))
              (assoc % :online? false)
              %) people))))

(defn received-rooms-list [state rooms]
  (assoc state :rooms rooms))

(defn room-added [state room]
  (update state :rooms conj room))

(defn message-received [state message]
  (update state :messages conj message))

(defn messages-received [state messages]
  (assoc state :messages messages))

(defn messages-cleared [state]
  (assoc state :messages []))
```

Without going into too much detail, the query functions allow us to look up a user by user-name or a room by ID. The transition functions handle most of the responses that we can expect from the API. One interesting piece of logic is the `person-joined` function, which either marks a previously seen user as "online" or adds a brand new user to the user list. Additionally, the `messages-cleared` function is one that will be invoked by our UI (rather than the API) whenever the user switches between rooms or conversations so that we do not see messages from the previous room/conversation while we wait for the server to send us a new message list. In roughly 40 lines of code we have defined the interface for interacting with application data.

UI State

Since this is a simple application, we only need to keep a few pieces of application state:

- The current "view" - i.e. the room or conversation that the user has focused
- A toggle determining whether to display the "Sign In" or "Sign Up" modal before the user has authenticated
- A flag indicating whether the "Create Room" input is open

Many applications keep input data in the UI state, but until we start building on top of React, this would introduce too much complexity to justify it. For this project, we will simply query the DOM to get the values of user input fields.

First, we will add these fields to the application state:

```
(def initial-state
  {;; ...
   :current-view nil
   ;; May be {:type :room, :id 123}
   ;;      or {:type :conversation, :username "user_abc"}

   :auth-modal :sign-in
   ;; May be :sign-in
   ;;      or :sign-up

   :create-room-input-open? false})
```

Next, we will add query and state transition functions, just like we did for the application
data:

```
;; UI state queries
(defn is-current-view-room? [state]
  (= ::room (get-in state [:current-view :type])))

(defn current-room-id [state]
  (get-in state [:current-view :id]))

(defn is-current-view-conversation? [state]
  (= ::conversation (get-in state [:current-view :type])))

(defn current-conversation-recipient [state]
  (get-in state [:current-view :username]))

(defn room-list [state]
  (let [current-room (when (is-current-view-room? state)
                       (get-in state [:current-view :id]))]
    (map (fn [room]
           (assoc room
             :active? (= current-room (:id room))))
         (:rooms state))))

(defn people-list [app]
  (let [current-username (when (is-current-view-conversation? app)
                           (get-in app [:current-view :username]))]
    (map (fn [person]
           (assoc person
             :active? (= current-username (:username person))))
         (:people app))))

;; UI state transition functions
(defn switched-to-room [state room-id]
  (assoc state :current-view {:type ::room
                              :id room-id}))

(defn switched-to-conversation [state username]
  (assoc state :current-view {:type ::conversation
```

```
                                     :username username})))

(defn auth-modal-toggled [state]
  (update state :auth-modal
    {:sign-up :sign-in                                    ①
     :sign-in :sign-up}))

(defn user-authenticated [state user]
  (assoc state :current-user user))

(defn create-room-input-opened [state]
  (assoc state :create-room-input-open? true))

(defn create-room-input-closed [state]
  (assoc state :create-room-input-open? false))
```

① Use a map itself as a function that maps the current auth model state to the next state

With our entire state interface defined, let's move on to the mechanism through which our components and API will interact with our state: the message bus.

Message Bus Pattern

Rather than mutating the application state directly from our components or the API, we will introduce a messaging layer that will allow us to more easily test our components and will give us the ability for one component to potentially react to a message from another. Building on the knowledge of `core.async` from the previous lesson, we will create a very simple messaging system. This messaging system will allow us to dispatch messages with a given type from anywhere in our app and subscribe functions to handle messages of a given type.

Listing 26.2: chat/message_bus.cljs

```
(ns learn-cljs.chat.message-bus
  (:require [cljs.core.async :refer [go-loop pub sub chan <! put!]]))

(def msg-ch (chan 1))                                     ①
(def msg-bus (pub msg-ch ::type))                         ②

(defn dispatch!                                           ③
 ([ch type] (dispatch! ch type nil))
 ([ch type payload]
  (put! ch {::type type
            ::payload payload})))

(defn handle! [p type handle]                             ④
  (let [sub-ch (chan)]
```

```
(sub p type sub-ch)
(go-loop []
  (handle (::payload (<! sub-ch)))
  (recur))))
```

① Channel on which messages will be dispatched
② Publication that will allow consumers to receive messages from msg-ch
③ Function for dispatching a typed message
④ Function for registering a handler for a type of message.

Figure 26.2: Architecture of the messaging layer

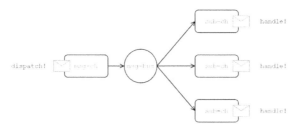

This simple messaging layer provides pub/sub capability where we can use dispatch! to emit messages onto the msg-ch channel and handle! to subscribe a callback to be called whenever messages of a given type are dispatched. While we could have hard-coded dispatch! to put messages on msg-ch and handle! to subscribe to msg-bus, but once again, this would make our code much more difficult to test and much less modular.

26.2 Building Components

Our application is fairly simple, but it consists of several distinct layout components:

- header
- sidebar
- message list
- message composer
- authorization modal

We will break out each of these high-level layout components into a namespace, and we will also include a top-level "app" component that initializes the rest of the layout.

Figure 26.3: Application layout

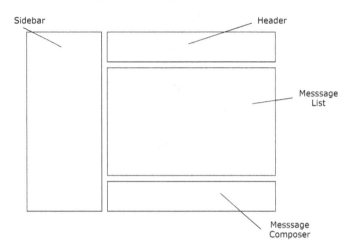

Most of our components will follow the same pattern: they will mount into a parent DOM node, watch a portion of the application state (or some value computed from the state) for change, and re-render themselves the a change occurs. Let's go ahead and create a function that will allow us to initialize a component that follows this pattern:

Listing 26.3: chat/components/component.cljs

```
(ns learn-cljs.chat.components.component
  (:require [learn-cljs.chat.state :as state]))

(defn init-component
  "Initialize a component.
  Parameters:
  el - Element in which to render component
  watch-key - Key that uniquely identifies this component
  accessor - Function that takes the app state and returns the
             component state
  render - Function that takes the parent element and component
           state and renders DOM"
  [el watch-key accessor render]
  (add-watch state/app-state watch-key                    ①
    (fn [_ _ old new]
      (let [state-old (accessor old)                      ②
            state-new (accessor new)]
        (when (not= state-old state-new)                  ③
          (set! (.-innerText el) "")
          (render el state-new)))))
  (render el (accessor @state/app-state))                 ④
  el)                                                     ⑤
```

① Watch the app state for all changes
② Use the supplied `accessor` function to compute the old and new app state
③ Only re-render if the component state changed
④ Perform an initial render
⑤ Return the parent component

The use of this utility function will become clear as we start building components in the next section.

Application Chrome

We will build the UI for this application in a top-down fashion, starting with the application container, followed by the "chrome" components - that is the header and sidebar - before moving on to lower level pieces. For the moment, let's create an app container that simply loads the header and renders it into the DOM:

Listing 26.4: chat/components/app.cljs

```
(ns learn-cljs.chat.components.app
  (:require [learn-cljs.chat.components.header :refer [init-header]]
            [goog.dom :as gdom])
  (:import [goog.dom TagName]))

(defn init-main []
  (gdom/createDom TagName.SECTION "content-main"
    (init-header)))

(defn init-app [el msg-ch]
  (let [wrapper (gdom/createDom TagName.DIV "app-wrapper"
                  (init-main))]
    (set! (.-innerText el) "")
    (.appendChild el wrapper)))
```

This application container code is fairly straightforward: we create a basic shell with a couple of DOM nodes then call `render-header` to create and return the DOM necessary for the header. Before this code does anything useful, we will need to create a `learn-cljs.chat.components.header` namespace that exposes the `init-header` function. We'll do that now:

Listing 26.5: state/components/header.cljs

```
(ns learn-cljs.chat.components.header
  (:require [goog.dom :as gdom]
            [learn-cljs.chat.components.component :refer [init-component]]
            [learn-cljs.chat.state :as state])
  (:import [goog.dom TagName]))
```

```clojure
(defn display-name [person]                          ①
  (if person
    (->> person
      ((juxt :first-name :last-name))
      (s/join " "))
    "REMOVED"))

(defn accessor [app]                                 ②
  (cond
    (state/is-current-view-room? app)                ③
    {:icon "meeting_room"
     :title (-> app
              (get-in [:current-view :id])
              (->> (state/room-by-id app))
              :name)
     :current-user (:current-user app)}

    (state/is-current-view-conversation? app)
    {:icon "person"
     :title (-> app
              (get-in [:current-view :username])
              (->> (state/person-by-username app))
              display-name)
     :current-user (:current-user app)}

    :else                                            ④
    {:title "Welcome to ClojureScript Chat"}))

(defn render [header {:keys [icon title current-user]}]   ⑤
  (doto header
    (.appendChild
      (gdom/createDom TagName.H1 "view-name"
        (gdom/createDom TagName.I "material-icons" icon)
        title))
    (.appendChild
      (gdom/createDom TagName.DIV "user-name"
        (when (some? current-user)
          (display-name current-user))))))

(defn init-header []                                 ⑥
  (init-component
    (gdom/createDom TagName.HEADER "app-header")
    :header accessor render))
```

① Helper function for displaying a formatted version of a user's name
② Accessor function that takes the app state and computes our component state
③ Use the functions that we wrote in `learn-cljs.chat.state` to access the relevant data
④ Provide a fallback if the user is not in a chat room or a conversation
⑤ Render function that updates the `header` element based on app state

⑥ Create the header component and return its DOME element

Here we see the `init-component` function in action: within `init-header`, we create an element to render the header content into, and we pass that element, along with an accessor function that computes component state from application state and a render function that will update our header whenever the component state changes. One nice feature of the way that we designed our `init-component` helper is that the render function will only be called if the app state changes in a way that affects how the header renders. When we get to the next section, we will rely on React to optimize the rendering cycle for us, but it is instructive to see how easily we can build a UI without any framework.

Before moving on, let's clean things up a bit. First, the `display-name` function will be useful for rendering user names in several places, so we can go ahead and refactor that function into a `render-helpers` namespace:

Listing 26.6: chat/components/render_helpers.cljs

```
(ns chat.components.render-helpers
  (:require [clojure.string :as s]))

(defn display-name [person]
  (if person
    (->> person
         ((juxt :first-name :last-name))
         (s/join " "))
    "REMOVED"))
```

Listing 26.7: chat/components/header.cljs

```
(ns chat.components.header
  (:require ; ...
            [chat.components.render-helpers :refer [display-name]])
  ; ...
)
```

Additionally, the syntax for the `goog.dom` library can be a bit verbose, so we will create another `dom` helper namespace that will allow us to write code like this:

```
(dom/h1 "title" "Hello world!")
```

instead of this:

```
(gdom/createDom TagName.H1 "title" "Hello world!")
```

We will create this helper namespace as `learn-cljs.chat.components.dom`.

Listing 26.8: chat/components/dom.cljs

```clojure
(ns learn-cljs.chat.components.dom
  (:require [goog.dom :as gdom])
  (:import [goog.dom TagName]))

(defn dom-fn [tag-name]                              ①
  (fn [& args]
    (apply gdom/createDom tag-name args)))

(def div (dom-fn TagName.DIV))
;; ...                                               ②

(defn with-children [el & children]                  ③
  (doseq [child children]
    (.appendChild el child))
  el)
```

① Higher-order function returning a function that creates a DOM element
② Define a function for each DOM element that we will use. Most of the elements have
   been omitted for brevity.
③ Define another helper that cleans up repeated use of .appendChild

Then, back in `header.cljs`, we can update our render and initialization functions to use this
new DOM utility:

```clojure
(ns learn-cljs.chat.components.header                ①
  (:require ; ...
            [learn-cljs.chat.components.dom :as dom]))

;; ...

(defn render [header {:keys [icon title current-user]}]
  (dom/with-children header
    (dom/h1 "view-name"
      (dom/i "material-icons" icon) title)
    (dom/div "user-name"
      (when (some? current-user)
        (display-name current-user)))))

(defn init-header []
  (init-component (dom/header "app-header")
    :header accessor render))
```

① Remove require of `[goog.dom :as gdom]` and import of `[goog.dom TagName]`

Now that we have refactored our code to make it more readable and concise, let's move on to the sidebar. The sidebar will display a list of rooms, a list of users that we can converse with, and a control for creating a new room. Clicking on either a room name or a user's name should switch to that room or conversation respectively. Unlike the header, the sidebar contains elements that the user should be able to interact with in order to update the application state. For this reason, we will pass the message channel down through the component hierarchy to all components that need it, and we will call the `learn-cljs.chat.message-bus/dispatch!` function to send off our messages. The messages will be processed by any handler that we have registered, and eventually, some of them will trigger API requests.

There is not anything that is novel in this code: we initialize components that receive application state, manage their own portion of the DOM, and add event listeners. Without further ado, the entire code for the sidebar is listed below:

Listing 26.9: chat/components/sidebar.cljs

```clojure
(ns learn-cljs.chat.components.sidebar
  (:require [learn-cljs.chat.components.dom :as dom]        ①
            [learn-cljs.chat.components.component :refer [init-component]]
            [learn-cljs.chat.components.render-helpers :as helpers]
            [learn-cljs.chat.message-bus :as bus]
            [goog.events :as gevents]
            [learn-cljs.chat.state :as state]))

(defn sidebar-header [title]
  (dom/div "sidebar-header" title))

(defn render-room [msg-ch room]
  (let [class-name (str "sidebar-item" (when (:active? room)
                                         " active"))
        text (:name room)]
    (doto (dom/div class-name text)
      (gevents/listen "click"                                ②
        #(bus/dispatch! msg-ch :switch-to-room
           {:id (:id room)})))))

(defn render-create-room [msg-ch el open?]                   ③
  (if open?
    (let [add-room-input (dom/input "add-room-input")]
      (dom/with-children el
        (doto add-room-input
          (gevents/listen "keyup"
            #(when (= (.-key %) "Enter")
               (bus/dispatch! msg-ch
                 :create-room (.-value add-room-input))))
          (gevents/listen "blur"
            #(bus/dispatch! msg-ch
               :close-create-room-input)))))
      (.focus add-room-input))                               ④
    (dom/with-children el
```

```
      (doto (dom/div "add-room" "Add")
        (gevents/listen "click"
          #(bus/dispatch! msg-ch :open-create-room-input))))))

(defn render-create-room-item [msg-ch]
  (init-component
    (dom/div "sidebar-item no-highlight")
    :sidebar-create-room
    :create-room-input-open?
    (partial render-create-room msg-ch)))

(defn render-rooms [msg-ch el rooms]
  (apply dom/with-children el                      ⑤
    (conj
      (mapv #(render-room msg-ch %) rooms)
      (render-create-room-item msg-ch))))

(defn sidebar-rooms [msg-ch]
  (init-component
    (dom/div "sidebar-rooms")
    :sidebar-rooms
    state/room-list
    (partial render-rooms msg-ch)))

(defn render-person [msg-ch person]
  (let [class-name (str "sidebar-item" (when (:active? person)
                                         " active"))
        text (helpers/display-name person)]
    (doto (dom/div class-name text)
      (gevents/listen "click"
        #(bus/dispatch! msg-ch :switch-to-conversation
          {:username (:username person)})))))

(defn render-people [msg-ch el people]
  (dom/with-children el
    (map #(render-person msg-ch %) people)))

(defn sidebar-people [msg-ch]
  (init-component
    (dom/div "sidebar-people")
    :sidebar-people
    state/people-list
    (partial render-people msg-ch)))

(defn init-sidebar [msg-ch]
  (dom/aside "sidebar"
    (sidebar-header "Rooms")
    (sidebar-rooms msg-ch)
    (sidebar-header "People")
    (sidebar-people msg-ch)))
```

① Require the UI helpers that we just factored out of the header code

② Add an event listener to each room in the list that we render

③ Render the "Add Room" widget that turns into an input on click

④ Automatically focus the input field whenever "Add Room" is clicked

⑤ Since dom/with-children expects a variadic argument list of children, we use apply to "unwrap" the vector of elements that we are passing in

We need to initialize this sidebar in components/app.cljs as well:

```
(ns learn-cljs.chat.components.app
  (:require ;; ...
            [learn-cljs.chat.components.sidebar            ①
             :refer [init-sidebar]]))

(defn init-app [el msg-ch]
  (let [wrapper (dom/div "app-wrapper"                    ②
                  (init-sidebar msg-ch)                   ③
                  ;; ...
                )]
    ;; ...
))
```

① Require the initialization function for the sidebar

② Refactor app.cljs to use our DOM helpers as well

③ init-sidebar will render the sidebar inside the app wrapper

Finally, we will create a learn-cljs.chat namespace that will load the DOM elements for both the header and the sidebar into the page itself:

Listing 26.10: chat.cljs

```
(ns learn-cljs.chat
  (:require [learn-cljs.chat.message-bus :as bus]
            [learn-cljs.chat.components.app                ①
             :refer [init-app]]
            [learn-cljs.chat.handlers]                     ②
            [goog.dom :as gdom]))

(defonce initialized?
  (do
    (init-app                                              ③
      (gdom/getElement "app")
      bus/msg-ch)
    true))
```

① Require the function that initializes the entire application UI

② Require the `learn-cljs.chat.handlers` namespace for the side effect of registering message handlers
③ Initialize the UI

We will continue to fill out this `learn-cljs.chat` namespace as we continue with this project, but one thing to notice is that it will be less pure and functional than most of the rest of our code. This is because, at some point, we need to actually load things for side effects, call stateful functions, make assumptions about the DOM on the page, or load global objects, such as the `msg-ch` channel. Rather than polluting our entire code base with this impurity, we will do as many impure operations in the core namespace as possible in the interest of making the *interesting* part of our code more modular.

One area in which we have not maintained functional purity in this application is in allowing UI components to access `learn-cljs.chat.state/app-state` directly, rather than constructing it in `learn-cljs.chat` and passing it down to each component explicitly. This is the sort of pragmatic trade-off that can sometimes be made to make the code easier to work with at the expense of testability and modularity. In a production application, we would usually be better served by a more constrained and explicit approach to accessing the state.

Message List

Now that we have the basic "shell" of the application in place, let's move on to the meat of the application: the message list. Even though the message feed is the core of our application, it is implemented as a single component. The state accessor takes the `:messages` collection off of the application, does a simple lookup in the `:users` collection to get the author of each message, and applies some formatting. The renderer simply creates some DOM for each of these messages. Since there is nothing in the message list that needs to respond to user input, we do not have to deal with attaching any event handlers.

Listing 26.11: chat/components/messages.cljs

```
(ns learn-cljs.chat.components.messages
  (:require [learn-cljs.chat.components.dom :as dom]
            [learn-cljs.chat.components.component :refer [init-component]]
            [learn-cljs.chat.components.render-helpers :as helpers]
            [learn-cljs.chat.state :as state]))


(defn message-state-accessor [app message]
  (let [sender (state/person-by-username app (:sender message))
        name (helpers/display-name sender)
        initial (-> name (.charAt 0) (.toUpperCase))
        formatted-timestamp (.toLocaleString
                              (js/Date. (* 1000 (:timestamp message))))]
    (assoc message :author {:name name
                            :initial initial}
                   :timestamp formatted-timestamp)))
```

```
(defn accessor [app]
  (->> app :messages (map #(message-state-accessor app %))))

(defn render-message [message]
  (dom/article "message"
    (dom/div "message-header"
      (dom/div "author-avatar" (get-in message [:author :initial]))
      (dom/div "author-name" (get-in message [:author :name]))
      (dom/div "message-timestamp" (:timestamp message)))
    (dom/div "message-content"
      (dom/p nil (:content message)))))

(defn render [el messages]
  (dom/with-children el
    (map render-message messages)))

(defn scroll-to-bottom [el]                        ①
  (let [observer (js/MutationObserver.
                   #(set! (.-scrollTop el)
                          (.-scrollHeight el)))]
    (.observe observer el #js{"childList" true})))

(defn init-messages []
  (dom/section "messages"
    (doto (dom/div "messages-inner")
      (scroll-to-bottom)
      (init-component :messages accessor render))))
```

① We use a Mutation Observer[1] to set the viewport to the bottom of the message list any time the message list changes. This way, the user always sees the most recent messages.

Since the message list will be rendered as a top-level component, we will need to initialize it within `components/app.cljs`:

```
(ns learn-cljs.chat.components.app
  (:require ;; ...
            [learn-cljs.chat.components.messages :refer [init-messages]]))

(defn init-main [msg-ch]
  (dom/section "content-main"
    ;; ...
    (init-messages)))
;; ...
```

With the message list done, let's move on to the message composer.

---

[1]https://developer.mozilla.org/en-US/docs/Web/API/MutationObserver

Message Composer

The composer will be the simplest component that we have seen yet. It is simply a textarea with an event listener that will dispatch a message and clear its content whenever the user hits the (Enter)/(Return) key:

```
Listing 26.12:  chat/components/compose.cljs

(ns learn-cljs.chat.components.compose
  (:require [learn-cljs.chat.components.dom :as dom]
            [learn-cljs.chat.message-bus :as bus]))

(defn init-composer [msg-ch]
  (let [composer-input (dom/textarea "message-input")]
    (.addEventListener composer-input "keyup"
      (fn [e]
        (when (= (.-key e) "Enter")
          (.preventDefault e)
          (let [content (.-value composer-input)]
            (set! (.-value composer-input) "")
            (bus/dispatch! msg-ch :add-message content)))))
    (dom/div "compose" composer-input)))
```

One thing to note before we move on is that we do not keep track of the message that the user is composing outside of the DOM itself. This means that in addition to our application state, we are relying on the DOM to hold some of our state. When we start building applications on top of React and Reagent, we will want to avoid this in favor of keeping all of our state in immutable data structures so that rendering is a simple, deterministic process of taking our app state and converting it to (virtual) DOM.

Like the message list, the composer will need to be mounted into the app and initialized within the main content area:

```
(ns learn-cljs.chat.components.app
  (:require ;; ...
            [learn-cljs.chat.components.compose :refer [init-composer]]))

(defn init-main [msg-ch]
  (dom/section "content-main"
    ;; ...
    (init-composer)))
;; ...
```

Authentication Modal

Since this is a multi-user chat application, we need to have some concept of users. We should then implement at least a simple sign up / sign in process so that users do not have to enter a first name, last name, and username every time they load the app. Additionally, we do not want users to impersonate each other. Below is the entire code listing for the authentication modal. We will walk through each section afterwards.

Listing 26.13: chat/components/auth.cljs

```clojure
(ns learn-cljs.chat.components.auth
  (:require [learn-cljs.chat.components.dom :as dom]
            [goog.dom.classes :as gdom-classes]
            [learn-cljs.chat.components.component :refer [init-component]]
            [learn-cljs.chat.components.render-helpers :as helpers]
            [learn-cljs.chat.message-bus :as bus]
            [learn-cljs.chat.state :as state]))

(declare accessor get-render sign-in-modal sign-up-modal
         auth-modal auth-form footer-link)

(defn init-auth [msg-ch]
  (init-component (dom/section "auth-modal")
    :auth
    accessor
    (get-render msg-ch)))

(defn accessor [state]
  (select-keys state [:current-user :auth-modal]))

(defn get-render [msg-ch]
  (fn [el {:keys [current-user auth-modal] :as s}]
    (if (some? current-user)
      (gdom-classes/add el "hidden")
      (doto el
        (gdom-classes/remove "hidden")
        (.appendChild
          (dom/div "auth-modal-wrapper"
            (if (= :sign-in auth-modal)
              (sign-in-modal msg-ch)
              (sign-up-modal msg-ch)))))))))

(defn sign-in-modal [msg-ch]
  (auth-modal msg-ch
    {:header-text "Sign In"
     :footer-text "New here? Sign up."
     :form-fields [{:label "Username" :type "text" :name "username"}
                   {:label "Password" :type "password" :name "password"}]
     :submit-action :sign-in}))

(defn sign-up-modal [msg-ch]
  (auth-modal msg-ch
    {:header-text "Sign Up"
     :footer-text "Already have an account? Sign in."
     :form-fields [{:label "First Name" :type "text" :name "first-name"}
                   {:label "Last Name" :type "text" :name "last-name"}
                   {:label "Username" :type "text" :name "username"}
```

```clojure
                        {:label "Password" :type "password" :name "password"}]
       :submit-action :sign-up}))

(defn auth-modal [msg-ch {:keys [header-text
                                 form-fields
                                 submit-action
                                 footer-text]}]
  (dom/div "auth-modal-inner"
    (dom/div "auth-modal-header"
      (dom/h1 nil header-text))
    (dom/div "auth-modal-body"
      (auth-form msg-ch form-fields submit-action))
    (dom/div "auth-modal-footer"
      (footer-link msg-ch footer-text))))

(defn auth-form [msg-ch form-fields submit-action]
  (let [form (dom/form nil
               (apply dom/with-children (dom/div)
                 (for [{:keys [label type name]} form-fields
                       :let [id (str "auth-field-" name)]]
                   (dom/div "input-field"
                     (dom/label #js {"class" "input-label"
                                     "for" id}
                       label)
                     (dom/input #js {"type" type
                                     "name" name
                                     "id" id})))))
               (dom/button #js {"type" "submit"} "Submit"))]
    (doto form
      (.addEventListener "submit"
        (fn [e]
          (.preventDefault e)
          (bus/dispatch! msg-ch submit-action
            (into {}
              (for [{:keys [name]} form-fields
                    :let [id (str "auth-field-" name)]]
                [(keyword name) (.-value (js/document.getElementById id))]))))))))

(defn footer-link [msg-ch footer-text]
  (doto (dom/a nil footer-text)
    (.addEventListener "click"
      (fn [e]
        (.preventDefault e)
        (bus/dispatch! msg-ch :toggle-auth-modal)))))
```

Right at the top of the file, we run into a ClojureScript feature that we have not yet encountered: the `declare` macro. As the name suggests, this macro declares vars that are not bound to any value yet. This allows us to refer to functions and other values within the namespace before they are physically defined in the source of the file. In our case, we declare these vars for convenience so that we can list the high-level functions first and the functions that implement the lower-level details later in the code. This is not very idiomatic ClojureScript, but it is useful for the purpose of walking through the code.

Next, we define our component that will manage the auth modal using the `init-component` helper that we created earlier. In order to render the authentication modal, we need to know only 2 things about the application state: whether there is an authenticated user, and which state the modal (if displayed) should be in - sign in or sign up. Before returning a render function for this component, we perform the side effect of adding or removing a "hidden" class from the parent component.

Next, we define both the "Sign In" and "Sign Up" states of the modal. For each state, we need to know what to display in the header and footer, what form fields to display, and what message to dispatch when the form is submitted. Since there are just a few things that vary between each modal state, we factor out the common code to the `auth-modal` function, which `sign-in-modal` and `sign-up-modal` call with different data.

The `auth-modal` function in turn uses a couple of additional lower-level functions for its implementation. First, we have `auth-form`, which creates a `form` element with all of the input elements specified within `form-fields`. It then attaches a `submit` event handler that queries each of the elements in the form and wraps them into a map of the field name to the field value. It then emits the appropriate message type with the field/value map as the payload. Second, we have `footer-link`, which displays a toggle link to switch between the two states of the modal. Since the form and the footer link both need to emit messages that the application should respond to, we pass the `msg-ch` down the component hierarchy to each of these lower-level components.

Finally, as before, we need to initialize the modal in `components/app.cljs`:

```
(ns learn-cljs.chat.components.app
  (:require ;; ...
            [learn-cljs.chat.components.auth :refer [init-auth]]))

(defn init-app [el msg-ch]
  (let [wrapper (dom/div "app-wrapper"
                  (init-auth msg-ch)
                  ;; ...
                )]
    ;; ...
  ))
```

With the UI complete, let's briefly look at how to hook up a WebSocket API.

26.3 Realtime Communication

Since our application is highly dynamic, and we want to send and receive messages in near-realtime, we will use a WebSocket API. The code for this ClojureScript Node.js API is beyond the scope of this book to cover, but it is available within the Learn ClojureScript GitHub repo[2]. Since we already have the ability to handle messages within the application, and since we talk with the API in terms of messages, there is surprisingly little that needs to be done. The API should expose a function for sending messages to the API, and it should also emit messages from the API back to our application. One interesting thing to note is that we do not have the concept of a request/response flow, only asynchronous messages that flow within the UI as well as between the UI and the API:

Listing 26.14: chat/api.cljs

```clojure
(ns learn-cljs.chat.api
  (:require [learn-cljs.chat.message-bus :as bus]
            [cljs.reader :refer [read-string]]))

(defonce api (atom nil))                              ①

(defn send!
  ([msg-type] (send! msg-type nil))
  ([msg-type payload]
   (.send @api
     (pr-str (if (some? payload)                      ②
               [msg-type payload]
               [msg-type])))))

(defn init! [msg-ch url]
  (let [ws (js/WebSocket. url)]
    (.addEventListener ws "message"
      (fn [msg]
        (let [[type payload] (read-string (.-data msg))]   ③
          (bus/dispatch! msg-ch
            (keyword (str "api/" (name type)))         ④
            payload))))
    (reset! api ws)))
```

① For convenience, we define the websocket API as a global atom
② `pr-str` serializes Clojure(Script) data
③ `read-string` de-serializes Clojure(Script) data
④ Prefix all API events with `api/` to distinguish them from UI events

In this API namespace, we define an extremely simple messaging protocol. Both the UI and the API emit messages to each other that are serialized ClojureScript data structures. The first element is a keyword identifying the message type, and the second element can be an optional payload of arbitrary type. We use the `pr-str` and `read-string` functions in the standard library to serialize/deserialize data structures using the Clojure-native EDN format[3].

---

[2]https://github.com/kendru/learn-cljs/tree/master/code/lesson-26/chat-backend
[3]https://github.com/edn-format/edn

We will first initialize the API within our core namespace:

```
(ns learn-cljs.chat.core
  (:require ;; ...
            [learn-cljs.chat.api :as api]))

(defonce initialized?
  (do
    (api/init! bus/msg-ch js/WS_API_URL)          ①
    ;; ..
    ))
```

① Read a global WS_API_URL from the page to determine the API url. This can be set within a build script.

Next, we will update our handlers namespace to both emit API messages in response to certain UI messages as well as handle the messages that come directly from the API. First of all, we will send the API notifications when the user activates a specific room or conversation so that it can send message updates that are relevant for that specific location:

```
(ns learn-cljs.chat.handlers
  (:require ;; ...
            [chat.api :as api]))

;; ...

(bus/handle! bus/msg-bus :switch-to-conversation
  (fn [{:keys [username]}]
    (api/send! :set-view {:type :conversation, :username username})
    ;; ...
  ))

(bus/handle! bus/msg-bus :switch-to-room
  (fn [{:keys [id]}]
    (api/send! :set-view {:type :room, :id id})
    ;; ...
  ))
```

Naturally, we will want to notify the server when we have sent a message. Since the server keeps track of what room or conversation we are currently in, all we need to send is the message itself.

```
(bus/handle! bus/msg-bus :add-message
  (fn [content]
    (api/send! :add-message {:content content})))
```

Since we let users create new rooms, we also need to send the server a message when this occurs.

```
(bus/handle! bus/msg-bus :create-room
  (fn [name]
    (api/send! :create-room {:name name})))
```

The auth modal emits events that should be used to sign in or sign up, so let's send those to the server as well.

```
(bus/handle! bus/msg-bus :sign-in
  (fn [data]
    (api/send! :sign-in data)))

(bus/handle! bus/msg-bus :sign-up
  (fn [data]
    (api/send! :sign-up data)))
```

That takes care of all of the messages that need to be sent *to* the API based on user inter-action. Now, let's handle the messages from the API to which the UI needs to react. First, let's handle authentication. Whenever a user successfully logs in or signs up, the API will send an `authenticated` message with user details. We should set this as the current user in the application state then request user and room lists to populate the sidebar:

```
(bus/handle! bus/msg-bus :api/authenticated
  (fn [user-info]
    (swap! state/app-state state/user-authenticated user-info)
    (api/send! :list-people)
    (api/send! :list-rooms)))
```

Once we have received the rooms list from the server, we should set the rooms list in the application state and switch to the first room in the list as the initial room.

```
(bus/handle! bus/msg-bus :api/rooms-listed
  (fn [rooms]
    (swap! state/app-state state/received-rooms-list rooms)
    (when-let [first-room (first rooms)]
      (bus/dispatch! bus/msg-ch :switch-to-room
        {:id (:id first-room)}))))
```

Next, let's handle the messages for when we receive the list of users, when a user joins, and when a user leaves. These handlers are simple because they simply pass the data from the API through to a state transition function that we wrote earlier.

```
(bus/handle! bus/msg-bus :api/people-listed
  (fn [people]
    (swap! state/app-state state/received-people-list people)))

(bus/handle! bus/msg-bus :api/person-joined
  (fn [person]
    (swap! state/app-state state/person-joined person)))
```

```
(bus/handle! bus/msg-bus :api/person-left
  (fn [username]
    (swap! state/app-state state/person-left username)))
```

Next, we will write handlers for receiving a single message as well as a list of messages - which will occur when the user switches rooms or conversations. Also, we will create a `should-set-message?` function that we can use to determine whether the message or messages from the API are still relevant for display. This will prevent us from accidentally posting a message from the previous room when the user switches to a new room before the API is aware of the switch.

```
(defn should-set-message? [username room]
  (let [app @state/app-state]
    (or
      (and (some? username)
           (state/is-current-view-conversation? app)
           (= username (state/current-conversation-recipient app)))
      (and (some? room)
           (state/is-current-view-room? app)
           (= room (state/current-room-id app))))))

(bus/handle! bus/msg-bus :api/message-received
  (fn [{:keys [message username room]}]
    (when (should-set-message? username room)
      (swap! state/app-state state/message-received message))))

(bus/handle! bus/msg-bus :api/messages-received
  (fn [{:keys [messages username room]}]
    (when (should-set-message? username room)
      (swap! state/app-state state/messages-received messages))))
```

Finally, we need one more handler for populating a new room on creation.

```
(bus/handle! bus/msg-bus :api/room-created
  (fn [room]
    (swap! state/app-state
      #(-> %
           (state/room-added room)
           (state/create-room-input-closed)))))
```

With that handler complete, we have a fully functional chat application!

Challenge

While this application is quite capable considering how few lines of code it contains, there are still many improvements that could be made. Try one or two of the following:

- Only render a certain number of messages at a time, rendering more only when the user scrolls to the point where they will be needed
- Display error messages from the server. Errors will follow the format: `[:error {:message "Some message"}]`
- Automatically reconnect the WebSocket if it closes

26.4   Summary

If you have reached this point, congratulations on creating a non-trivial application in ClojureScript! At this point, we have learned all of the core language features and idioms, and we have put them to practice in creating an interesting, useable chat app. While we ended up with a fully-functional app, we had to resort to some imperative code and manual DOM manipulation, similar to what we would do in JavaScript if we were not using a framework. In the next section, we will see how React's virtual DOM and Clojure Script's preference for immutability form a perfect marriage that will allow us to write declarative application UIs.

Part VI

ClojureScript Applications

We have covered a lot of ground since the very first lesson. In fact, we have covered almost the entire language, and from this point on, we will be focusing on strategies and tools that will help us master ClojureScript programming. We have discussed in depth the value of functional programming, but the DOM that we interact with as web programmers is intrinsically imperative and impure. As a result, the applications that we have written have fallen short of our ideal of pure(-ish) functional programming. That is about to change. In this section, we will use the Reagent[4] library to create simple, extensible, and pure applications.

- Lesson 27: React as a Platform
- Lesson 28: Using React via Reagent
- Lesson 29: Separate Concerns
- Lesson 30: Capstone 5 - Notes

---

[4]https://reagent-project.github.io/

Lesson 27

React as a Platform

In contrast to JavaScript's multi-paradigm nature, ClojureScript promises a functional programming experience. However, we have found that as soon as we need to interact with the DOM, our code becomes... less than functional. In this lesson, we will explore how React's declarative nature makes it a perfect platform for ClojureScript applications. We will be writing React applications, but instead of using JSX, hooks, and something like Redux or MobX for state management, we will be using ClojureScript data structures and the same tools and techniques that we have been learning about to this point.

_____

In this lesson:

- Understand why React is the perfect platform for functional web applications
- See how React's DOM diffing allows us to write declarative UIs
- Learn how immutability enables pure components out of the box

_____

27.1   Functional Programming Model

As its name suggests, React is built around the idea of *reactive programming*. The core concept behind reactive programming is that a program is a description of how data flows through a system. Certain values can also be computed from other values, so a change in one value may propagate to many additional values. As a concrete example, let's think about a spreadsheet with 3 cells: A, B, and C, where C is calculated from A and B.

Figure 27.1: Reactive spreadsheet cells

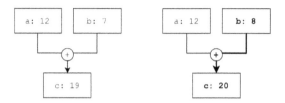

Whenever either A or B changes, C changes as well. There may be additional values downstream that depend on the value of C, in which case the change to A or B could continue propagating. Now imagine that the final value in that chain of data dependencies is a data structure that represents the entire user interface. We have a clean and conceptually simple way to describe a UI as a computation over a reactive application state.

This reactive data model plays well with functional programming. Think back to how we modeled state updates in the previous lesson: handlers would take the current state (which was data) and a message (which was also data), and they would produce a new state. Now think about the reactive model in which a state change flows through potentially many transformations to produce a new state. If we think about the graph of those transformations being applied at a discrete moment in time, then we end up with a model of computation in which we have an application that exists as a sequence of immutable values. Each of these values is represented by a data structure that can be rendered to the DOM.

When we use React from JavaScript, we represent that data structure as JSX, and when we use ClojureScript, we use regular Clojure(Script) data structures. The fact that we do not need to think about how to mutate the DOM means that we are free from the imperative style of DOM manipulation that we have had to resort to up to this point. Since we are just transforming data, we regain all of the advantages of testability, functional purity, and determinism that has been our goal.

27.2   DOM Diffing

Our job is to produce a data structure that represents the entire application. However, rerendering the entire DOM from scratch whenever anything changes is incredibly slow and inefficient for anything but the simplest apps. This is where React comes into play. Even if we re-compute the data structure that represents our DOM from scratch - the *virtual DOM* - React applies a diffing algorithm to determine what changes actually need to be made. So from our perspective, we are re-rendering from scratch on every state transition, but React is taking our virtual DOM and the previous virtual DOM and applying the necessary mutations to the actual DOM in order to bring it in sync with our virtual DOM.

As an example, we can think about a toggle switch. The toggle may be represented as a div that has an inner span with either the class `toggle-on` or `toggle-off`. We could represent it as the following:

```
(defn toggle-switch [on?]
  [:div {:class "toggle-switch"}
    [:span {:class (if on? "toggle-on" "toggle-off")}]])
```

When the application containing this switch first loads, let's assume that on the initial render, this toggle gets called with `on?` bound to `false`. React will see that it had no virtual DOM before, so it will run the imperative code to create these DOM nodes with the appropriate attributes. Suppose that at some later point, the user performs an action that sets `on?` to `true`. The virtual DOM generated will go from this:

```
[:div {:class "toggle-switch"}
  [:span {:class "toggle-off"}]]
```

to this:

```
[:div {:class "toggle-switch"}
  [:span {:class "toggle-on"}]]
```

Even though we are returning a new data structure, React will diff the two and find that the only difference is that the class name on the span changed, so it will intelligently update only that one piece that changed. Even as we start composing many components together that may all change in some way as the app state changes over time, we can think of rendering the whole world from scratch on each change and rely on React's diffing algorithm to calculate and make only the minimal change necessary to reconcile the actual DOM with the virtual DOM that we have declared.

27.3 Creating Fast Apps

React's functional reactive programming model and DOM diffing are not at all unique to ClojureScript, but there is one aspect of ClojureScript that makes it much more amenable to React's programming model: data is immutable by default. In the previous section, we talked about how we can render our application from scratch every time something changes. In a lot of cases, this is fast enough, and we can create even fairly sizeable apps that recreate an entire virtual DOM tree on every update. However - going back to the toggle case - if the toggle is part of a very large app, and its state is the only thing that changed, we do not need to re-render potentially hundreds of components.

Value Equality

We have already talked about the fact that ClojureScript's data structures are immutable, but they also have another very useful property: value equality. This means that two data structures are considered equal if they have the same contents, regardless of whether they point to the exact same structure in memory or not. This is not the case in JavaScript. For instance, consider the following code:

```javascript
const xs = [1, 2, 3];
const ys = [1, 2, 3];
xs === ys; // false

const dog1 = { name: 'Fido' };
const dog2 = { name: 'Fido' };
dog1 === dog2; // false
```

In terms of equality, JavaScript does not care whether two arrays or two objects happen to have the same contents or not. If they are not references to the exact same object in memory, then they are considered not equal. In contrast, ClojureScript considers data structures of the same type with the same contents to be equal. Translating the JavaScript example to ClojureScript yields a different result:

```clojure
(def xs [1 2 3])
(def ys [1 2 3])
(= xs ys) ;; true

(def dog1 {:name "Fido"})
(def dog2 {:name "Fido"})
(= dog1 dog2) ;; true
```

Two ClojureScript collections only differ if their contents differ. If we think about an arbitrarily nested data structure, we can see that a change to a nested property will cause its parent to no longer be equal to the parent element in the original structure. The changes will cascade all the way up to the top-level collection. However, properties that do not lie in the path from the element that changed back to the root will not be affected, and they will be equal across the original and updated structures. Let's illustrate this with an example.

```clojure
(def game {:players [{:id 1 :score 283}
                     {:id 2 :score 212}
                     {:id 3 :score 198}]
           :level {:name "Warehouse"
                   :tiles [[:empty :empty :crate :wall-v :empty]
                           ;; ...
                           ]}})
(def game-new (update-in game [:players 1 :score] inc))    ①

(= (get-in game [:players 1 :score])                       ②
   (get-in game-new [:players 1 :score]))
;; false
```

```
(= (get-in game [:players 1]) (get-in game-new [:players 1]))
;; false
(= (get-in game [:players]) (get-in game-new [:players]))
;; false
(= game game-new)
;; false

(= (get-in game [:level]) (get-in game-new [:level]))        ③
;; true
(= (get-in game [:players 0]) (get-in game-new [:players 0]))
;; true
```

① Update a nested property
② Everything between the updated property and the root is not equal
③ Everything outside the update path is equal

Additionally, testing two data structures for equality is a relatively cheap operation in Clojure. The reason for this has to do with the fact that ClojureScript uses *persistent* data structures that implement structural sharing. What this means is that when we have one data structure and apply some transformation to it, the resulting data structure will only recreate the portions of the original that have changed. Any collection within the data structure that does not change as a result of the update will refer to the exact same collection in memory. When ClojureScript does its equality check, it first tests to see whether two objects are both references to the same object in memory. This is an extremely fast test, and in the case that a portion of the data structure is shared, this check can elide a much more expensive deep equality check.

Figure 27.2: Persistent data structures

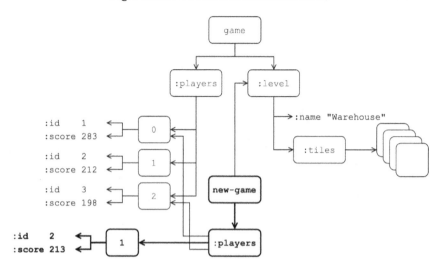

Pure Components

In React, an instance of React.Component will always re-compute its virtual DOM when React tries to re-render it. An instance of React.PureComponent, on the other hand, will only re-compute its virtual DOM if any of its props or state are not equal to their values on the previous render. Pure components achieve this optimization by implementing the shouldComponentUpdate() method. In ClojureScript, the components that we create will behave like React PureComponents. Since each component will be backed by an immutable data structure, we will only end up re-computing its virtual DOM when we know it is necessary.

While it is possible to hand-optimize the shouldComponentUpdate() method or use immutable data and pure components when using React with JavaScript, we get these optimizations for free with ClojureScript. As we will see in the next lesson, the Reagent framework optimizes things even farther.

27.4   Summary

In this lesson, we learned how React's reactive programming model fits well with pure functional programming practices and immutable data. We also saw how React's virtual DOM allows us to express our UI as a data structure and let React take care of rendering efficiently. Finally, we saw how immutable data, efficient equality checks, and pure components work together to provide an optimized rendering process out of the box.

Lesson 28

Lesson 28: Using React via Reagent

We have seen that React is a good platform for writing ClojureScript applications, but we have not yet written any code. While it is entirely possible to use the React API directly, we are going to be using Reagent, which provides a very simple API that lets us concern ourselves with writing components rather than fiddling with React lifecycle and complex state management. Reagent components use the same *hiccup*-style DOM representation that we used back in Lesson 20 when we wrote the Contact Book application. Reagent also comes with built-in state management, which uses atoms to keep track of data. Our process for writing Reagent applications will be similar to the process we used in Lesson 20, except we can rely on Reagent and React to automatically and efficiently re-render when our state is updated.

In this lesson:

- Defining a data model using (reactive) atoms
- Querying and updating application state
- Creating different types of Reagent components

28.1   Reactive Data

In the last lesson, we mentioned that React follows a reactive programming model. This is true of Reagent's state management as well. Reagent provides a specialized atom called a *reactive atom* that can keep track of when it is dereferenced (i.e, when `@atom` or `(deref atom)` is called). If it is dereferenced inside a Reagent component, it will signal to Reagent to re-render the component. To see how values can reactively flow through a system, we can create the spreadsheet cell example from the last chapter using some of Reagent's reactive primitives. First, we'll initialize a new Figwheel project:

```
$ clj -X:new :template figwheel-main :name learn-cljs/reagent-test :args '["+deps"]'
$ cd reagent-test
```

Next, we need to add reagent as a dependency in `deps.edn`:

Listing 28.1: deps.edn

```
:deps {;; Other deps...
       reagent/reagent {:mvn/version "1.0.0"}}
```

Now we can replace the body of the default HTML file that Figwheel generates with our HTML that contains a few inputs cells for the world's simplest spreadsheet:

Listing 28.2: resources/public/index.html

```
<h1>Reactive Cells</h1>
<div>
  <label for="cell-a">A: </label>
  <input id="cell-a" type="number" value="0" />
</div>
<div>
  <label for="cell-b">B: </label>
  <input id="cell-b" type="number" value="0" />
</div>
<div>
  <label for="cell-c">C: </label>
  <input id="cell-c" readonly type="number" />
</div>
```

Now we are ready to hook this page up to Reagent for state management. In the `learn-cljs.reagent-test` namespace, we will create 2 reactive atoms to represent the A and B cells and a `reaction` that represents the C cell, whose value will be updated whenever one of the other cells changes.

Listing 28.3: reagent_test/core.cljs

```
(ns learn-cljs.reagent-test
    (:require [reagent.core :as r]          ①
              [reagent.ratom :as ratom]     ②
              [goog.dom :as gdom]
              [goog.events :as gevents]))
```

```
(def a-cell (r/atom 0))                              ③
(def b-cell (r/atom 0))
(def c-cell
  (ratom/make-reaction                               ④
    #(+ @a-cell @b-cell)))

(def a (gdom/getElement "cell-a"))
(def b (gdom/getElement "cell-b"))
(def c (gdom/getElement "cell-c"))

(defn update-cell [cell]
  (fn [e]
    (let [num (js/parseInt (.. e -target -value))]
      (reset! cell num))))

(gevents/listen a "change" (update-cell a-cell))     ⑤
(gevents/listen b "change" (update-cell b-cell))

(ratom/run!                                          ⑥
  (set! (.-value c) @c-cell))
```

① `reagent.core` provides the reactive version of `atom`
② `reagent.ratom` provides several reactive programming utilities
③ `a-cell` and `b-cell` are reactive atoms
④ `c-cell` is a reaction, which acts like an atom whose value is derived from other reactive atoms
⑤ Update the corresponding cell when the input for A or B changes
⑥ Use `ratom/run!` to update the C input whenever `c-cell` changes

If we run this example, we will see a page with 3 inputs labeled A, B, and C. A and B are normal number inputs, and C is a read-only input that displays the result of adding A and B together. We create reactive atoms for the A and B cells using `reagent.core/atom`, which act like regular atoms that can propagate changes to other computations the rely upon them. We then create the C cell as a *reaction* to the other 2 cells. Since we dereference the `a-cell` and `b-cell` atoms within this reaction, Reagent creates a dependency relationship between Both A → C and B → C such that the value of C is updated reactively upon any change to A or B. As a reaction, C itself acts as a read-only reactive atom, and it could be used inside another reaction, which could be used inside another reaction, etc. A whole system of reactive atoms and reactions form a directed acyclic graph (DAG) such that any "upstream" changes automatically propagate "downstream" as far as they are able.

Figure 28.1: A directed acyclic graph

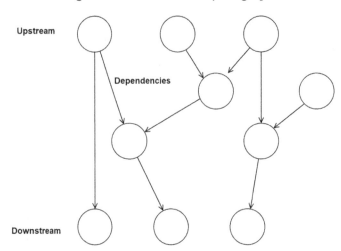

We will come back to the concept of reactive data later when we see how to apply it to creating data-driven components, but first, we'll look at components themselves.

28.2 Building Components

Reagent components are a very simple, declarative way to build up a virtual DOM structure to hand to React for rendering. A component is simply a function that returns a hiccup-like data structure. In the interest of sticking to tradition, we'll create a component that prints the text "Hello World" inside a p tag:

```
(defn hello []
  [:p "Hello World"])
```

That's it. That is our first Reagent component that defines a single element. An element represents a tag where the first element is a keyword version of the tag name, an optional second element can contain a map of attributes, and the remaining items are children, which can be text, other elements, or other Reagent components.

We have a component, so now what? We need some way to render this component to the actual DOM. We can do this with the `reagent-dom.render` function, which takes just 2 arguments: a Reagent component and a DOM node to render it to. First, let's create a new Reagent project that we will use for the rest of this lesson. This will be a very simple app that allows us to enter how many minutes we exercised on a given day, and it will chart our exercise over time.

```
$ clj -X:new :template figwheel-main :name learn-cljs/exercise-tracker :args '["+deps"]'
$ cd exercise-tracker
```

Next, we'll add Reagent as a dependency just like we did in the previous section (not shown). Now, let's update the `learn-cljs.exercise-tracker` namespace with the `hello` component, and we will also render this component to the DOM.

Listing 28.4: exercise_tracker/core.cljs

```
(ns learn-cljs.exercise-tracker
  (:require [reagent.dom :as rdom]
            [goog.dom :as gdom]))

(defn hello []
  [:p "Hello World"])

(rdom/render
  hello                           ①
  (gdom/getElement "app"))        ②
```

① Component to render
② DOM node to mount our component into

If we run `clj -A:fig:build`, we can see the Hello World printed to the screen:

Figure 28.2: Reagent hello world

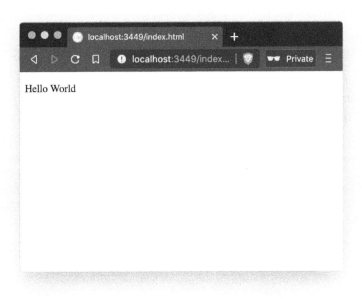

While this is far from interesting in what it does, something *is* interesting about the structure: we have a single entry point (the call to `rdom/render`) that performs a side effect, and our UI itself - currently a single tag - is completely declarative. We can expand on this structure to create a simple form for accepting the input that we need. Once again, the CSS for this project can be found in the book's repository, but we will not cover styling as part of the lesson.

```
(defn date-input []
  [:div.input-wrapper                                  ①
    [:label "Day"]
    [:input {:type "date"}]])                          ②

(defn time-input []
  [:div.input-wrapper
    [:label "Time (minutes)"]
    [:input {:type "number" :min 0 :step 1}]])

(defn submit-button []
  [:div.actions
    [:button {:type "submit"} "Submit"]])

(defn form []
  [:form.input-form
    [date-input]                                       ③
    [time-input]
    [submit-button]])

(defn app []
  [form])

(rdom/render
  [app]
  (gdom/getElement "app"))
```

① A class name can be added to an element directly
② HTML attributes can be given as a map following the tag name
③ A Reagent component can be provided instead of a tag name

Now that we have a form in place, let's add a chart above it that will display the data points that the user enters. Since we do not have any real data in state yet, we can just stub out a data structure that has the shape that we want, and we will worry about transforming the actual input into this shape via a `reaction` later.

```
(defn- random-point []
  (js/Math.floor (* (js/Math.random) 100)))

(defonce chart-data
  (let [points (map random-point (range 30))]         ①
```

```
      (r/atom {:points points
               :chart-max (reduce max 1 points)}))))

(def chart-width 400)
(def chart-height 200)
(def bar-spacing 2)

(defn chart []
  (let [{:keys [points chart-max]} @chart-data        ②
        bar-width (- (/ chart-width (count points))
                     bar-spacing)]
    [:svg.chart {:x 0 :y 0
                 :width chart-width :height chart-height}
     (for [[i point] (map-indexed vector points)       ③
           :let [x (* i (+ bar-width bar-spacing))      ④
                 pct (- 1 (/ point chart-max))
                 bar-height (- chart-height (* chart-height pct))
                 y (- chart-height bar-height)]]
       [:rect {:key i                                   ⑤
               :x x :y y
               :width bar-width
               :height bar-height}])])))

;; ...
;; Change the app function to render the chart too
(defn app []
  [:div.app
   [chart]
   [form]])
```

① Generate a random number between 0 and 99 for each point
② Dereferencing `chart-data` makes this component reactive
③ `(map-indexed vector xs)` will produce a sequence of vectors of `[idx x]`
④ Calculate the data needed to draw each bar
⑤ Like in React, each item in a sequence should have a unique key

28.3 Updating State

Unlike the chat application, which queried the DOM to get the value of its inputs, we are going to invert the responsibility here by putting our input data in state and letting the components render the value from state. Whenever the user makes a change in the input, we want to propagate that change back to state, which will cause our component to re-render. Both React and Reagent refer to this type of input handling as *controlled inputs* because the value of an input is controlled by UI state. The simplest way to create a controlled input component is to use a slight variation of a Reagent component.

```clojure
(defn- current-date-string [d]
  (let [pad-zero #(.padStart (.toString %) 2 "0")
        y (.getFullYear d)
        m (-> (.getMonth d) inc pad-zero)
        d (pad-zero (.getDate d))]
    (str y "-" m "-" d)))


(defonce state
  (r/atom {:inputs {:date (date-string (js/Date.))
                    :minutes "0"}}))
```

Now we simply need to dereference the `state` atom within our input components, and they
will automatically re-render whenever the state changes.

```clojure
(defn date-input []
  [:div.input-wrapper
   [:label "Day"]
   [:input {:type "date"
            :value (get-in @state [:inputs :date])}]])
```

If we load the app, it will now populate the date input with today's date, and it will populate
the time input with 0. If you try to update either of these inputs, you will see that they
cannot be changed. This is because their value is being set by the UI state, and React will
not allow us to update the value of a controlled input. The solution is to add an `on-change`
handler to each of the components that will update the appropriate value within the state
with the new value of the input.

```clojure
(defn date-input []
  [:div.input-wrapper
   [:label "Day"]
   [:input {:type "date"
            :value (get-in @state [:inputs :date])
            :on-change #(swap! state assoc-in [:inputs :date]
                          (.. % -target -value))}]])
```

Components with Setup

Now we can update the inputs. When we change an input, the value in state is updated,
which causes the component to re-render (because it dereferences `state`) with the updated
value. Although this works, it is not ideal for performance because every time `state` changes,
Reagent will try to re-render this component. In a larger app, this can cause serious performance problems if every stateful component tries to re-render whenever any piece of state
changes. What we want instead is a reaction that only changes when a portion of the app
state changes - in this case, only when the appropriate input value changes. Since this is a
very common use case, Reagent provides a utility called a *cursor*. A cursor acts like a reactive atom that points to a specific location inside another reactive atom. When the value at

that location is updated, the cursor is updated, and any component that dereferences the cursor is updated. Additionally, the cursor can also be updated with `swap!` or `reset!`, and the changes will be reflected in the underlying state.

We could create these cursors as vars at the level of our namespace, but since their use is effectively scoped to a single component, we can create them as a set-up step for our inputs. The components that we just created are the simplest type supported by Reagent - they are functions that evaluate to the DOM (expressed as hiccup) that we want to render. In React terms, these components are simple render functions. However, Reagent allows us to perform some set-up of our component by having our component function *return* a render function. This will allow us to create a cursor to the input state then return a render function that makes use of this cursor.

```
(defn date-input []
  (let [val (r/cursor state [:inputs :date])]       ①
    (fn []
      [:div.input-wrapper
        [:label "Day"]
        [:input {:type "date"
                 :value @val                          ②
                 :on-change #(reset! val              ③
                               (.. % -target -value))}]])))
```

① Create a cursor once before the component is mounted
② Dereference the cursor to make this component reactive
③ Update the state via the cursor

When we use a component with setup, the setup step is run only when the component is mounted, whereas the render function that it returns will be called any time the component's state is updated. The setup step is the rough equivalent of the `componentWillMount()` lifecycle method in React.

You Try It

- We have made several updates to the `date-input` component: displaying a value from state, updating state, and optimizing rendering using a cursor. Try making the equivalent changes to the `time-input` component.

Finally, we will deal with form submissions. When the user submits the form, we will set an entry in a `data` map whose key is the date string and whose value is the number of minutes of exercise done on that day. Upon submission, the form input should also revert to their default state. Let's go ahead and write a function that makes these changes to state and invoke it as an on-submit handler for the `form` component.

```
(defn initial-inputs []
  {:date (date-string (js/Date.))
   :minutes "0"})

(defonce state
  (r/atom {:inputs (initial-inputs)
           :entries {}}))

;; ...

(defn submit-form [state]
  (let [{:keys [date minutes]} (:inputs state)]
    (-> state
        (assoc-in [:entries date] (js/parseInt minutes))
        (assoc :inputs (initial-inputs)))))

(defn form []
  [:form.input-form {:on-submit (fn [e]
                                  (.preventDefault e)
                                  (swap! state submit-form))}
   ;; ...
   ])
```

Now that we have all of the user input handling done, we will next see how to use reactions to write live queries that provide a component with a computed view over the UI state that is automatically kept in sync.

28.4   Writing Reactive Queries

So far, the state that we have wanted to render (the input values) has had a one-to-one mapping to the components that we render, but for the chart, we want to re-shape the data before rendering the chart. When we created fake data to use as a stub for the chart, we supplied a sequence of points that should be rendered from left to right as well as a maximum value to determine the height of the y-axis. However, the state contains a map from date to number. We can write a function to generate a sequence of the last 30 days of data, using the user-entered number if available and 0 otherwise. We can then create a reaction that will recalculate the chart data any time the underlying :entries map changes.

```
(defn get-points [entries]
  (let [ms-in-day 86400000
        chart-days 30
        now (js/Date.now)]
    (map (fn [i]
           (let [days-ago (- chart-days (inc i))
                 date (date-string (js/Date. (- now (* ms-in-day days-ago))))]
             (get entries date 0)))
         (range chart-days))))
```

```
(defn chart []
  (let [entries (r/cursor state [:entries])          ①
        chart-data (ratom/make-reaction             ②
                    #(let [points (get-points @entries)]
                       {:points points
                        :chart-max (reduce max 1 points)}))]
    (fn []                                           ③
      ;; ...
      )))
```

1. Get a cursor so that our reaction only re-runs when :entries changes
2. Create a reaction that re-calculates the chart data whenever :entries changes
3. Return the render function that dereferences our chart-data reaction

Here we update the chart component to use the more advanced form of Reagent component that includes component setup. In the setup, we first get a cursor to the :entries key of the state. This is not strictly necessary, but it allows us to run our reaction only when an entry is changed rather than any time the state is updated. Next, we create a reaction using reagent.ratom/make-reaction. Since the function that we supply dereferences the entries cursor, Reagent re-calculates the value of this reaction whenever the cursor changes. One critical piece to note is that the body of the render function *did not change at all*. Since the shape of the data that we are querying out of state matches what the component expects, there is no change necessary.

Now the app is fully functional, and if we add an entry using the form, the changes will propagate through the entries cursor, into the chart-data reaction, and finally into the render function of the chart component. We can think of these reactions as live queries into state. We set them up once, and they will provide a flow of data into our components automatically. This data-centric approach that Reagent encourages is a perfect fit with idiomatic ClojureScript.

Figure 28.3: The exercise tracker app

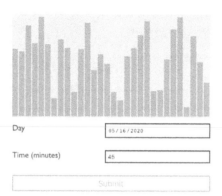

Challenge

This application has no persistence and will be reset if the page is reloaded. Try adding simple persistence using `localStorage`.

28.5 Summary

In this lesson, we learned how to use Reagent for both UI rendering and state management. We saw how Reagent enables declarative components and reactive programming for keeping those components in sync with the application state without any imperative "glue" code. With just a few simple primitives - reactive atoms, cursors, and reactions - we were able to create a stateful application easily and with very few lines of code. We also saw a couple of different types of Reagent components that we can choose between depending on whether a component needs any set-up or not.

Lesson 29

Lesson 29: Separate Concerns

Two broad strategies can be used when building a Reagent application. The first is to keep all state in a single atom, which is the approach that we used in the last lesson. The second is to keep different pieces of state separate and to use asynchronous communication between them. The first approach is simpler and easier to reason about, but the second is useful in creating large UIs that may be developed by multiple teams. It lends itself to the idea of micro-frontends, in which different teams maintain different components that are tied to separate business initiatives or functional areas, and these components can interact with other teams' components via messaging. Since we have already had a look at the first approach, this lesson will cover the basics of the second approach.

In this lesson:

- Create decoupled components
- Explore different messaging patterns for communicating within a UI
- Moving business logic into a frontend API

29.1 Connecting Components With Channels

ClojureScript provides us with all of the mechanisms that we need for quick and simple messaging in `core.async`, so we will take advantage of that. There are two cases in which we may want to use component-local state and messaging instead of shared state and reactive programming: creating modular components that can be re-used and integrated across multiple applications, and providing components that serve an auxiliary - even service-like - function, such as notifications, tours/onboarding widgets, and progress bars. In this lesson, we'll implement a notification component that manages its state but uses `core.async` channels to communicate.

First, we will use a similar message bus pattern to what we used in Lesson 26 to enable components to be able to publish and subscribe to a single common message bus:

```
(ns learn-cljs.notifications
    (:require [cljs.core.async :refer [go-loop pub sub chan <! put!]]))

(defonce msg-ch (chan 1))
(defonce msg-bus (pub msg-ch ::type))

(defn dispatch!
 ([type] (dispatch! type nil))
 ([type payload]
  (put! msg-ch {::type type
                ::payload payload})))
```

Namespaced Keywords

Standard ClojureScript keywords start with a single colon followed by one or more characters that are valid in an identifier, e.g. `:i-am-a-keyword`. However, keywords may also contain a namespace to distinguish them from other keywords that may have the same name. For example, `:genre/rock` and `:terrain/rock` have the same name - `"rock"` - but different namespaces. There are two ways to create a namespaced keyword: by prefixing the keyword name with the namespace followed by a forward slash or starting the keyword with a double-colon. The double-colon version uses the current ClojureScript namespace as the keyword namespace, so a keyword that is referenced as `::type` within a namespace called `learn-cljs.notifications.pubsub` could also be referenced as `:learn-cljs.notifications.pubsub/type`. Namespaced keywords are especially common in larger projects with multiple contributors.

Unlike the message bus that we used in Lesson 26, we hard-code the `dispatch!` function to emit to the `msg-ch` channel. Similarly, our components will rely on the `msg-bus` being in scope. Now we can write our notification component:

```
(def initial-state
 {:messages []
  :next-id 0})
```

```
(defn add-notification [state id text]
  (-> state
      (update :messages conj {:id id
                              :text text})
      (assoc :next-id (inc id))))

(defn remove-notification [state id]
  (update state :messages
    (fn [messages]
      (filterv #(not= id (:id %)) messages))))        ①

(defn notifications []
  (let [state (r/atom initial-state)]               ②
    (listen-for-added! state)                        ③
    (fn []
      [:div.messages
        (for [msg (:messages @state)                 ④
              :let [{:keys [id text]} msg]]
          ^{:key id}
          [:div.notification.is-info
            [:button.delete {:on-click #(swap! state remove-notification id)}]
            [:div.body text]])])))
```

① `filterv` acts just like `filter`, but it returns a vector
② load the initial state into a reactive atom at component set-up
③ we will implement this function next
④ dereferencing this atom causes the component to be reactive

The state for this component is quite simple: a collection of messages and an increment-ing counter to keep track of the next id. We also have a pair of functions for adding and removing a message from state. Next, we'll define the `listen-for-added!` function that will subscribe this component to `::add-notification` messages:

```
(defn listen-for-added! [state]
  (let [added (chan)]
    (sub msg-bus ::add-notification added)
    (go-loop []
      (let [text (::payload (<! added))
            id (:next-id @state)]
        (swap! state add-notification id text)
        (js/setTimeout #(swap! state remove-notification id) 10000)
        (recur)))))
```

The `go-loop` created by this function will consume messages from the `::add-notification` topic and add them to the messages vector using the `add-notification` function that we already defined. It will also set a timer to remove the message after `10000` milliseconds.

Note that although we will consume messages from a message bus to add notifications to the component's state, the render function of this component is agnostic to how that data gets into its state. It would be trivial to take this notification component and plug it into an application that manages its entire state in a single atom. The render function would remain untouched, and we would only need to modify the command handler functions and the component setup function.

Now that we have a pluggable notification component, we can hook up another component to publish notifications. For the sake of example, we will create a simple form that accepts a user's first and last name and then emits a greeting when the form is submitted.

```
(defonce form-state (r/atom {:first-name ""                  ①
                             :last-name ""}))

(defn update-value [e field]                                 ②
  (swap! form-state assoc field (.. e -target -value)))

(defn submit-form []                                         ③
  (let [{:keys [first-name last-name]} @form-state]
    (dispatch! ::add-notification
      (str "Welcome, " first-name " " last-name)))
  (swap! form-state assoc :first-name ""
                          :last-name ""))

(defn input-field [key label]                                ④
  [:div.field
    [:label.label label]
    [:div.control
      [:input.input {:value (get @form-state key)
                     :on-change #(update-value % key)}]]])

(defn input-form []
  [:div.form
    [input-field :first-name "First Name"]
    [input-field :last-name "Last Name"]                     ⑤
    [:div.field
      [:button.button {:on-click submit-form}
        "Add"]]])
```

① Reactive atom for managing form state
② Event handler for input fields
③ Event handler for submit button click
④ Input field component
⑤ Arguments are passed as the elements immediately after the component function

After the previous lesson, this should look like a pretty standard Reagent component. We create a reactive atom to hold the state of the form, and we create components for inputs and a submit button. The interesting piece about this code is that the `submit-form` function is decoupled from the notification component. The downside of creating decoupled components like this is that it is more difficult to trace the result of some action through the code to know exactly what the outcome will be. The outcome depends on what (if anything) is subscribed to the `::add-notification` topic.

You Try It

Try factoring out this example into separate namespaces for each of the following:

- input form
- notifications component
- messaging layer

Remember that prefixing a keyword with a double-colon gives it a namespace with the same name as the namespace it appears in.

29.2   Message Patterns

There are many different ways to structure asynchronous messaging that achieve the goal of decoupling components from each other and from coordination logic, so we will turn to examine several of the broad categories of messaging: direct pubsub, command/event, and actors. Each one of these approaches takes a different approach to the trade-off between simplicity and modularity.

Direct Publish/Subscribe

The direct publish/subscribe (or pubsub) pattern is the one that we used in the example above: there is a message bus that accepts messages from a single channel and broadcasts them to any subscriber channels that are registered to that topic. With this approach, we maximize flexibility such that any component can publish a message, and any component can listen. This pattern replaces direct function calls with message dispatch.

Figure 29.1: Direct pubsub messaging

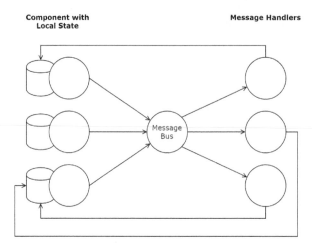

This flexibility is also the downside of this pattern. Function calls are highly constrained, and we can easily trace execution from one function to another. When we think about the pure substitution model of execution that we have discussed several times, a program looks like one large function. Asynchronous messaging breaks this paradigm such that we have to think of our program as multiple programs that can all observe the actions of others and react accordingly. While the complexity of direct pubsub is easy enough to manage in small applications, we often need a pattern that imposes a few constraints, which brings us to the Command/Event pattern.

Command/Event

In the notification component example, the form dispatched an `:: add-notification` message. If there were some other action that needed to take place (such as submitting the form to an API), then we would be faced with the awkward choice of whether to have our API handler listen for this specific `:: add-notification` message or make the form submission handler aware of the new action that needs to be performed. Since the goal of messaging is to decouple components from one another and to separate presentation logic from business logic, we would prefer to keep our components agnostic of the actions that they need to trigger. One way to achieve this is with the Command/Event pattern.

With this pattern, our components will dispatch *commands*, but another layer will be responsible for handling each command and emitting zero or more *events* that other systems may react to. For the notification example, we could replace the `dispatch!` function with one that explicitly delegates each type of command to a dedicated handler.

Figure 29.2: Command/event messaging

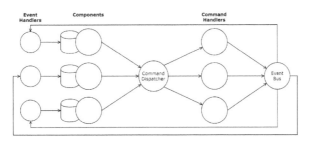

```
(defonce evt-ch (chan 1))
(defonce evt-bus (pub evt-ch ::type))

(defn emit!
  ([type] (emit! type nil))
  ([type payload]
   (put! evt-ch {::type type
                 ::payload payload})))

;; ... Other handlers

(defn handle-user-form-submit! [form-data]
  (let [{:keys [first-name last-name]} form-data]
    ;; ... emit other events
    (emit! :notification/added (str "Welcome, " first-name " " last-name))))

(defn dispatch! [command payload]
  (case command
    ;; ... handle other commands
    :user-form/submit! (handle-user-form-submit! payload)))
```

Our new `dispatch!` function is a normal, synchronous function that will delegate handling of each specific command to a specialized handler function. Here, the `:user-form/submit!` command is handled by `handle-user-form-submit!`. In a real application, this handler would likely do other things like make API calls or emit additional events, but we will keep it simple and only emit an event for the notifications component to display.

Although we have replaced the pubsub pattern for commands with a direct function dispatch, we have kept it for events. In fact, `evt-ch`, `evt-bus`, and `emit!` are just renamed versions of `msg-ch`, `msg-ch`, and `dispatch!` from the pubsub version, except that their purpose is to convey event messages only and not commands. The only piece of the UI that needs to change in this version is that the notification component should subscribe to the `:notification/added` topic on `evt-bus`:

```
(defn listen-for-added! [state]
  (let [added (chan)]
    (sub evt-bus :notification/added added)
```

```
  ;; ...
))
```

The trade-off that we must make when using the command/event pattern over direct pub-
lish/subscribe is boilerplate code. Instead of embedding all message handling logic inside
our components, we must now maintain a command handler layer. The advantage is that
when we need to modify the messages that are sent or received in our application, there is a
single place that we need to modify, whereas there is not a bound to how many subscribers
may need to be identified and modified.

Actor System

Before we wrap up, it is worth looking at one more messaging pattern that is borrowed from
Erlang/Elixir and the Akka framework: actors. Actors are conceptual entities that have a
mailbox where they can receive messages to act on at some point. Actors can send messages
to other actors' mailboxes as well, and they can be created and destroyed programmatically.
Unlike Erlang and Elixir, Clojure does not have *native* support for actors, but they can be
trivially emulated using the CSP model of concurrency provided by core.async. For example,
we can create a simple system of actors using only a few functions.

Listing 29.1: A basic actor system

```
(defn actor-system []                                    ①
  (atom {}))

(defn send-to! [system to msg]
  (when-let [ch (get @system to)]
    (put! ch msg)))

(defn actor [system address init-state & {:as handlers}]
  (let [state (r/atom init-state)                        ②
        in-ch (chan)]
    (swap! system assoc address in-ch)                   ③
    (go-loop []
      (let [[type & payload] (<! in-ch)]
        (when-let [handler (get handlers type)]
          (apply handler state payload))                 ④
        (recur)))
    state))
```
---

① We represent an actor system as a mutable map of addresses to channels
② Each actor holds state in a reactive atom
③ Register the actor with the system
④ Dispatch to a specific handler based on the message type

With this actor system, we can create actors that manage each distinct piece of the application state. With this simple implementation, we can create a single actor system using the `actor-system` function then declare any number of actors using the `actor` function. Unlike most actor implementations, our actor function will return the reactive atom representing the actor's state, which we can then dereference in our Reagent components. The actor itself will live as a `go` loop that will continually read messages from its mailbox and dispatch them to the handler functions that we declare. Let's see how to apply this to the notification example.

```
Listing 29.2: Using our actor system

(defonce sys (actor-system))                          ①

;; ...                                                 ②

(defonce notification-state
  (actor sys 'notifications                            ③
    {:messages []
     :next-id 0}

    :add-notification
    (fn [state text]
      (let [id (:next-id @state)]
        (swap! state add-notification id text)
        (js/setTimeout
          #(send-to! sys 'notifications
            [:remove-notification id])
          10000)))

    :remove-notification
    (fn [state id]
      (swap! state remove-notification id))))

(defonce form-state
  (actor sys 'input-form
    {:first-name ""
     :last-name ""}

    :update
    (fn [state field value]
      (swap! state assoc field value))

    :submit
    (fn [state]
      (let [{:keys [first-name last-name]} @state]
        (send-to! sys 'notifications
          [:add-notification (str "Welcome, " first-name " " last-name)]))
      (swap! state assoc
        :first-name ""
        :last-name ""))))

(defn notifications []
```

```
[:div.messages
  (for [msg (:messages @notification-state)          ④
        :let [{:keys [id text]} msg]]
    ^{:key id}
    [:div.notification.is-info
      [:button.delete
        {:on-click #(send-to! sys 'notifications   ⑤
                      [:remove-notification id])}]
      [:div.body text]])])

;; ...                                                ⑥
```

① Declare a single actor system
② `add-notification` and `remove-notification` are unchanged
③ Declare an actor with the symbol `'notifications` as its address
④ `notification-state` is just a reactive atom that we can dereference
⑤ Updating state is now done by sending a message to an actor
⑥ The remaining components are omitted because they do not demonstrate any new concepts

Figure 29.3: Actor system messaging

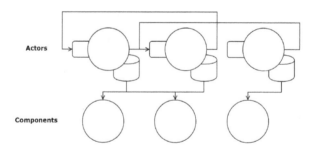

One clear advantage of this pattern is that we can declare the state right next to all of the functions that may update it, which makes tracing business logic trivial. For state that is only going to be used by a single component, this pattern does not offer a significant advantage over creating an atom when setting up the component, but for shared state, this pattern can simplify how we manage state.

Quick Review

- In the Command/Event pattern, where should side effects (like API calls) be performed?

- Which messaging pattern is the simplest for small applications?
- Is the Actor pattern more appropriate for state that is accessed by a single component or many components?

29.3 Client/Server Architecture

When we start to decouple our view components from the business logic of updating state, we can start to think of state management as an API that lives on the client. This way of programming gives us a clear boundary for separating presentation and business logic concerns, and it leads to much more maintainable code. Additionally, if we factor our state management from our UI, then we can also deal with getting data to and from a backend API layer outside our components. This additional level of separation gives us much more flexibility since we are free to vary how the backend API and components work independently. For instance, if we need to re-shape the data that comes from a back-end before rendering it, that can be done in our frontend API layer.

This front-end API looks slightly different in each of the messaging patterns. In the direct pubsub pattern, the message handlers provide this API layer, although there is no distinction between messages that originate in the UI from those that originate from a back-end API, so this pattern can lead to spaghetti code in larger codebases. In the command/event pattern, the same command handler will generally handle a command originating in the UI and control and back-end API calls that need to be made within a single function, so the logic is more centralized. Finally, in the actor pattern, we can create a dedicated actor whose responsibility is running back-end API requests - and perhaps keeping track of things like what requests are in progress or have failed in order to display loading/error indicators in the UI. In any case, using messaging to decouple components from each other and core business logic makes our code more flexible at the cost of added complexity.

29.4 Summary

In this lesson, we considered the example of a notification component to discuss the need for communication between components. In previous lessons, we had looked at using a single reactive atom and allowing communication via shared access to that single atom. In this lesson, we looked at an alternative way of communication using messaging. We considered three patterns - direct pubsub, command/event, and actor systems - which each serve to provide constraints around how components can communicate with each other as well as with backend APIs. Finally, we considered how messaging allows us to treat our business logic as a front-end API and how decoupling state management from presentation leads to more flexible code.

Lesson 30

Capstone 5 - Notes

In this section, we have been learning how to use the Reagent framework to apply our ClojureScript knowledge to web applications. In this final capstone lesson, we will once again use a project to synthesize what we have learned about Reagent and modular application design. As in the previous capstone lessons, this one will draw on all that we have learned so far - from working with sequences to state management and asynchronous communication. At this end of this lesson, we will have created a note-taking application from scratch. As was the case in the previous capstone, we will only be building the front-end. In order to follow along, you can use the API running at `https://notes.learn-cljs.com/api` with a set of credentials that can be obtained by issuing a POST request to `https://notes-api.learn-cljs.com/accounts`.

In This Lesson:

- Create a flexible component-based UI
- Handle state management with Reagent
- Interact with a RESTful API

Figure 30.1: Screenshot of CLJS Notes

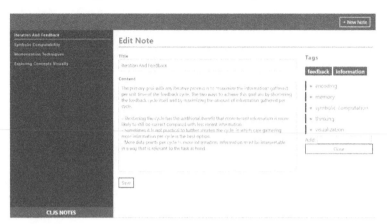

30.1   What We Are Building

The motivation for this capstone came from the author's own desire to have a simple note-taking application that could easily be extended as his needs evolved. A user should be able to use this app to take notes, classify them via tags, and edit their collection of notes. The back-end API for this application is deliberately uninteresting for two reasons:

1. It is designed to look like most of the APIs that we as web developers interact with at our jobs.
2. The primary focus of this lesson is on building UIs, so the less noise introduced by the API, the better.

This app is designed to be used by a single user and does not require any authentication or authorization.

30.2   State Management

Now that we know what we are building, it is time to model the data and uncover the patterns that the UI components can use to access that data.

We will start with a basic model for the UI state: notes, tags, and the relationships between them. Since we will be getting the data from a server, we need to consider its data model when deciding how to store and access that data from the UI. We will make use of two primary endpoints: /notes to list all notes, and /tags to list all tags. However - as is the case in most real-world apps - the data will not be in the ideal format for the UI's consumption, so we will reshape it with a process commonly called normalization.

Data Normalization

One of the main ideas that relational database technology has brought us is the concept of normalization. While normalization does have a technical definition, we can use an informal description: in the canonical application state, data should be shared via references rather than copies. For our purpose, this means that we should store notes and tags separately and maintain a list of the links between them. Additionally, we will structure them in a way that makes lookups efficient. For example, we could receive an API response like the following:

Listing 30.1: Data shape: source

```
[{:id 1
  :title "Books to Read"
  :content "..."
  :tags [{:id 2 :name "list"}
         {:id 3 :name "reading"}]}
 {:id 2
  :title "Groceries"
  :content "..."
  :tags [{:id 1 :name "food"}
         {:id 2 :name "list"}]}]
```

The first difficulty with this data structure is that the tags are nested under each note. For note-centric views this is fine, but if we are viewing or editing tags, this structure is less than ideal. We could leave the notes as-is and maintain a separate collection of tags. However, when we edit a tag, we would have to apply the same edit to every copy of that tag that is nested under the notes. The solution here is to do the same thing that we would do if we had a many-to-many relationship in a relational database management system: create separate collections for notes, tags, and the relationships between them. The goal is to transform the data into a shape like the following:

Listing 30.2: Data shape: result

```
{:notes                            ①
  {1 {:id 1
      :title "Books to Read"
      :content "..."}
   2 {:id 2
      :title "Groceries"
      :content "..."}}
 :tags
  {1 {:id 1 :name "food"}
   2 {:id 2 :name "list"}
```

```
     3 {:id 3 :name "reading"}}}

 :notes-tags
   {:by-note-id                                    ②
     {1 [2 3]
      2 [1 2]}
    :by-tag-id
     {1 [2]
      2 [1 2]
      3 [1]}}}}
```

---

① Each entity is stored in a map indexed by its ID for easy retrieval.

② References are stored in a separate map for each direction (note → tags and tag → notes) for easy lookup.

You may see that this code does not completely live up to the promise of avoiding duplication. Each reference is effectively stored twice - once for the `:by-note-id` collection and another time for the `:by-tag-id` collection. In practice, however, this duplication can be handled in a localized manner so that adding/removing tags from notes is still a simple operation.

To re-shape this data, we need to create several indexes that will enable the following operations to be performed efficiently:

1. Look up any note or tag by ID
2. Given any note, look up its corresponding tags.
3. Given any tag, look up its corresponding notes.

In the case of the tag and note resources, we need a map from ID to resource. Since each ID is unique, there will only be one resource for any given ID. ClojureScript's `group-by` function is almost what we want... but not *quite*:

```
cljs.user=> (def items [{:id 1 :title "foo"}
                        {:id 2 :title "bar"}])
#'cljs.user/items

cljs.user=> (group-by :id items)
 {1 [{:id 1, :title "foo"}],
  2 [{:id 2, :title "bar"}]}
```

The `group-by` function takes a group function `f` and a collection `xs`, and it returns a map of (`f x`) to a vector of all items that yielded the same (`f x`). A keyword is commonly used as the group function so that all items with the same keyword property are grouped together. Since we know that each IDs will have a single element in its group, we can take the first element from every value. The ClojureScript library does not come with a function for transforming every value in a map, but we can write one trivially:

```
(defn map-values [f m]
  (into {} (for [[k v] m] [k (f v)])))
```

This function uses a `for` sequence comprehension to iterate over every entry in `m`, yielding another entry that has the same key but a value that has had `f` applied. These key, value vectors are then collected into a new map. We can now use this to write a new indexing function:

```
cljs.user=> (defn make-index [f coll]
              (->> coll
                   (group-by f)
                   (map-values first)))
#'cljs.user/make-index

cljs.user=> (let [items [{:id 1 :title "foo"}
                         {:id 2 :title "bar"}]]
              (make-index :id items))
{1 {:id 1, :title "foo"},
 2 {:id 2, :title "bar"}}
```

This function works for the primary note and tag indexes, but we need a slightly different strategy for handling the `:notes-tags` indexes. First, these are not unique indexes, so each group will contain multiple elements. Additionally, these indexes need only sequences of IDs as their values - not full note or tag maps. Therefore, we need to map over the elements in each group and extract a single property from each one. Consider the following:

```
cljs.user=> (def links [{:note-id 1 :tag-id 2}
                        {:note-id 1 :tag-id 3}
                        {:note-id 2 :tag-id 1}
                        {:note-id 2 :tag-id 2}])
#'cljs.user/links

cljs.user=> (group-by :note-id links)
{1 [{:note-id 1, :tag-id 2} {:note-id 1, :tag-id 3}],
 2 [{:note-id 2, :tag-id 1} {:note-id 2, :tag-id 2}]}
```

Once again, `group-by` gives us almost what we want. Instead of applying a function to each group (as we did above), we need to apply a function to each item within the group. This is slightly more complicated, but it still requires only the familiar sequence functions that we are used to working with:

```
cljs.user=> (->> links
                 (group-by :note-id)
                 (map-values #(mapv :tag-id %)))       ①
{1 [2 3],
 2 [1 2]}
```

① For each group, map the `:tag-id` function over every element, yielding a vector.

We can modify the `make-index` function so that it handles both of the cases that we need by allowing it to take optional functions for transforming each group and transforming each element in the group. One way to handle optional arguments is the "kwargs" (keyword args) pattern. A function's parameter vector can end with an & followed by a map destructuring pattern. The function will then accept zero or more pairs of arguments that are interpreted as keyword/value pairs. We can now write our final `make-index` function:

Listing 30.3: Final `make-index`

```
(defn make-index [coll & {:keys [index-fn value-fn group-fn]
                          :or {value-fn identity
                               group-fn identity}}]
  (->> coll
       (group-by index-fn)
       (map-values #(group-fn (mapv value-fn %)))))

;; Example usage:
cljs.user=> (make-index items
                        :index-fn :id
                        :group-fn first)
{1 {:id 1, :title "foo"},
 2 {:id 2, :title "bar"}}
cljs.user=> (make-index links
                        :index-fn :note-id
                        :value-fn :tag-id)
{1 [2 3],
 2 [1 2]}
```

With this function written, we need only to write a function to extract all `:note-id`/`:tag-id` pairs and a final response normalization function.

Listing 30.4: Final `normalize-notes`

```
(defn get-links [notes]
  (mapcat (fn [note]
            (for [tag (:tags note)]
              {:note-id (:id note)
               :tag-id (:id tag)}))
          notes))

(defn normalize-notes [notes]
  (let [links (get-links notes)
        notes-without-tags (mapv #(dissoc % :tags) notes)
        all-note-tags (mapcat :tags notes)]
    {:notes (make-index notes-without-tags
                        :index-fn :id
                        :group-fn first)
     :tags (make-index all-note-tags
```

```
                    :index-fn :id
                    :group-fn first)
    :notes-tags
    {:by-note-id
     (make-index links
                    :index-fn :note-id
                    :value-fn :tag-id)
     :by-tag-id
     (make-index links
                    :index-fn :tag-id
                    :value-fn :note-id)}}}))
```

Now that the data normalization is working as we expect, it is time to move on to the architecture that we will use for state management and coordination.

Quick Review

- What is the benefit of normalizing data?
- What is the *kwargs* pattern? Are there other ways to pass optional parameters to a function?
- Given the normalized data format, how could you reconstruct a note with its tags nested under it?

UI State

In addition to the data that we retrieve from the server, there are a few more pieces of state that we will maintain:

Listing 30.5: notes/state.cljs

```
(ns learn-cljs.notes.state
  (:require [reagent.core :as r]))

(def initial-state
  {:current-route [:home]                              ①
   :notifications {:messages []                        ②
                   :next-id 0}
   :data {:notes {}
          :tags {}}})

(defonce app (r/atom initial-state))
```

① Route parameters for the current route. The state will serve as the source of truth for routing, and we will be using a routing library to keep the URL in sync with the state.

② Notifications for display using a component adapted from Lesson 29.

This minimal state is all that we need to build the capstone project, so let's move on to the architecture that we will use to coordinate updates to state.

Coordination Architecture

The architecture that we will use follows the *command/event* pattern from Lesson 29. The flow will be as follows:

1. The UI issues a command by calling a `learn-cljs.notes.command/dispatch!` function with a command name and optional payload.
2. A command handler performs any side effects needed for the command (including calling an API) and may emit events to an event bus.
3. State update functions listen for events and update the global application state accordingly.

Another departure from Lesson 29 is that we will not be using `core.async` for the messaging. While `core.async` would work here, it is overkill for the simple case where we have one function that emits events and one place where we dispatch to event handlers.

First up is the command dispatcher. This is a simple function that takes a command name and an optional command payload and dispatches to some other function to perform side effects and/or emit events:

Listing 30.6: notes/command.cljs

```clojure
(ns learn-cljs.notes.command
  (:require [learn-cljs.notes.events :refer [emit!]]))

(defn handle-test-hello! [name]
  (println "Hello" name)                              ①
  (emit! :test/greeting-dispatched {:name name}))     ②

(defn dispatch!
  ([command] (dispatch! command nil))
  ([command payload]
   (js/setTimeout                                     ③
    #(case command
       :test/hello (handle-test-hello! payload)

       (js/console.error (str "Error: unhandled command: " command)))
    0))
)
```

① The handler function may perform side effects.
② It should also emit events to which other portions of the app can react.
③ Run dispatcher asynchronously so that the call stack can clear before events are han-
    dled.

The UI can issue commands by calling _command/dispatch!directly. For example, a
component could call(notes.command/dispatch!   :test/hello "world"), and the textHello
worldwould be printed to the console. To support more commands, we will add conditions to
thecaseexpression indispatch¡ and a corresponding handler function.

Next, we need to implement the emit! function that is responsible for delivering events to
subscribers. Any code can register a listener function that will be called whenever an event
is emitted so that it can have a chance to react to it.

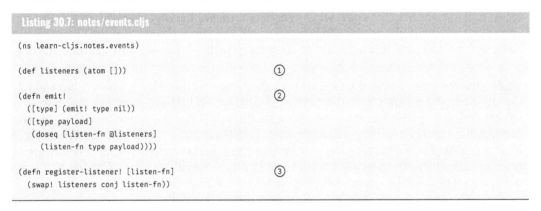

Listing 30.7: notes/events.cljs

```
(ns learn-cljs.notes.events)

(def listeners (atom []))                                ①

(defn emit!                                              ②
  ([type] (emit! type nil))
  ([type payload]
   (doseq [listen-fn @listeners]
     (listen-fn type payload))))

(defn register-listener! [listen-fn]                     ③
  (swap! listeners conj listen-fn))
```

① Keep track of the functions to notify when an event is emitted.
② Call each listener function in succession with the event type and payload.
③ Allow other code to register a listener.

Note that when we declare listeners, we use def rather than defonce. This is intentional and
will allow us to re-register listeners every time the app is reloaded. The result is that when
we update event handlers, we do not need to perform a full refresh of the app for the change
to be effective.

Finally, we will register a listener that is responsible for performing any necessary updates
to the app state when an event occurs.

Listing 30.8: notes/state.cljs

```
(ns learn-cljs.notes.state
  (:require ;; ...
            [learn-cljs.notes.events :as events]))
```

```
;; ...

(def handlers (atom {}))

(defn register-handler! [event-type handler-fn]
  (swap! handlers assoc event-type handler-fn))

(events/register-listener!
 (fn [type payload]
   (when-let [handler-fn (get @handlers type)]
     (swap! app #(handler-fn % payload)))))
```

Now, from anywhere in the code, we can register an event handler that will update the app state whenever an event occurs. That handler will be passed the state of the database and the event payload; and it is expected to return a (possibly updated) state for the database.

We created the event bus in such a way that many listeners could be registered, but we only register a listener for state updates. Why the extra layer of indirection rather than allowing the command dispatcher update the app state directly? The main reason is to designate one place to tap into if we want to log events, save them in localStorage to send to a server in an automated bug report, or integrate with a third-part component that is not aware of our state structure. Decoupling the act of emitting an event from updating the app state buys us a lot of flexibility in the long run for very little effort up-front.

To recap to flow of our state management:

1. A UI component dispatches a command using command/dispatch!.
2. The command dispatcher invokes a handler function, which can emit events and may also perform side effects, such as making API calls.
3. The event bus emits the event to listeners.
4. The state listener handles the event by passing the event and the current state of the database to any handlers registered for that event.
5. An event handler will take the event and the current state of the database and will return an updated state.
6. The update state will propagate to any components that depend on it, and they will re-render.

Figure 30.2: State coordination

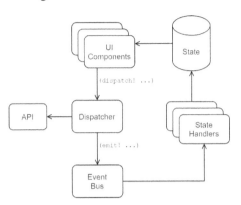

30.3 Building the Application

In the first part of this lesson, we focused on a "horizontal slice" of functionality - state management. Since state management is such a core concern to any front-end app, it is important that it is well-designed. However, we will now turn to a "vertical slices" approach to building the rest of the application. That is, we will focus on one feature at a time and develop the UI components, state handlers, API functions, etc. that are related to that feature. After all, that is how most real-world applications are built.

The first "feature" that we will build is the layout. The layout is fairly simple, with a header containing a "New Note" button, a sidebar with a list of notes, and a main content area where the user will create and edit notes.

Figure 30.3: Layout shell

We will add most of this structure in our top-level `notes.cljs` file:

Listing 30.9: notes.cljs

```clojure
(ns learn-cljs.notes
  (:require [learn-cljs.notes.ui.header :refer [header]]
            [learn-cljs.notes.ui.main :refer [main]]
            [learn-cljs.notes.ui.sidebar :refer [sidebar]]
            [learn-cljs.notes.ui.footer :refer [footer]]
            [reagent.dom :as rdom]
            [goog.dom :as gdom]))

(defn app []
  [:div.app
   [header]
   [main]
   [sidebar]
   [footer]])

(rdom/render
 [app]
 (gdom/getElement "app"))
```

We have not created the `header`, `main`, `sidebar`, or `footer` components yet, so let's do that now, starting with the header.

Listing 30.10: notes/ui/header.cljs

```clojure
(ns learn-cljs.notes.ui.header)

(defn header []
  [:header.page-header])
```

The main file will be a similar skeleton for now:

Listing 30.11: notes/ui/main.cljs

```clojure
(ns learn-cljs.notes.ui.main)

(defn main []
  [:div.main])
```

We will then follow the same pattern for the sidebar:

Listing 30.12: notes/ui/sidebar.cljs

```clojure
(ns learn-cljs.notes.ui.sidebar)

(defn sidebar []
  [:nav.sidebar])
```

Next, we will create the footer, which will simply display the name of the application. Since the footer is a static layout component, we will not revisit it for the rest of the lesson.

```
Listing 30.13: notes/ui/footer.cljs
```

```
(ns learn-cljs.notes.ui.footer)

(defn footer []
  [:footer.footer "CLJS Notes"])
```

Now that we have a little structure in place, let's start by letting the user create a new note. We will add a button to the header that navigates to a view where the user can fill in their note and save it. Although this seems like a small feature, it will involve:

1. adding a few UI components, including the concept of a *view*
2. introducing a router for managing navigation
3. creating an API namespace that will control communication with the server

First, we will add the "New Note" button to the header. In the header component, we will require a single button component from _ui.common' (which we will create shortly):

```
Listing 30.14: notes/ui/header.cljs
```

```
(ns learn-cljs.notes.ui.header
  (require [learn-cljs.notes.ui.common :refer [button]]))

(defn header []
  [:header.page-header
   [button "+ New Note"
    {:route-params [:create-note]           ①
     :class "inverse"}]])
```

① The :route-params option will control the target of the link.

Before we implement the button component, let's take a brief detour to discuss routing.

Routing

Like most single-page applications, we will use URL routing to determine which view should be displayed. This presents a challenge, since we the state atom - not the URL - to hold the canonical state of our application, including routing information. In order to manage routing state, we will use the bide[1] library to act as a source of events. Whenever

---

[1]https://github.com/funcool/bide

the URL of our application changes, we will treat it as a :route/navigated event that contains the route and any parameters (e.g. the note ID for an :edit-note view). This flow allows us to treat the browser itself as a source of events that may update the application's state, which remains the single source of truth. One consequence of this method of routing is that we need to allow links and buttons to invoke the router, which will in turn update the URL and emit a :route/navigated event. Thankfully, we already have a command dispatcher abstraction, so our components can just dispatch commands, including routing commands.

Figure 30.4: Routing flow

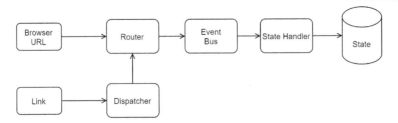

We will now create a router and hook it up to the relevant pieces of the application. Let's start by creating a routes namespace that contains the router and related code.

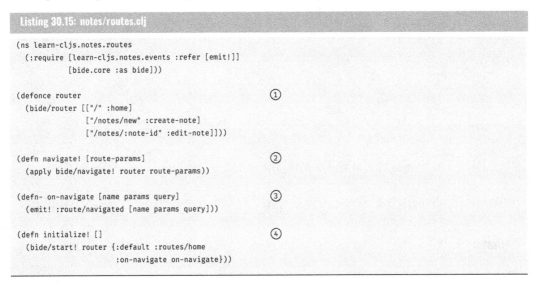

Listing 30.15: notes/routes.clj

```clojure
(ns learn-cljs.notes.routes
  (:require [learn-cljs.notes.events :refer [emit!]]
            [bide.core :as bide]))

(defonce router                                          ①
  (bide/router [["/" :home]
                ["/notes/new" :create-note]
                ["/notes/:note-id" :edit-note]]))

(defn navigate! [route-params]                           ②
  (apply bide/navigate! router route-params))

(defn- on-navigate [name params query]                   ③
  (emit! :route/navigated [name params query]))

(defn initialize! []                                     ④
  (bide/start! router {:default :routes/home
                       :on-navigate on-navigate}))
```

① Create the router only once
② Side-effecting function that the command dispatcher will call to update the current route

③ Callback that will be run whenever the a route change completes

④ Initialize the router on startup

Next, we will expose a command in the dispatcher that calls the `navigate!` function that we just defined:

```
Listing 30.16: notes/command.cljs

(ns learn-cljs.notes.command
  (:require ;; ...
            [learn-cljs.notes.routes :as routes]))

(defn handle-navigate! [route-params]
  (routes/navigate! route-params))
;; ...

(defn dispatch
  ;;...
  :route/navigate (handle-navigate! payload))
```

Now that we have exposed the router to our UI via the dispatcher, let's initialize the router when the application starts up.

```
Listing 30.17: notes.cljs

(ns learn-cljs.notes
  (:require ;; ...
            [learn-cljs.notes.routes :as routes]))
;; ...
(defonce initialized?
  (do
    (routes/initialize!)
    true))
```

The reason that we expose an `_routes/initialize!`rather than initialize the router immediately when `_routes` is evaluated is that the router will call the `on-navigate` callback as soon as it is initialized; and if that happens before the event handlers are registered, the state will not be updated. By deferring loading until our core file and all of its imports have been evaluated, we ensure that the initial route event will be handled appropriately. Next, we will create and register the handler for the `:route/navigated` event.

```
Listing 30.18: notes/event_handlers/routes.cljs

(ns learn-cljs.notes.event-handlers.routes
  (:require [learn-cljs.notes.state :refer [register-handler!]]))

(register-handler!
 :route/navigated
 (fn [db route-params]
```

```
(assoc db :current-route route-params)))
```

We will need to evaluate this namespace on startup so that the handler is registered, so let's take care of that in two steps:

1. Create a _event-handlers.core' that requires all event handler namespaces for side effects.
2. Require the _event-handlers.core in our top-level _core namespace.

Listing 30.19: notes/event_handlers/core.cljs

```
(ns learn-cljs.notes.event-handlers.core
  (:require [learn-cljs.notes.event-handlers.routes]))
```

and

Listing 30.20: notes.cljs

```
(ns learn-cljs.notes
  (:require ;; ...
            [learn-cljs.notes.event-handlers.core]))
```

With all of the plumbing in place, we will update our `main` component to load different views depending on what route the user is on.

Listing 30.21: notes/ui/main.cljs

```
(ns learn-cljs.notes.ui.main
  (:require [learn-cljs.notes.state :as state]
            [learn-cljs.notes.ui.views.home :refer [home]]))

(defn not-found []                                          ①
  [:section.hero
   [:h1.title "Page Not Found!"]])

(defn main []
  (let [[route params query] (:current-route @state/app)]   ②
    [:div.main
     (case route
       :home [home]
       [not-found])]))
```

① Fall back to a generic `not-found` component if the app is at an unknown route
② Pull the route parameters out of state to call the appropriate view

As the final step before we return to the feature of creating a new note, we will create the simple home view that we referenced above.

```
Listing 30.22: notes/ui/views/home.cljs

(ns learn-cljs.notes.ui.views.home)

(defn home []
  [:div.home.hero
   [:h1.title "Welcome to Notes"]
   [:h2.subtitle "Select a note or create a new one to get started."]])
```

That was quite an effort to get routing working correctly, but it was worth it! We now have a very clean routing architecture that allows us to easily add views as well as keep our UI components decoupled from the routing mechanism.

Challenge

Update the router to use HTML5 History-based routing instead of hash-based. In order to have this work with the Figwheel dev server, you will need to write a bit of server-side Clojure code.

Creating a New Note

With the length of that detour, I would not blame you if you forgot that we were in the middle of creating a button for adding a new note. Within the ui.header.cljs file, we had added a require for [learn-cljs.notes.ui.common :refer [button]], which we will create now.

```
Listing 30.23: notes/ui/common.cljs

(ns learn-cljs.notes.ui.common
  (:require [learn-cljs.notes.command :refer [dispatch!]]))

(defn handle-navigate [route-params]
  (fn [_]
    (dispatch! :route/navigate route-params)))

(defn button [text {:keys [route-params class]
                    :or {class ""}}]
  [:button {:class (str "button " class)
            :on-click (handle-navigate route-params)}
   text])
```

For now, our button component acts like a link, which is exactly the behavior that we want. Here is the complete flow of routing that we have just enabled with this button:

1. The button will now use the `button` component to dispatch a `:route/navigate` command with the route params `[:create-note]` as its payload.
2. The command dispatcher will pass this command to the router, which will cause the browser's URL to change.
3. The route change will in turn cause the router to emit a `:route/navigated` event with the new route parameters.
4. The event handler in `event_handlers/routes.cljs` will respond to this event by updating the `:current-route` parameter in the application state.
5. Finally, the `main` component will re-render due to the state change and will load a view associated with the `:create-note` route and will render a "Not Found" route as a fallback.

Checkpoint

λ

The app loads with a home page, an empty sidebar, and a button in the header that reads "+ New Note". Clicking this button navigates to a "Page Not Found" view.

Next, we will create the view for the `:create-note` route.

Listing 30.24: notes/ui/views/note_form.cljs

```
(ns learn-cljs.notes.ui.views.note-form
  (:require [reagent.core :as r]
            [learn-cljs.notes.state :refer [app]]
            [learn-cljs.notes.ui.common :refer [button]]))

(defn update-data [data key]                          ①
  (fn [e]
    (swap! data assoc key (.. e -target -value))))

(defn input [data key label]                          ②
  (let [id (str "field-" (name key))]
    [:div.field
     [:div.label
      [:label {:for id} label]]
     [:div.control
      [:input {:id id
               :type "text"
               :on-change (update-data data key)
               :value (get @data key "")}]]]))

(defn textarea [data key label]
  (let [id (str "field-" (name key))]
    [:div.field
     [:div.label
      [:label {:for id} label]]
     [:div.control
```

```
        [:textarea {:id id
                    :on-change (update-data data key)
                    :value (get @data key "")}]]])))

(defn submit-button [data text]
  [button text {:dispatch [:notes/create @data]}])          ③

(defn note-form []
  (let [form-data (r/cursor app [:note-form])]             ④
    (fn []
      [:section.note-form
       [:h2.page-title "Edit Note"]
       [:form
        [input form-data :title "Title"]
        [textarea form-data :content "Content"]
        [submit-button form-data "Save"]]])))
```

① Constructor for an event handler that will set a specific key in the `data` atom
② Helper components for the input and textarea
③ Re-use the `button` component used in the header, but with a `:dispatch` option
④ Use a Reagent cursor to select only the state this component needs

Since nothing in this file is particularly novel, let's return to the button component to add support for a `:dispatch` option. The intent is that when the button is clicked, it will call the command dispatcher with the command name and payload specified in the value of the option. We can also add an `:on-click` option that will simply call the provided callback, since we will make use of that option later.

Listing 30.25: notes/ui/common.cljs

```
;; ...
(defn handle-dispatch [command-data]
  (fn [e]
    (.preventDefault e)
    (apply dispatch! command-data)))

(defn button [text {:keys [route-params dispatch on-click class]
                    :or {class ""}}]
  [:button
   {:class (str "button " class)
    :on-click (cond
                route-params (handle-navigate route-params)
                dispatch (handle-dispatch dispatch)
                on-click on-click
                :else #(js/console.error "No action provided for button"))}
   text])
```

Now the behavior of the button will vary depending on whether the `route-params`, `dispatch`, or `on-click` option is provided. Remember that `cond` will evaluate the right-hand side of the first truthy clause in encounters, so the behavior when `route-params` is specified will not change. However, if `dispatch` is provided, it will call _command/dispatch¡ with the arguments provided.

You Try It

- There is quite a bit of duplication between the `input` and `textarea` components. Try factoring out the common code into one or more helpers to DRY it up.

The next thing that we need to add is a command handler for `:notes/create`. This handler will call a function in the API (which we will implement next).

```
(defn handle-create-note! [note]
  (api/create-note! note))

(defn dispatch!
  ;; ...
  (case command
    ;; ...
    :notes/create (handle-create-note! payload))
)
```

Since this is the first bit of server interaction that we are implementing, we could use a couple of utilities - one for performing requests in a consistent manner and one for emitting error notifications that will be displayed in the UI.

Listing 30.26: notes/api.cljs

```
(ns learn-cljs.notes.api
  (:require [learn-cljs.notes.events :refer [emit!]]
            [learn-cljs.notes.errors :as err]
            [camel-snake-kebab.core :as csk]
            [camel-snake-kebab.extras :as cske]))

(defn do-request!
  ([method path cb] (do-request! method path nil cb))
  ([method path body cb]
   (let [serialized-body (when body
                           (->> body                                    ①
                                (cske/transform-keys csk/->camelCaseString)
                                (clj->js)
                                (js/JSON.stringify)))]
     (-> (js/fetch (str js/API_URL path)                                ②
                   (cond-> {:method (name method)
                            :headers {"Authorization" (str "Bearer " js/API_TOKEN)}
                            :credentials "include"}
```

```
                    (some? body)
                    (->
                     (assoc :body serialized-body)
                     (update :headers merge {"content-type" "application/json"}))

                    :always
                    clj->js))
          (.then (fn [res]
                   (if (.-ok res)
                     (when (= 200 (.-status res))
                       (.json res))
                     (throw (ex-info "API Request Failed"
                                     {:status-code (.-status res)
                                      :status (.-statusText res)}
                                     :api-failure)))))
          (.then #(->> %
                       (js->clj)                              ③
                       (cske/transform-keys csk/->kebab-case-keyword)
                       (err/ok)
                       (cb)))
          (.catch #(cb (err/error %)))))))            ④

(defn- display-error [err]                           ⑤
  (emit! :notification/added
         {:type :error
          :text (str "API Error: " (ex-message err))}))

(defn create-note! [note]                            ⑥
  (do-request! :post "/notes" note
               (fn [res]
                 (->> res
                      (err/map
                       #(emit! :note/created %))
                      (err/unwrap-or display-error)))))
```

① Convert request body to idiomatic JSON
② Read global variables from the page to determine the API endpoint and credentials
③ Convert the response body from JSON to ClojureScript data structures
④ Convert any errors that were thrown into error objects
⑤ Helper for emitting error notifications
⑥ At least the code to perform a single request is nice and simple now, right?

There is a lot going on in this file, but the bulk of it is related to the implementation of the `do-request!` helper. Let's quickly look at what it is doing. First, it allows client code to specify the HTTP method, URL relative to the API base, an optional body, and a response callback. If a body is supplied, it uses the `camel-snake-kebab` library to convert Clojure-style *snake-case* keyword keys to *camelCase* strings, and it does the inverse to the response body (don't forget to add `camel-snake-kebab/camel-snake-kebab {:mvn/version "0.4.2"}` to the project dependencies). It also uses the errors-as-values technique discussed in Lesson 24 to pass either a successful or error result to the callback. The _errors' namespace is taken verbatim from Lesson 24, so it will not be repeated here.

Since we need to read a couple of global variables, let's open `index.html` and add these.

Listing 30.27: index.html

```html
<!-- ... -->
<script type="text/javascript">
  window.API_URL = "https://notes-api.learn-cljs.com";
  window.API_TOKEN =
    "Get an API token with: curl -X POST https://notes-api.learn-cljs.com/tenant";
</script>
<!-- ... -->
```

The notification component that is used is adapted from Lesson 29 and will not be covered explicitly here. Please see the code in the accompanying repository for reference.

As the final step in creating a new note, we will need to register an event handler for the `:note/created` event.

Listing 30.28: notes/event_handlers/api_data.cljs

```clojure
(ns learn-cljs.notes.event-handlers.api-data
  (:require [learn-cljs.notes.state :refer [register-handler!]]
            [learn-cljs.notes.command :refer [dispatch!]]))

(register-handler!
 :note/created
 (fn [db payload]
   (let [{:keys [id title]} payload]
     (dispatch! :notification/add
                {:type :info
                 :text (str "Note created: " title)})
     (dispatch! :route/navigate                      ①
                [:edit-note {:note-id id}])
     (assoc-in db [:data :notes id]                  ②
               (dissoc payload :tags)))))
```

① Dispatch a navigation event so that the edit view for this note will load.
② Insert the returned note into the notes index in the application state.

Don't forget to require this namespace in `notes/event_handlers/core.cljs` so that it will be evaluated on startup.

Checkpoint

You are able to fill in the title and content on a new note form, and the note is saved to the server when you click the "save" button. You are also redirected to the note edit URL, although there is no view to display yet.

Challenge

This capstone is already massive. You don't need an extra challenge on this one. Go get yourself a cup of tea!

Listing notes

In comparison to the code that we have added so far, adding a list of notes will be a minor task. For the initial feature of creating a new note, we started from the UI components and worked back to the API. For this feature, let's do the opposite - focus on how to get the data into the UI, then build the components to display it.

First, we will add a function to the API that calls the "/notes" endpoint to get the full notes list.

Listing 30.29: notes/api.cljs

```
;; ...
(defn get-notes! []
  (do-request! :get "/notes"
               (fn [res]
                 (->> res
                      (err/map
                       #(emit! :notes/received %))
                      (err/unwrap-or display-error)))))
```

Yes, 7 lines of code is all we need for this API. The hard work of writing the `do-request!` helper id paying off. In fact, we can refactor this code a bit more, since the response callback shares a lot of logic with the callback for `create-note!`. In fact, the only difference is in the function that emits the event. Let's create another helper function that takes care of the error handling logic.

```
(defn- with-error-handling [f]
  (fn [res]
    (->> res
         (err/map f)
         (err/unwrap-or display-error))))
```

```
;; create-note! can also be refactored.

(defn get-notes! []
  (do-request! :get "/notes"
               (with-error-handling #(emit! :notes/received %))))
```

Next, we will add a command to the dispatcher that invokes this API function.

Listing 30.30: notes/command.cljs

```
;; ...
(defn handle-get-notes! [_]
  (api/get-notes!))
;; ...
(defn dispatch
  ;;...
  :notes/get-notes (handle-get-notes! payload))
```

The next piece is the handler for :notes/received event that the API emits. Although there is quite a bit of work that goes into normalizing the API response, the good news is that we did that work at the beginning of the lesson, and what remains is trivial:

Listing 30.31: notes/event_handlers/api_data.cljs

```
;; ...

;; Paste the final code from the Data Normalization section here

(defn update-normalized-notes [db notes]
  (let [{:keys [learn-cljs.notes tags notes-tags]} (normalize-notes notes)]
    (update db :data #(-> %
                          (update :notes merge notes)
                          (update :tags merge tags)
                          (assoc :notes-tags notes-tags)))))

(register-handler!
 :notes/received
 (fn [db payload]
   (update-normalized-notes db payload)))
```

Now everything other than the UI is wired up, so let's open the sidebar file and add a component for listing the notes that came back from the API.

Listing 30.32: notes/ui/sidebar.cljs

```
(ns learn-cljs.notes.ui.sidebar
  (:require [reagent.core :as r]
            [reagent.ratom :as ratom]
            [learn-cljs.notes.state :refer [app]]
            [learn-cljs.notes.command :refer [dispatch!]]
```

```
                [learn-cljs.notes.ui.common :refer [link]]))

(defn created-at-sorter [a b]                         ①
  (> (:created-at a)
     (:created-at b)))

(defn notes-list []
  (let [notes (r/cursor app [:data :notes])
        notes-list (ratom/make-reaction              ②
                     #(->> @notes
                           (vals)
                           (sort created-at-sorter)))]
    (dispatch! :notes/get-notes)                      ③
    (fn []
      [:nav
       [:ul.notes-list
        (for [note @notes-list
              :let [{:keys [id title]} note]]
          ^{:key id}
          [:li [link title [:edit-note {:note-id id}]]])]])))

(defn sidebar []
  [:nav.sidebar
   [notes-list]])
```

① Function for sorting notes with the newest at the top
② Define the notes list as a reaction over the raw data
③ Request notes when the component mounts

For the notes list, we want to display the newest notes first, but our application state only has the notes in a map, where no order is defined. In order to get the sorted list, we can create a reaction that is recomputed only when the underlying notes data changes. Recall the analogy of spreadsheet cells where reactions are like the formulas that connect the cells. The one piece that we are missing is the `link` component, so let's add that now.

Listing 30.33: notes/ui/common.cljs

```
(ns learn-cljs.notes.ui.common
  (:require ;; ...
            [learn-cljs.notes.state :as state]
            [learn-cljs.notes.routes :as routes]))
;; ...
(defn link [text route-params]
  [:a {:href (routes/get-url route-params)
       :on-click (handle-navigate route-params)
       :class (if (routes/matches? route-params (:current-route @state/app))
                "active" "")}
   text])
```

The link component behaves similar to the button, but it also adds an `active` class when the current route matches the link's target. This helps us achieve the typical navigation bar functionality where the current link is highlighted. This component relies on two new functions in the _routes namespace -get-url and matches¿, so let's add them now.

```
Listing 30.34: notes/routes.cljs
```

```
;; ...
(defn get-url [route-params]
  (str "#"
       (apply bide/resolve router route-params)))

(defn matches? [route-params current-route]
  (= (get-url route-params)
     (get-url current-route)))
```

The `get-url` function will generate a URL string from route params - exactly the inverse of what happens when we navigate to a new URL and need to infer the route. The `matches?` function will compare two route parameters to test whether they generate the same URL. This function is used to determine if the browser is currently on some link's target.

Editing Existing Notes

Since we already have a form for authoring new notes, we now need to generalize it a bit so that it can handle both creating new notes and editing existing ones. The strategy that we will take is to hook into the routing logic to determine whether to set the form data to an empty state or load in some note when the user navigates to the form. Within the form itself, we will make several labels conditional upon whether it is in a creating or editing state, and we will dispatch a different action for create versus update. Since we are re-using the same view, let's add another entry to the main component's view switcher.

```
Listing 30.35: notes/ui/main.cljs
```

```
;;...
(defn main []
  ;; ...
  (case route
    :edit-note [note-form]
    ;; ...
  ))
```

Next, let's add the pieces that we need in the API and command dispatcher. First, the API needs two functions - one to perform the update and another to fetch a single note. The update endpoint does not return the updated note, so we follow up the update with a fetch to ensure that our copy is up to date.

```
Listing 30.36: notes/api.cljs

(defn update-note! [note]
  (do-request! :put (str "/notes/" (:id note)) note
               (with-error-handling
                 #(emit! :note/updated note))))

(defn get-note! [id]
  (do-request! :get (str "/notes/" id)
               (with-error-handling #(emit! :note/received %))))
```

...then the dispatcher:

```
Listing 30.37: notes/command.cljs

;; ...
(defn handle-update-note! [note]
  (api/update-note! note))

(defn handle-get-note! [id]
  (api/get-note! id))
;; ...
(defn dispatch
  ;;...
  :notes/update (handle-update-note! payload)
  :notes/get-note (handle-get-note! payload))
```

Since we want any updates that we make to the note to be reflected in the application state immediately, we need to add an event handler for the :note/updated event. In this handler, we will also dispatch an action to fetch the newly-updated note in its entirety. We will also add the handler to merge this note into our state when the response comes back.

```
Listing 30.38: notes/event_handlers/api_data.cljs

(register-handler!
 :note/updated
 (fn [db payload]
   (let [{:keys [title id]} payload]
     (dispatch! :notification/add
                {:type :info
                 :text (str "Note saved: " title)})
     (dispatch! :notes/get-note id)              ①
     (assoc-in db [:data :notes id] payload))))

(register-handler!
 :note/received
 (fn [db payload]
   (update-normalized-notes db [payload])))      ②
```

① On update, re-fetch the note

② Re-use the same merging logic that we use for the bulk `:notes/received` event

The last piece of state management that we need for this feature is the hook into the routing event handler.

Listing 30.39: notes/event_handlers/routes.cljs

```clojure
;;...
(defn- note-for-edit-route [db route-params]              ①
  (let [note-id (get-in route-params [1 :note-id])
        note-id (js/parseInt note-id)]
    (get-in db [:data :notes note-id])))

(register-handler!
 :route/navigated
 (fn [db route-params]
   (cond-> db
     true (assoc :current-route route-params)            ②

     (= :create-note (first route-params))               ③
     (assoc :note-form {})

     (= :edit-note (first route-params))                 ④
     (assoc :note-form (note-for-edit-route db route-params)))))
```

① Given a route to some note's edit view, return that note from state
② Always update the current route
③ When navigating to a create route, clear the form state
④ When navigating to an edit route, duplicate the corresponding note as the initial form state

Previously, this handler only updated the `:current-route` in state, but we just added conditional updates to be performed depending on the route.

Now, let's go back to the note form and update it so that the appropriate labels are displayed, and dispatch uses the appropriate save action based on whether the user is creating or editing a note. We introduce an `is-new?` helper that checks the form data for the presence of an ID to determine whether it is a new note.

Listing 30.40: notes/ui/views/note_form.cljs

```clojure
(defn is-new? [data]
  (-> data :id nil?))

(defn submit-button [data]                               ①
  (let [[action text] (if (is-new? @data)
                        [:notes/create "Create"]
```

```
                         [:notes/update "Save"])]
       [button text {:dispatch [action @data]}]]))

(defn note-form []
  (let [form-data (r/cursor app [:note-form])]
    (fn []
      [:section.note-form
       [:h2.page-title
        (if (is-new? @form-data) "New Note" "Edit Note")]
       [:form
        [input form-data :title "Title"]
        [textarea form-data :content "Content"]
        [submit-button form-data]]])))
```

① Bind two symbols at once based on some condition

With some relatively minor changes, our app now supports editing notes!

Challenge

Instead of dispatching to either :notes/create and :notes/update, try using a generic :notes/save command that calls a different API endpoint based on whether the note is new.

Tagging Notes

The final feature that we will support in our note-taking app is the ability to apply tags to notes as well as add new tags to the system. There will be three API endpoints that we need to support:

- Listing all tags
- Creating a new tag
- Tagging a note

Let's go ahead and add commands for each of these actions, followed by the necessary API functions, then the event handlers.

Listing 30.41: notes/command.cljs

```
;; ...
(defn handle-get-tags! [_]
  (api/get-tags!))

(defn handle-create-tag! [tag-name]
```

```
  (api/create-tag! tag-name))

(defn handle-tag-note! [{:keys [note-id tag-id]}]
  (api/tag-note! note-id tag-id))
;; ...
(defn dispatch
  ;;...
  :tags/get-tags (handle-get-tags! payload)
  :tags/create (handle-create-tag! payload)
  :notes/tag (handle-tag-note! payload))
```

Now we'll move on to the API functions.

Listing 30.42: notes/api.cljs

```
(defn get-tags! []
  (do-request! :get "/tags"
               (with-error-handling #(emit! :tags/received %))))

(defn create-tag! [tag-name]
  (do-request! :post "/tags" {:name tag-name}
               (with-error-handling #(emit! :tag/created %))))

(defn tag-note! [note-id tag-id]
  (do-request! :put (str "/notes/" note-id "/tags/" tag-id)
               (with-error-handling
                 #(emit! :note/tagged {:note-id note-id
                                       :tag-id tag-id}))))
```

We added three command and three API functions, so it should come as no surprise that we will add three event handlers next.

Listing 30.43: notes/event_handlers/api_data.cljs

```
(register-handler!
 :tags/received
 (fn [db payload]
   (update-in db [:data :tags]
              merge (make-index payload
                                :index-fn :id
                                :group-fn first))))

(register-handler!
 :tag/created
 (fn [db payload]
   (assoc-in db [:data :tags (:id payload)] payload)))

(register-handler!
 :note/tagged
 (fn [db payload]
   (let [{:keys [note-id tag-id]} payload]
```

```
(-> db
    (update-in [:data :notes-tags :by-note-id note-id] conj tag-id)
    (update-in [:data :notes-tags :by-tag-id tag-id] conj note-id)))))
```

When we receive the list of tags, we use the `make-index` function that we wrote at the beginning of the lesson to index them by id then merge them on top of any tags that may already be in state. When we create a tag, we simply add it to the indexed tags in state. Finally, when we tag a note, we add entries to both the notes-by-tag and tags-by-notes indexes.

The last piece that we need to add is the UI for managing tags. We will add this as part of the note create/edit form.

Listing 30.44: notes/ui/views/note_form.cljs

```
(ns learn-cljs.notes.ui.views.note-form
  (:require ;; ...
            [learn-cljs.notes.ui.tags :refer [tag-selector]]))
;; ...
(defn note-form []
  ;; ...
      [:section.editor
       [:form.note ;;...
       ]
       [:div.tags
        [:h3 "Tags"]
        (if (is-new? @form-data)
          [:p.help "Please save your note before adding tags."]
          [tag-selector])]]]))
```

The main change here is the use of the `tag-selector` component, which we are about to write. We did restructure some of the DOM here in order to add a level of nesting so that the note form and the tag selector can sit on the page side by side. In order to keep things as simple as possible, we will only support adding tags to notes that have been saved. Otherwise, we would have to keep track of what notes we wanted to add to a new note and add them only once we knew the ID of the note that was created.

Below is the listing for the entire tag-selector component and all of its dependencies. There is a lot going on here, so take you time understanding it. A good portion of the file is dedicated to creating reactions that join data between the tags, indexes, and the note that is being edited.

Listing 30.45: notes/ui/tags.cljs

```
(ns learn-cljs.notes.ui.tags
  (:require [reagent.core :as r]
            [reagent.ratom :as ratom]
            [learn-cljs.notes.state :refer [app]]
            [learn-cljs.notes.ui.common :refer [button]]
            [learn-cljs.notes.command :refer [dispatch!]]))
```

```
(defn name-sorter [a b]
  (< (:name a) (:name b)))

(def all-tags
  (r/cursor app [:data :tags]))

(def tags-by-note-index
  (r/cursor app [:data :notes-tags :by-note-id]))

(def editing-note-id
  (r/cursor app [:note-form :id]))

(def note-tags
  (ratom/make-reaction
    #(get @tags-by-note-index @editing-note-id)))

(def attached-tags
  (ratom/make-reaction
    #(->> (select-keys @all-tags @note-tags)
          (vals)
          (sort name-sorter))))

(def available-tags
  (ratom/make-reaction
    #(->> (apply dissoc @all-tags @note-tags)
          (vals)
          (sort name-sorter))))

(defn attached-tag-list []
  [:div.attached
    (for [tag @attached-tags
          :let [{:keys [id name]} tag]]
      ^{:key id}
      [:span.tag name])])

(defn available-tags-list []
  [:div
    (for [tag @available-tags
          :let [{:keys [id name]} tag]]
      ^{:key id}
      [:div.tag {:on-click #(dispatch! :notes/tag {:note-id @editing-note-id
                                                   :tag-id id})}
        [:span.add "+"] name])])

(defn create-tag-input []
  (let [tag-name (r/atom "")]
    (fn []
      [:div.create-tag
        "Add: "
        [:input {:value @tag-name
                 :on-key-up #(when (= (.-key %) "Enter")
                               (dispatch! :tags/create @tag-name)
                               (reset! tag-name ""))
```

```
                 :on-change #(reset! tag-name (.. % -target -value))}]]))))

(defn available-tag-selector []
  (let [is-expanded? (r/atom false)]
    (dispatch! :tags/get-tags)
    (fn []
      [:div.available
       (if @is-expanded?
         [:div.tag-selector
          [available-tags-list]
          [create-tag-input]
          [button "Close" {:class "block"
                           :on-click #(reset! is-expanded? false)}]]
         [button "+ Add Tags" {:class "block"
                               :on-click #(reset! is-expanded? true)}])])))

(defn tag-selector []
  [:div.tag-selector
   [attached-tag-list]
   [available-tag-selector]])
```

This `tag-selector` component displays a collection of all of the tags that have been applied to the note that the user is currently viewing. It also contains a drawer with the remaining labels that can be expanded or collapsed, and a label can be applied by clicking on it. Finally, the user can type the name of a new label in the text box and hit Enter to create a new label.

30.4 Summary

Now that we have added the last feature to this capstone project, it is time to congratulate yourself. Not only have you completed this capstone, but you have made it through this journey into learning ClojureScript. We started this book with basic lessons on syntax, using somewhat contrived examples to take small steps towards familiarity. We then advanced to projects that synthesized the basic concepts into more useful patterns and constructs. Finally, in this last capstone, we created a well-structured and extensible UI application. This application has an intentional architecture that embraces functional programming, declarative UIs and immutable state management - it is not a toy project.

Thank you, fellow ClojureScript programmer, for joining me on this journey from the basics to real-world programming in this weird and wonderful language. Now go and build some amazing things!

Index

accumulator, 194
add-watch, 251
AJAX, 82
Akka, 340
Alan Perlis, 232
arguments
    default values, 204
array access, 143
assembly language, 12
associative collections, 184
async/await, 8, 284

batteries included, 12
bide, 357
binding, 90, 128
bottom-up programming, 134, 160
browser compatibility, 3, 17, 148
Bulma CSS, 222

call stack, 118, 135
channel, 277, 284, 293
clj, 46
clj-new, 49, 255
Clojars, 50
Clojure, 4, 16, 46, 259, 361
clojure.spec, 201
closure, 132, 241
CoffeeScript, 10
cohesion, 260
collection operations
    assoc, 206
    assoc-in, 211

dissoc, 208
get-in, 209
merge, 202
select-keys, 208
update-in, 211
collections, 169
comp, 234
compile-to-JavaScript, 9
conditional expressions
    cond, 107
    condp, 107
    if, 99
    when, 101
conditions, 272
constructor function, 201, 241
controlled inputs, 327
core.async, 277, 333, 352
coupling, 260
CSP, 8, 277, 285
cursor, 328

DAG (directed acyclic graph), 323
Dart, 10
data binding
    1-way, 81
    2-way, 80
data types
    atom, 78
    atoms, 248
    booleans, 27
    converting to/from JavaScript, 138
    functions, 125

keywords, 27, 334
lists, 28
maps, 29, 174
nil, 30
numbers, 26
primitives, 25
seq, 185
sets, 30, 176
strings, 26
symbols, 28, 91
vectors, 29, 173
declare, 306
def, 93
defonce, 60
deps.edn, 46
design by contract, 130
Design Patterns, 240
destructuring, 94
dirty-checking, 7
DOM Manipulation, 316
DOM manipulation, 148, 160, 312

EDN (extensible data notation), 46, 308
Eiffel, 130
Electron, 20
Elixir, 340
Eric Normand, 284
Erlang, 340
error values, 269, 366
ES2015, 9
evaluation
    of function calls, 39, 131
    of sequences, 40
event handler, 154, 161, 221, 307, 354,
        371
ex-info, 267
expressions, 33

failjure, 272
Figwheel, 46, 49, 57, 255, 322
    clj-new template, 50
    connecting to browser, 58
    CSS reloading, 60

function composition, 234
functional programming, 5, 13, 316
functions
    anonymous shorthand, 127
    arities, 128
    definition, 126
    docstrings, 129
    parameters, 131

garbage collection, 93
generators, 8
global state, 13
Go (programming language), 8
go block, 280
go-loop, 281
Google Closure Compiler, 256
Google Closure compiler, 8
Google Closure Library, 6, 12, 18, 149
group-by, 348

hiccup, 220, 324, 329
HTML5 History, 361
huccup, 321

idempotency, 62
identity, 248
IDEs, 53, 60
immer, 18
immutability, 7, 89, 238, 304, 316
    persistent data structures, 239, 319
Immutable.js, 18, 240
initialization code, 63

Java Virtual Machine, 4, 19, 21, 49, 266
JavaScript
    standard library, 17
    this, 132
jQuery, 17
jquery, 6
juxt, 223

kwargs pattern, 350

let, 93

lexical scope, 132
    shadowing, 133
libspec, 257
Light Table, 20
Linux, 48
Lisp, 33, 240
lisp, 272
live reloading, 353
Lodash, 17
lodash, 172
looping constructs
    `dorun`, 120
    `doseq`, 121
    `for`, 112
    `loop/recur`, 117
    recursion, 135
loops, 111

macros, 259
`map-values`, 349
message bus, 292
messaging
    actors, 340
    command/event, 338, 343, 352
    pubsub, 337
Microns icon font, 222
middleware, 244
minification, 18
mobile clients, 17
module loading, 8
monad, 270

namespace, 53
namespaces, 8, 128, 255
nested data, 209
Node.js, 21
normalization, 347, 351, 368

object prototype, 12
object-oriented programming, 5, 180, 200, 232, 244, 260
OpenWeatherMap, 82
operator precedence, 35

OSX, 48

`partial`, 235
Peter Norvig, 240
predicate function, 187
priomise, 277
process, 277
promise, 284
promises, 8
property access, 141
PureScript, 10

Ramda, 172
Raspberry Pi, 21
React.js, 297
    DOM diffing, 316
    JSX, 315, 316
reaction, 322, 326, 331
reactive atom, 322, 328, 336, 341
reactive programming, 315
Reagent, 50, 61, 75, 304
reduce, 192
    short form, 196
referential transparency, 237
REPL
    alternatives, 69
    browser connection, 68
    definition of, 67
    workflow, 70
repl, 263
require, 256
`reset!`, 250
routing, 357

s-expression, 33
s-expressions, 24
scaling issues, 6, 200, 333
Scheme, 13, 126
sequence comprehension, 112
sequence operations, 179
    `concat`, 219
    `conj`, 169
    `filter`, 186

    `first`, 170

    `into`, 185

    `map`, 181

    `reduce`, 193

    `rest`, 170

sequences, 40, 169

side effects, 236

    within`do`, 161

    within functions, 124

    within `let`, 93

    within loops, 119

    within `when`, 102

spreadsheet, 322, 369

standard library, 4

Starbase Lambda, 103

state transition, 289

strategy, 244

`swap!`, 249

tail recursion, 118

ternary operator, 100

third-party libraries, 17

threading macros, 216, 223

timeout, 281

Tony Hoare, 277

tooling

    JavaScript, 45

    javascript, 6

transients, 252

truthiness, 106

try/catch, 265

TypeScript, 10

UI frameworks, 3

Unix, 48

`update`, 226

value equality, 318

vars, 89, 128

virtual DOM, 6, 7, 312, 316, 320, 324

Vue, 80

WebSocket, 72, 307